CRITICALLY READ
THEORY AND METHODS
OF ARCHAEOLOGY

CRITICALLY READING THE THEORY AND METHODS OF ARCHAEOLOGY

An Introductory Guide

GUY GIBBON

ALTAMIRA PRESS
A Division of Rowman & Littlefield
Lanham • Boulder • New York • Toronto • Plymouth, UK

Published by AltaMira Press
A division of Rowman & Littlefield
4501 Forbes Boulevard, Suite 200, Lanham, Maryland 20706
www.rowman.com

10 Thornbury Road, Plymouth PL6 7PP, United Kingdom

British Library Cataloguing in Publication Information Available

Library of Congress Cataloging-in-Publication Data
Gibbon, Guy E., 1939–
  Critically reading the theory and methods of archaeology : an introductory guide / Guy Gibbon.
    pages cm
  Includes bibliographical references and index.
  ISBN 978-0-7591-2340-3 (cloth : alk. paper) — ISBN 978-0-7591-2341-0 (pbk. : alk. paper) — ISBN 978-0-7591-2342-7 (electronic)
  1. Archaeology—Study and teaching. 2. Archaeology—Methodology. 3. Critical thinking—Study and teaching. 4. Report writing. I. Title.
  CC83.G53 2014
  930.1072—dc23   2013016869

Printed in the United States of America

CONTENTS

Introduction   1

Part I: Foundations   5

CHAPTER 1

What Kind of Archaeology Is It?   7

Descriptions of the aim of archaeology • Two missteps: flatland modernism and skeptical postmodernism • The tasks of archaeology from a four quadrants perspective • Cultural resource management • What *is* the aim of archaeology?

CHAPTER 2

What Kind of Investigation Is It?   17

The research cycle • Investigations within the research cycle • Additional considerations

CHAPTER 3

What Are the Issue and the Claim?   27

What is the issue? • What is the claim? • Thinking critically about questions • What is the historical context of the issue and claim?

CHAPTER 4

What Is the Argument?   35

Is there an argument? • Why is it necessary to evaluate arguments? • Is it a good argument? • A checklist for evaluating arguments • Evaluating arguments fairly

CHAPTER 5

What Are the Assumptions?   45

Types of assumptions and their function in arguments ▪ Hints for
locating assumptions ▪ Research programs: an introduction

CHAPTER 6

Is the Writing Clear?   55

Organization and style ▪ Ambiguous words and phrases ▪ Spotting
ambiguities ▪ Clarifying ambiguity ▪ Vague claims and puzzling
comparisons ▪ Unfamiliar words and phrases

CHAPTER 7

Are (Deceptive) Rhetorical Devices Used?   67

Euphemisms and dysphemisms ▪ Persuasive comparisons, definitions,
and explanations ▪ Stereotypes, innuendo, and loaded questions ▪
Weaselers, downplayers, and sarcasm ▪ Hyperbole and proof surrogates

CHAPTER 8

Is There a Fallacy in the Reasoning?   75

Errors in reasoning ▪ Fallacies that violate the relevance criterion ▪
Fallacies that violate the acceptability criterion ▪ Fallacies that violate
the sufficiency criterion ▪ Fallacies that violate the rebuttal criterion

CHAPTER 9

Are There Skeptical Postmodern Themes in the Argument?   85

Unmasking the foundations of science ▪ The influence of
postmodernism in scholarly research ▪ Six responses to
skeptical postmodernism

Part II: From Observations to Population Estimates   95

CHAPTER 10

Are Facts Clearly Distinguished from Opinions and Other Claims?   97

How factual are factual claims? ▪ The credibility of evidence ▪
Recognizing factual claims in your reading ▪ Major kinds of
evidence ▪ Intuition, authority, and testimonials ▪ Personal
observation, case studies, and analogies ▪ Research studies
as evidence

CHAPTER 11

How Are the Observations Summarized?   107

What are data? ▪ Tabular and pictorial methods of displaying data ▪
Measures of position: the average ▪ Measures of variability: the spread

CHAPTER 12

Is There an Inductive Argument?   119

Deductive and inductive arguments ▪ Inductive generalizations ▪
Analogical arguments ▪ Fallacies of inductive reasoning

CHAPTER 13

Is There a Population Estimate from a Sample?   129

Statistical inference ▪ Hypothesis testing ▪ An example
of formal hypothesis testing

Part III: Interpreting the Archaeological Record   139

CHAPTER 14

Is There a Theory in My Reading?   141

Making sense of the archaeological record ▪ Two views
of the structure of a theory ▪ The empiricism–social
constructivism–scientific realism dispute

CHAPTER 15

Which Research Program Is My Reading an Example Of?   151

Trait-centered archaeology ▪ Systems-centered archaeology ▪
Agency-centered archaeology ▪ Integral archaeology ▪ Must
archaeologists work within a single research program?

CHAPTER 16

Is an Explanation Offered?   161

Identifying explanations ▪ Three targets of explanation in
archaeology ▪ Argument to the best explanation ▪ Common
errors in framing explanations ▪ Using an analogy to explain

CHAPTER 17

Is There a Causal Argument?   171

Causation among specific events ▪ Common mistakes in causal
reasoning ▪ Causation in populations ▪ Use of anecdotal evidence
in causal reasoning

Part IV: Evaluating Interpretations of the Archaeological Record   181

CHAPTER 18

Are Deductively Valid Conclusions Drawn?   183

Deductive versus inductive strength of arguments ▪ Some common patterns of deductive arguments ▪ An example of deductive reasoning in archaeology

CHAPTER 19

Are Concepts Given Archaeological Interpretations?   193

Preparing predictions for testing ▪ The reliability and validity of indicators ▪ Evaluating archaeological indicators

CHAPTER 20

Are the Conclusions Reasonable?   203

Are the conclusions true? ▪ Assessing the truth value of conclusions: a four-step approach ▪ Common errors in drawing conclusions ▪ Remember: The research cycle is a cycle

Coda: Is Critical Reading Worth the Effort?   213

Notes   215

Bibliography   229

Index   237

About the Author   245

Introduction

Books on the archaeological research process typically focus on separate topical issues, such as dating, excavation, or the reconstruction of diet or political systems, or consider the archaeological process as a humanistic practice in which the evaluation of the interpretations of archaeologists has only a secondary—if any—role. While these books provide useful overviews of the archaeological enterprise, they do not emphasize the interrelated nature of the issues they introduce or critically examine the topics they review. *Critically Reading the Theory and Methods of Archaeology* asks readers to think about what they read within this broader context. It addresses such questions as the following: What kind of archaeology am I reading? Are (deceptive) rhetorical devices used? Is an explanation offered? Is there a causal argument? Are concepts given archaeological interpretation? Are the conclusions reasonable?[1]

In *Critically Reading the Theory and Methods of Archaeology*, thinking about what you read means thinking critically about what you read. To think critically is first to think logically and second to know where and how to challenge the arguments that you come across when you read archaeology. In universities and colleges, the study of logic has become a highly technical discipline taught within departments of philosophy. Our focus here is on informal logic or what is sometimes called the logic of everyday discourse. Those who consciously read critically become more adept at reading comprehension, at figuring out the logic of an argument, and at skillfully challenging defective arguments when they are confronted. A defective argument may be something simple, like basing a conclusion on inadequate information, or something more complex, like not interrelating all of the multiple factors that must be weighed when evaluating a hypothesis, model, or theory. Traditional critical thinking issues of this "rigorous reasoning" type are reviewed in chapters 3–8, 10, 12, and 16–18.

Today, the critical thinking enterprise also includes an examination of the assumptions and values that guide schools of thought within a discipline and the basic, shared procedural framework of that discipline. The guiding principle is that all aspects of a discipline should be subject to critical analysis. Chapter 15 reviews the major research orientations in archaeology (which I call research programs in this book). Archaeology's four main research orientations—trait-centered archaeology, systems-centered archaeology, agency-centered archaeology, and integral archaeology—are all based on different foundational assumptions about the aim of archaeology. Chapter 9 discusses issues raised by skeptical postmodernists that are relevant to that discussion. A trial formulation of the basic procedural framework that underlies all schools of archaeology is laid out in chapters 2, 11, 13, 14, 19, and 20. Chapter 1 introduces a broader conceptual framework—the four quadrants perspective—that will help readers think more holistically about the differing aims and procedures of archaeological research when they read archaeology.

From an organizational perspective, there are twenty chapters divided into four parts. Part I introduces issues that are tangential to the research cycle itself. These issues include the aim of archaeology, the identification of arguments and assumptions, and the recognition of fallacies and rhetorical devices, such as a "red herring." As you will see, each of these issues can and does affect the nature and results of your reading. Part II reviews the roles of descriptive and inferential statistics in the research cycle. Part III examines the four main research approaches used today in archaeology and their underlying assumptions and values, as well as the nature of theories, explanations, and causal arguments. Some of the many problems that archaeologists face in evaluating knowledge claims about past people, cultures, and social systems are introduced in part IV. As specialists in the field will recognize, each part and each chapter is a gentle introduction to complex issues. For readers interested in exploring the field of critical reading more thoroughly, recommended readings and additional comments are included in notes at the back of the book.

All of this is a prelude to suggestions for reading this book. *Critically Reading the Theory and Methods of Archaeology* is written on two levels. Down at the level of the trees within a forest, each part and each chapter within a part can be read on its own. Feel free to enter the book at any part or in any chapter. Like the research cycle itself, there is no privileged or essential starting point. At the level of the forest as a thing in itself, an argument runs through the book: the cyclical research process in archaeology is composed of a series of six sequential transformations of information (perhaps it is safer to say *at least* six). Stated another way, research in archaeology does not produce a single type of archaeological information, but multiple kinds of information. An essential task in reading archaeology, then, is to clearly recognize these transformations (and the kinds of information they result in) and to comprehend how they are made. As you will learn, the way a particular transformation is made (poorly or with sophistication) affects all other transformations in the research cycle.

This book can and will be read for different reasons. Many readers of archaeology—students, professionals, and committed nonprofessionals—will read the book on their own in order to learn how to read archaeology more critically. The book is appropriate supplemental reading for undergraduate and graduate courses in archaeology or as stand-alone reading in undergraduate-level and graduate-level seminars. Students writing a thesis and professional archaeologists will find the book useful in improving the clarity, coherence, and open-mindedness of their writing. Finally, the book can be used as a guide to indicate what the basic critical reading and writing skills are that everyone entering the teaching profession in archaeology in the twenty-first century should have. It should be the responsibility of their senior mentors that they have these skills before they begin their teaching career.

Like books written for introductory courses, *Critically Reading the Theory and Methods of Archaeology* concentrates for the most part on prehistoric archaeology, where the word "prehistory" refers to the past of people who lack a written record that includes detailed information about their lifeways. While historical archaeology is a growing and lively discipline, its practice involves issues that go beyond the limited intent of this book.

FOUNDATIONS I

A COMMON MISCONCEPTION among nonprofessional readers of archaeology is that archaeology is archaeology is archaeology—that is, that all archaeologists do the same things for the same reasons. In reality, while the methods employed by archaeologists are in most cases indistinguishable (C-14 dating, screening during excavation, and so forth), archaeologists have widely varying goals that they pursue using a smorgasbord of different research strategies. Even more fundamental are the incongruent rationales for doing archaeology that underlie the goals and research strategies they adopt. While goals, research strategies, and rationales may seem like airy, abstract topics, understanding the agendas archaeologists adopt is an essential endeavor in understanding what you read when you pick up a book or an article written by an archaeologist. Part I explores many of these important background issues.

We begin then by asking this question: Why do the agendas of archaeologists vary? One reason is that many archaeologists develop an expertise in one kind of research in archaeology, such as site excavation, plant identification, or stone tool knapping. Consequently, they concentrate their research in that area of expertise. Archaeologists also differ in their strategies of explaining and of reasoning to theories, and in whether their goals are those of cultural historians, social scientists *sensu stricto*, or humanists.

Perhaps most importantly, archaeologists differ in the assumptions they make about the natural world, human beings, culture, the archaeological record, and other aspects of the world around us. That is, they have different views about what exists, of what the characteristics of the things that exist are, and of how those things and their characteristics should be studied and understood. These divergent sets of assumptions result in the development of competing research programs or ways of doing archaeology.

Part I considers each of the above reasons for the existence of diversity in strategies of research in archaeology—that is, differing aims, kinds of investigation, issues, questions, and assumptions (chapters 1, 2, 3, and 5). Part I also reviews two integral but often neglected issues in reading archaeology: the nature of reasoned argument and the identification of deceptive rhetorical devices and fallacies (chapters 4, 7, and 8). Chapter 6 considers how fuzzy writing affects our understanding of what we read. The last chapter in part I, chapter 9, visits the so-called culture wars, for these debates situate books and articles in archaeology within the broader cultural landscape of contemporary Euro-American society. Together, these nine chapters provide an introduction to reading archaeology.

What Kind of Archaeology Is It? 1

A REASONABLE PLACE TO START is with questions about the aim of archaeology. What is the aim of archaeology, then? Do all archaeologists share the same aim? If they do not, how do their aims differ—and how do these differences affect what they write and what we read? Although these questions may seem simplistic, they are of fundamental importance in reading archaeology.

We begin our search for the aim of archaeology with a review of definitions of archaeology drawn from archaeology texts, dictionaries, and encyclopedias. As you will see, the more detailed definitions point to diverse and seemingly conflicting definitions of the aim of archaeology. As a critical reader, your first question should be this: What does this diversity mean? (For, as a critical reader, you do not read passively.) One possibility is that some archaeologists are practicing archaeology incorrectly or perhaps in a less sophisticated way than other archaeologists. Another is that archaeologists have different tasks to perform, and these diverse definitions simply point to these different tasks.

Active readers of archaeology will be familiar with the acrimonious science versus humanities debates that have gone on among archaeologists since the 1980s. Proponents of both sides of the debate maintain that their opponents are practicing archaeology in a wrongheaded way. These arguments support the first possibility mentioned above. My position on this controversy is apparent in the title of the second section of this chapter, "Two Missteps: Flatland Modernism and Skeptical Postmodernism." The third section introduces what I think is a more useful (and accurate) way of understanding the diverse definitions of archaeology that we encounter in our reading when we read archaeology. In contrast to the science contra humanities literature, a four quadrants approach assumes that the study of human beings can and must be approached from multiple perspectives, all of which—while only partial when each is applied as the sole research orientation—have their own unique forms of knowledge, scholarly approaches, versions of truth, and means of knowledge validation.

Another aim of many archaeologists, cultural resource management, is not even mentioned in everyday definitions of archaeology. This aim is discussed in the fourth section. In the summary section, I return to the question "Does archaeology have an aim?" and draw an unusual conclusion.

My goals in this chapter are straightforward. They are to make the point that archaeologists have different legitimate aims in doing archaeology; to show the value of a four quadrants perspective when thinking about the tasks of archaeology; to begin to explore what it means to practice archaeology in each of the four quadrants; and to endorse the idea that archaeology can (and should) be practiced as a discipline from a holistic, integral perspective, a perspective that includes the diverse kinds of archaeology we commonly encounter when we read archaeology.

Descriptions of the Aim of Archaeology

Descriptions of the aim of archaeology vary widely in precision and detail. Consider the following rather simple descriptions of the aim of archaeology:

- The aim of archaeology is the "study of the human past, principally through material culture."[1]
- The aim of archaeology is the "scientific study of material remains (as fossil relics, artifacts, monuments) of past human life and activities."[2]
- The aim of archaeology is the "study of human existence through unwritten, material remains."[3]

Descriptions like those below contain more detail and in their detail emphasize a particular view of archaeology:

- The aim of archaeology "is the study of prehistoric and historic cultures through the analysis of material remains."[4]
- Archaeology, which is a subdivision of anthropology, involves "the study of the human past through its material remains." Anthropology is "the study of humanity—our physical characteristics as animals

and our unique non-biological characteristics we call *culture.*" *Culture* is a "term used by anthropologists [to refer to] the non-biological characteristics unique to a particular society."[5]

- Archaeology is a special "form of anthropology that uses material remains to study extinct human societies. The objectives of archaeology are to construct culture history, reconstruct past lifeways, and study cultural process."[6] (Reconstructing culture history consists of arranging cultural units in a way that accurately reveals their generic affinities. Reconstructing past lifeways refers to the reconstruction of the lifeways of extinct peoples. The study of cultural process refers to the "dynamic relationships operating among cultural systems."[7])

To see that these descriptions of archaeology have a specific emphasis, compare them with the following descriptions:

- The defining purpose of archaeology is "the discovery of the meanings of things."[8]
- "Archaeologists need to find out what people thought about the world—to understand them as agents."[9]
- "The aim of archaeology is to provide exciting and versatile interpretations that lead us closer to understanding what was going on in the past and, through this process, to understanding ourselves better in the present."[10]

The above descriptions are representative of opposing views of the aim of archaeology in mainstream archaeology today. Still other views of the aim of archaeology were once popular but have faded from use. Compare the following outdated descriptions to those mentioned above: the aim of archaeology is to illustrate history, which historians write about (the now notorious "handmaiden to history" view); the aim of archaeology is to look backward in history for inspiration in the present (for models of proper behavior, the good life, and so on); the aim of archaeology is to gather relics for a personal collection or for a museum collection.

Manuscripts are written within these general intellectual orientations for many reasons, of course, besides the pure promotion of scholarship. Some articles are written for newspapers and popular journals like *Archaeology*. Others are someone's doctoral dissertation or a professor's tenure book. As in other disciplines, some archaeologists write in a quest for prestige and self-promotion—and the content of what you read is second-ary to this endeavor. The preface or acknowledgment section of a book will often contain clues to the presence of these and other secondary aims.

Two Missteps: Flatland Modernism and Skeptical Postmodernism

Archaeologists have been engaged in a nasty quarrel since the 1980s, with some favoring a strictly scientific approach and others a more humanistic, postmodern perspective. Both modern science (that is, science as defined from a modernist perspective) and postmodernism have made valuable contributions to our understanding of human beings and the world more generally. On one hand, science has maintained that knowledge claims must be validated against empirical (that is, observable) data (the rallying cry of the Enlightenment was "No more myths!"). On the other hand, postmodernism introduced the valuable insights that "every actual occasion has an interpretive component" and "all perspectives need to be given a fair hearing." However, both perspectives result in distorted approaches to the study of human beings when carried to extremes.

Science has been a key component of the modern worldview that resulted from the debates of Enlightenment thinkers like Thomas Paine, Voltaire, Jean-Jacques Rousseau, David Hume, and others in the eigh-teenth century as influenced by natural philosophers like Isaac Newton, Galileo, and Robert Boyle. In part because of the context of the debate, especially the confrontation between reason contra religious beliefs as ways of knowing, empirical science became scientific materialism, the belief that there is no reality save what can be registered by the eye and empirical instruments. All that exists in the universe is matter (or matter and energy). Notions like meaning, consciousness, culture, intention, and values were considered epiphenomena (at best) of material things like the brain. This position, which is still a dominant discourse in archaeology and the West-ern world more generally, has been called the "disaster of modernity" and "flatland modernism" because it collapses mental experiences like thought and culture into material objects.[11]

As its name implies, postmodernism is a revolt against flatland modern-ism. At its core, postmodernism is based on three useful and most likely accurate assumptions: much of what we take to be innocently given to us by the senses (an outlook called the "myth of the given") is in some significant ways a construction of the mind, an interpretation (this view is commonly referred to as constructivism); meaning is context dependent (a view called contextualism); and cognition must (therefore) privilege no single perspective. In skeptical postmodernism, each of these assumptions is blown radically out of proportion. The principle that "all perspectives need to be given a fair hearing" becomes "no perspective whatsoever is better than any other," "every actual occasion has an interpretative component" becomes "there is nothing but interpretation," and "meaning is context dependent" becomes a denial that any sort of meaning actually exists or can be conveyed at all.[12] Since skeptical postmodernism is a component of some schools of agency-centered archaeology, I dedicate chapter 9 to a discussion of its recognition when we read archaeology.

The Tasks of Archaeology from a Four Quadrants Perspective

Philosopher Ken Wilber has argued contra the scientific materialism versus skeptical postmodern debate that the study of human beings is more usefully approached from an integral four quadrants perspective that combines positive aspects of each of these positions.[13] The four quadrants are four perspectives on human beings, each of which has its own distinctive kind of reality, type of valid knowledge, mode of study, version of truth, and means of validation. According to this approach, no quadrant is more important than another, and each is open to scientific inquiry.

In the four quadrants approach, the left side is interior, the right side is exterior, the upper parts are individual, and the lower parts are communal or collective (see figure 1.1). The upper left quadrant is the quadrant of all individual subjective consciousnesses, of an individual's thoughts, feelings, intentions, sensations, understandings, and experiences. It is the quadrant of "I" and can be recognized in your reading as a focus on the study of individual experiences inside a person who lived in the past.

The lower left quadrant is the quadrant of intersubjective understandings, of what anthropologists call culture. It is closely related to the upper left quadrant, for people derive the meaning of their interior experiences from their cultural background. The cultural background of individuals provides a context in which mutual understanding (which is not the same as mutual agreement) can occur. A culture in this intersubjective sense is most often associated with a common language, a set of some sort of morals and ethics, and a shared worldview. The lower left quadrant is the quadrant of "We" and can be recognized in your reading as a focus on

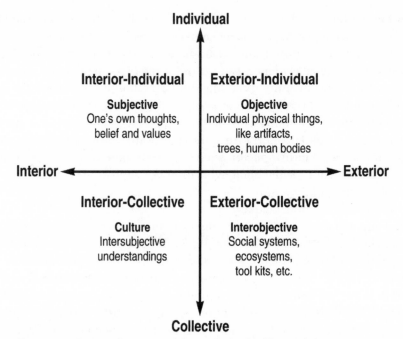

Figure 1.1.   Four quadrants perspective on the study of human beings.

the interior of human social systems, on culture, worldview, and other intersubjective understandings.

The upper right quadrant is the quadrant of "It" and can be recognized in your reading as a focus on individual physical things, such as a person's body, brain, skeleton, or behavior, or individual types of artifacts like an arrowhead, a pottery vessel, or a flint chip. It is also the realm of individual living plants and animals, and of the earth and planets. For human beings, it is the realm of physical conditions, such as available food sources and water.

The lower right quadrant is the quadrant of the exterior of collectives like human societies and ecosystems. In the lower right quadrant, the members of social groups are linked together by social fields that help to coordinate their activities in such a way that the society acts like a single organism. For human beings, it is the realm of social organization and of techno-economic bases like gathering and farming, and of information channels, feedback loops, and processes. The lower right quadrant is the quadrant of "Its" and can be recognized in your reading as a focus on systems of social organization, such as bands, tribes, chieftains, and states; on techno-economic bases like hunter-gatherer and horticulturalist; and on the exterior of systems in general.

From a four quadrants perspective, each quadrant has its own distinctive kind of reality, type of valid knowledge, mode of study, and means of validation. Each makes truth claims that are falsifiable through its own kind of experiential evidence, and thus each is subject to scientific inquiry. From this perspective, the three strands of all valid knowledge are (1) instrumental injunction: a research program, practice, or experiment of the form "If you want to know this, do this"; (2) direct apprehension: a direct experience or apprehension of data brought forth by the injunction; and (3) communal confirmation (or rejection): a checking of the results (the data, the evidence) with others who have the appropriate skills to carry out the injunction.[14]

Note that scientific inquiry from this perspective applies to all four quadrants and that "data" refers to direct and immediate experience in any quadrant, not just to the sensory empirical in the upper right quadrant. Scientists in this broad sense test the validity (truth) claims of each quadrant as a way of testing views of reality and of curbing misunderstandings. Validity claims in the upper left quadrant in the social sciences in general are about what an individual person thought or experienced, or is thinking or experiencing. The most direct way to get at the thoughts and experiences of a person is to talk to that person or to read what that person said about his or her thoughts and experiences in a diary or other manuscript. Of course, the person could be lying or perhaps confused. Academic approaches to the interior of individuals include structuralism, phenomenology, interpretive theories of psychoanalysis, and psychology in general.

Validity claims in the lower left quadrant are about cultural fit, about understanding the meaning of something like a cockfight in a community. The validity criterion is mutual understanding. Participant observers (cultural anthropologists, for example) seek to understand the cultural fit of the cockfight within the context of the community's cultural and linguistic practices.

Validity claims in the upper right quadrant are about representational truth—that is, truth about the objective world of physical things. The question is, does the truth claim accurately represent the facts (where the facts refer to observable, empirical things that can be seen)? This is the realm of physical sciences like physics, chemistry, and biology, and the cognitive sciences and neurophysiology.

Validity claims in the lower right quadrant are about functional fit, about how well (and how) the parts fit together in an overall system or whole. While researchers in the lower left quadrant ask "What does it mean?" those working in the lower right quadrant ask "What does it do?"

Where one kind of anthropologist is interested in the meaning of cock-fighting in a community, another kind of anthropologist is interested in the function of cockfighting in a social system. An appropriate answer might be that cockfighting promotes social cohesion within the social system. But both approaches are correct and useful, if partial. No quadrant is more important than another.

Regardless of the diverse aims of archaeologists, it should be stressed that the medium of archaeology remains material culture, whether a con-temporary building, for instance, or the ruins of one used in the past.[15] This raises problems unique to the discipline. Like all artifacts made by individuals or social groups, the defining pattern and meaning of a build-ing (an upper right object) does not come from itself. It is a product of creative human thought (the upper left quadrant) and shared cultural patterns (the lower left quadrant). How do archaeologists, especially prehistoric archaeologists, develop testable knowledge about the interior thoughts of individuals and the cultural understandings they share? As you will see, even the accurate modeling of social systems (lower right quadrant) can be problematic because of the fragmentary and partial na-ture of the archaeological record.

Chapter 2 lays out a model of scientific inquiry that is unique to archae-ology and that is applicable to all four quadrants as viewed through the lens of the archaeological record. Part III of the book reviews major research approaches in archaeology, their relationships to the four quadrants, and the kinds of validity claims they typically make. Part IV reviews a few is-sues involved in the testing of these claims.

Cultural Resource Management

If I asked for a show of hands, I would find that most readers are familiar with the expression *cultural resource management* (CRM). I would also prob-ably find that only a few readers are able to write a short essay that accu-rately describes the history and intent of CRM. However, if we stacked all the academic books and articles about archaeology written in the last forty years in one pile, all of the popular books and articles in another, and all CRM manuscripts in another, the CRM stack would tower high above the other two.

In the United States, the meteoric rise of cultural resource management has resulted from federal and state legislation that requires an assessment of cultural resources whenever federal or state land is modified or federal or state funds are used on private land. Examples of preservation legislation in the United States include the National Historic Preservation Act of 1966 (amended in 1976 and 1980), the National Environmental Policy Act of 1969, Executive Order 11593 in 1971, the Archaeological and Historic Preservation Act of 1974, and the Archaeological Resources Protection Act of 1979. During a typical year in the early twenty-first century, millions of dollars are allocated to carry out the mandate of this legislation, with only a small portion of that amount for archaeological research.

Since its primary intent is preservation, the typical CRM manuscript is an unpublished report of a field investigation. Furthermore, it usually takes a good bit of effort to get copies of this "good gray" literature, for the few copies that are printed are normally on file in governmental agencies that may limit access to them. Still, the sheer volume of CRM projects each year makes these manuscripts an invaluable information source for people with a serious interest in archaeology. Equally important, since the vast majority of professional positions in archaeology today are in some branch of CRM, aspiring archaeologists are likely to spend their professional careers in this increasingly dominant branch of the discipline. Consequently, I include examples drawn from the CRM literature throughout this book.

As a clue, the presence of a CRM orientation in what you are reading can generally be recognized by the presence of two or more of the following terms: *historic context, enforcement, National Register, mitigation, heritage, review and compliance, license, 106 process, impacted, cultural recourses, regulations, evaluation criteria, property, mandated, statute, significance, integrity,* and *management.*

What *Is* the Aim of Archaeology?

Can we say, then, that archaeology has *an* aim? The obvious, qualified conclusion is "certainly not." The message of chapter 1 is clear: multiple voices speak through the archaeological literature. As a reader, one of your many tasks is to identify those voices, for understanding what you are reading depends in large part on distinguishing among these voices.

Accepted. Nonetheless, chapter 1 has a more important message: In order to obtain a full and accurate understanding of human beings, it is necessary to integrate the results of diverse perspectives. Each perspective pursued alone, while capable of producing valid and useful knowledge, is incomplete. The four quadrants approach provides one glimpse of what an integral understanding of human beings in the past would look like. Of course, archaeology is a young discipline, and archaeologists usually focus on one quadrant or one side of the four quadrants—and many still argue that this quadrant or side is more important than the other quadrants or side. Furthermore, archaeologists have formidable problems in accessing and validating information in the left-hand quadrants. However, as a critical reader, your task is the simpler one of recognizing the perspective (the aim) of the writer whose work you are reading, whether it is from one side or the other of the flatland modernism–skeptical postmodernism debate or from one of the quadrants, and of evaluating what you are reading.

What Kind of Investigation Is It? **2**

AS A GLANCE AT THE ABSTRACTS in any archaeological journal will show, there is a bewildering variety of types of investigations in archaeology. Is there pattern in this diversity—or is it truly bewildering? Chapter 2 raises the question "What kind of investigation is it?" and suggests several frameworks for answering this question.

The Research Cycle

This section introduces a schematic reconstruction of the research process in archaeology. Although its purpose in this chapter is to help us understand the variety of types of investigations in archaeology, it will serve as a framework, too, for issues raised in parts II, III, and IV of this book. Following the diagram in figure 2.1, research in archaeology cycles through six information components, none of which can be ignored.[1] The six components are observations, sample summaries, empirical generalizations, theories, predictions, and empirical interpretations.

In the research cycle, information components are transformed into one another by methods like defining, measuring, theory building, and sampling. The solid-line ovals in figure 2.1 encircle the main methods that control each of these transformations. Parts II through IV of this book demonstrate that each transformation produces a distinctive and different kind of information. As the diagonal lines in figure 2.1 illustrate, information transformations link aspects of the archaeological record to statements that situate them in a proposed past sociocultural and physical context. Simple examples are the identification of a worked piece of ground stone as a "grinding stone" and a concentrated group of large square features

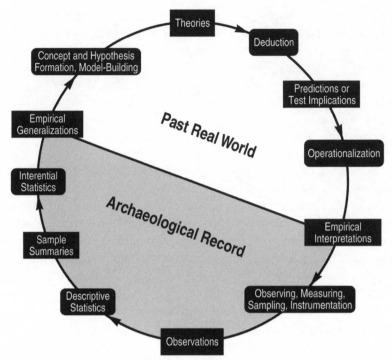

Figure 2.1. Schematic diagram of an idealized version of the research cycle in archaeology.

as a "village." The movement back and forth across the diagonal line in figure 2.1 is a defining characteristic of archaeology. In archaeology, how well the transformations are made can and most often does determine the success of a project.

Since each segment of the research cycle involves a different research task, an article written about the task of one segment of the cycle will look different from those written from other positions within the cycle. If you understand the cycle, however, you understand a great deal about archaeology—and unity is given to what otherwise appears to be a set of unconnected writings. This section describes the research cycle. The following section provides labels for some of the more common kinds of investigations associated with the cycle.

Transforming Observations into Empirical Generalizations

Like all scholars who deal with matter, archaeologists must decide what to observe in the archaeological record, for an infinite number of observations can (in theory) be made on any artifact or feature. Although it is commonly assumed that archaeologists simply make observations, deciding what to observe and what to record in the archaeological record can be quite problematic. Even the notion of an observation is controversial, as we will learn in chapters 9, 10, and 19. Here, however, we concentrate on the transformation of observations already made (the bottom information component) into sample summaries and empirical generalizations. This series of transformations takes place in the bottom left quarter of the research cycle.

Given a set of observations on some aspect of the archaeological record, two kinds of description are possible: description of patterns in a sample of observations and description of patterns in the population from which the sample was drawn. Description of patterns in the sample of observations is summarized through the methodological controls of measurement, scaling, and descriptive statistics. Descriptive statistics reduce unwieldy-looking masses of data—that is, pages of numbers—to a few group measures. Examples are the average weight of thirty-three grinding stones, the range in length of twenty projectile points, and the most common house type in a site. The end product is a new information component called a sample summary.

The second kind of description, the description of patterns in the population from which the sample was drawn, involves claims about populations that are incompletely known. These kinds of descriptive statements in archaeology, which are called empirical generalizations because they generalize about some unknown measurement or relationship in the observable (empirical) archaeological record, are made by induction, which is a thought process that (among other things) derives general principles or information from particular instances or facts. In archaeology, this process transforms descriptions of the attributes of samples of artifacts and other things encountered in the archaeological record, such as plant and animal remains, into generalizations about the attributes of all things of that particular type in a particular context.

Empirical generalizations are about the objective patterns that exist in and between populations of artifacts, sites, and features, such as the length of all projectile points of a particular kind and the association of all sites of a particular kind that contain similar kinds of projectile points. Archaeologists more often than not make inspired guesses about the characteristics of unknown populations. Nonetheless, the most reliable method available for making accurate inferences to the characteristics of unknown populations is statistical inference. Statistical inference is the process of reasoning from a sample description to a population description using the principles of probability. An example in archaeology is estimating the average length of all Clovis projectile points from an available sample of two hundred Clovis points, in which the two hundred points are the sample and "all Clovis projectile points" is the population.

The transformation of observations into sample summaries and empirical generalizations is the topic of chapters 11 and 13, respectively.

Theory Building

Although archaeologists may differ in their aims, they share the goal of making sense of the material remains they study by relating them to past people and their lifeways. They do this by making different kinds of conjectures about these material remains. In figure 2.1, these different kinds of conjectures are called theory for short, though they could be called interpretations of the past or some other such term.[2] In contrast to statements about artifacts and other material things in the archaeological record, theories in archaeology are statements about a past people when viewed through the lens of one or more of Wilber's four quadrants. Theories are constructed through a process of abstraction, which is an imaginative leap from notions about the archaeological record to notions about some past real-world context, such as daily life in a Neolithic village or the intersubjective understandings (the culture) of the people who lived in that village. The transformation of sample summaries and empirical generalizations into theories is controlled by the principles of concept formation and model building, among other theory-building methods.[3]

In archaeology, the abstract terms in theories generally refer to properties and characteristics of concepts associated with past human societies and cultures—to concepts like axe, projectile point, house, surrounding natural environment, understanding of the cosmos, and degree of centralized political power—rather than to flint chips or pottery sherds. A shift has been made during this transformation from a focus on archaeological contexts to a focus on past real-world sociocultural, psychological, and material culture contexts, from a discussion of sites and artifacts to a discussion of communities of people and tools in social and environmental settings. This transformation is discussed in part III of this book.

Theory Testing

Since theories claim—if only hypothetically—that something was the case in the past, they are claims to knowledge. A distinguishing characteristic of archaeology as a social science discipline is the necessity of justifying knowledge claims by pitching them back upon the material world of the archaeological record. This is generally accomplished in archaeology by devising confrontations between the implications of knowledge claims like these and fresh observations on the archaeological record.

Every theory makes some predictions about the content of the world. For example, the simple theory that this artifact was once the projectile tip of an arrow implies that the artifact was once bound to a shaft and propelled through the air when used. These two predictions, which are test implications of the theory, are contained in the definition of "projectile point." The statement that a certain set of archaeological sites are the remains of a chiefdom level of social organization contains test predictions, even if implicit, about the past hierarchical relationship of the sites as communities and of the people who lived in those communities.

In archaeology, terms within test implications typically refer to characteristics of past sociocultural systems and human groups, such as "bound to a shaft," "propelled through the air," and "a ranked society." These abstract notions must be given empirical, archaeological interpretations through the methodological control of operationalization. Operationalization is a long and awkward word that simply refers to the process of transforming statements about the past-in-itself into statements about the present archaeological record using the methodological controls of instrumentation, scaling, and sampling.

The fit of a theory with reality is evaluated by comparing the empirical interpretations of sociocultural and other past real-world concepts with these fresh observations. If the tests demonstrate a satisfactory fit between observed and expected observations, a prediction is considered supported or confirmed. However, demonstrating that a theory "fits" some proposed past real world is nearly always a complex process whose success is uncertain before it starts, for many reasons. These reasons include the existence of cultural and natural transformation processes that may "distort" the archaeological record, a too small sample of the archaeological record, and the difficulty of generalizing from a sample to larger but unobservable populations of that record. Because of these problems, procedures for decision-making in uncertain situations are reviewed in chapter 20. The process of evaluating theories is the subject of part IV of this book.

Research proceeds repeatedly around the research cycle in this manner, constantly confronting conjectures and observations.

Investigations within the Research Cycle

Although movement around the research cycle is emphasized in this book, individual archaeologists generally focus their research on particular phases of the research cycle. In the majority of cases, they do this because they are best at or most interested in a particular kind of research, such as faunal analysis, site excavation, or theory construction, or they are hired to do that kind of investigation. When grouped by their position within the cycle of research, the intent of these various interests should become clear.

As used here, the notion of an internal project refers to a research activity that transforms one information component in the research cycle into another. An external project is a reflection on that research, such as an evaluation of the methods archaeologists use in the transformation of one information component into another. That is, external considerations stand outside or above the research cycle, while internal projects take place within the cycle. Both sorts of projects lead to distinctive kinds of investigations in archaeology, though both may be concentrating on the same part of the research cycle.

A first step in asking "What kind of investigation is it?" is to determine which section of the research cycle is being emphasized. For instance, some archaeologists emphasize the bottom half of the cycle and pursue problems that require excavation, measurement, and the construction of sample summaries; this is generally called empirical research or analysis. Others emphasize the top part of the cycle and concentrate on theory building and testing. Still other archaeologists—or the same archaeologists in a different project—concentrate on the left side (the context of discovery) or on the right side (the context of justification) of the cycle. These research concentrations can be grouped into major types of investigation.

The goal of *descriptive studies* is usually the systematic description and classification of a sample of the archaeological record. This sample is often obtained through the excavation of a site. Descriptive studies are fact-finding expeditions that attempt to answer the questions of what, where, and when. The main methodological controls of descriptive studies are sampling, mechanical instruments of observation (including those used in excavation), and descriptive and inferential statistics.

Exploratory investigations account for sample summaries and empirical generalizations by generating theories of various kinds. They produce theories about some part of the past within a context of discovery. The following abstract is an example of this type of investigation.

Paleocoastal Marine Fishing on the Pacific Coast of the Americas: Perspectives from Daisy Cave, California

Analysis of over twenty-seven thousand fish bones from strata at Daisy Cave, dated between about 11,500 and 8500 cal B.P., suggests that early Channel Islanders fished relatively intensively in a variety of habitats using a number of distinct technologies, including boats and the earliest evidence for hook-and-line fishing on the Pacific Coast of the Americas. The abundance of fish remains and fishing-related artifacts supports dietary reconstructions that suggest fish provided more than 50 percent of the edible meat represented in faunal samples from the early Holocene site strata. The abundance and economic importance of fish at Daisy Cave, unprecedented among early sites along the Pacific Coast of North America, suggest that early maritime capabilities on the Channel Islands were both more advanced and more variable than previously believed. When combined with a survey of fish remains from several other early Pacific Coast sites, these data suggest that early New World peoples effectively used watercraft, captured a diverse array of fish, and exploited a variety of marine habitats and resources.[4]

Interpretive and theoretical studies synthesize sets of data, theories, and other types of already existing information about past sociocultural contexts in new ways. The goal of this type of investigation is to suggest new interpretations of already existing information through the adoption of new concepts, new relationships, and new theories. The following abstract is an example of this type of investigation.

A Preliminary Analysis of Functional Variability in the Mousterian of Levallois Facies

In this classic paper, Sally and Lewis Binford suggest a new interpretation of the vertical alteration of artifact industries in the Mousterian levels in sites in France. Earlier interpretations had suggested that (1) each type of Mousterian represents the remains of a different group of people, with each group being characterized by its own traditional way of making tools, or (2) each assemblage represents a slightly different adaptation to a different environment, the alteration of industries being determined by environmental variation through time. Sally and Lewis Binford suggest that the different types of Mousterian are associated with a seasonal pattern of living, with each type representing the remains of activities carried out at different seasons of the year.[5]

Hypothesis testing as a research strategy compares the empirical implications of theories with new observations. In a theory, a hypothesis is a statement that is either speculative or lacks sufficient support to call it a fact. It may also be a statement derived from a theory through the process of deduction (see chapters 14, 18, and 20). An emphasis on hypothesis testing compels archaeologists to specify just what (if anything) is being tested. It also forces archaeologists to distinguish between testable hypotheses, assumptions (see chapter 5), and vague generalizations like "The climate changed, so a new cultural adaptation appeared" (but how and why did a new cultural adaptation appear?).

While the preceding types of investigation are examples of internal projects, the following two types of investigation are examples of external projects:

Instrumental-nomological investigations (another unwieldy expression) develop theoretical constructs—that is, they construct, standardize, and validate instruments of measurement. This type of external investigation can involve the creation of measurement systems and of instruments for making measurements within these systems. It can also involve the creation of new theoretical and operational definitions of concepts like "intensive agriculture," "band-level society," and "ethnic identity" (see chapter 19). The following abstract is an example of this kind of investigation.

Identification of Horse Exploitation by Clovis Hunters Based on Protein Analysis

Positive results were obtained from protein residue analysis on three Clovis points from Wally's Beach, southwestern Alberta. Two tested positive for *Equus*, the third for bovid, probably *Bison* or *Bootherium*. All genera are present on the site remains. This finding clearly demonstrates use of *Equus* by Clovis hunters. Four C-14 dates indicate that the site was in use between 11,000 and 11,300 B.P.[6]

External projects are also concerned with the best way to conduct research, the value of contending assumptions, and the aim of archaeology, among other abstract issues. Research program debates in which archaeologists argue over the basic assumptions that archaeologists should adopt when studying the archaeological record are common examples. Other meta-analyses attempt to show why a particular strategy of research cannot produce the results it was designed for or why a particular kind of explanation or argument is inadequate. The following abstract illustrates the flavor of this kind of investigation.

The Archaeology of Place

Some archaeologists have suggested that if archaeologists are to be successful at understanding the organization of past cultural systems, they must understand the organizational relationships among places which were differentially used during the operation of past systems. This point is illustrated by observations made among the Nunamiut Eskimo. Against this background it is demonstrated that the two most common forms of archaeological systematics, "assemblage" versus "type"-based systematics, are not appropriate for the study of places. In the later case, it is not possible to analyze places as such, while one cannot see places with different "content" as part of a single system in the former. It is concluded that current archaeological systematics are totally inappropriate for studying past systems of adaptation and their evolutionary modification.[7]

Additional Considerations

In asking "What kind of investigation is it?" other considerations must also be kept in mind. Two are mentioned here to illustrate what these additional considerations are like.

Publication Outlet

You should note the medium in which the writing occurs. Was the author writing an article for a magazine, a newspaper, or a professional journal? Was a book published by an academic publisher, such as the University of Chicago Press; by a mass-market publisher; by a small-scale regional journal, such as *The Minnesota Archaeologist*; or by the author herself? These different publication outlets generally have a particular tone, style of organization, degree of scholarship, purpose, and other dimensions that the critical reader will find informative.

Primary or Secondary Analysis

In my usage here, a primary analysis refers to new excavations or surveys or measurements or readings—that is, to fresh kinds of evidence or understandings. A secondary analysis comments on or reworks an existing reading or existing evidence. A secondary analysis might also be a replication study that duplicates an earlier study to retest a hypothesis or to demonstrate that the same kinds of material are present in similar kinds of sites. These latter kinds of studies are particularly important in compliance research, where there is an emphasis on producing robust results and generalizations that have broad application. This made-up abstract is an example of this latter kind of study.

Have Gophers Severely Disturbed Prairie Region Sites?

Replication studies funded by a State Transportation Department demonstrated that 90 percent of the small activity sites in an exposed but widespread landscape feature in the prairie region of the state have been severely disturbed by gophers. Therefore, decision-makers decided that they can save considerable amounts of money each year (in a shrinking state budget) by requiring less expensive patterns of artifact retrieval in this landscape feature than full excavation, if field checks verify the presence of disturbed conditions.

Still other kinds of considerations can affect the length, content, and medium of a publication. Among these are whether a project was planned or opportunistic (for instance, workers grading a road uncover burials that are quickly studied before reburial and a brief report is written); whether a study is a freestanding project or a component of a larger interdisciplinary project; whether a study is a preliminary pilot project or a full-length project; and whether the writing is intended for students or professionals. With a little effort, active readers can think of other considerations of this nature that shape the publications they read.

Despite the rhetoric of special-interest archaeologists, no one type of investigation in archaeology is inherently inferior or superior to others. Each plays a role in the discipline of archaeology. Consequently, one of the many attributes of a critical reader is being open to recognizing and reading different types of investigations. Is an investigation external or internal? If it is internal, which information component or components is it focused on? This is important information, for answers to these questions alert the reader to the pattern of argument that might be present, the type of question that might be asked, and many other issues of which a critical reader should be aware.

What Are the Issue and the Claim? 3

A RCHAEOLOGY IS A DISCIPLINE of constant inquiry, for we know far less about past people and their lifeways than we realize. In fact, much of what we think we know remains uncertain, for the archaeological record is fragmentary and partial and must be interpreted. More likely than not, then, what you read when you read archaeology will address an issue of some kind, if by the word "issue" we mean any matter that is in doubt or open to dispute. Typical examples are the settlement history of Grasshopper Pueblo, the location of the fortified Spanish mission at Santa Catalina, and the contents of an unexcavated archaeological site.

Most of your reading in archaeology will also make one or more claims about the issue, if by the word "claim" we mean something that is asserted to be true. In the above examples, the claim would be something about the settlement history of Grasshopper Pueblo, the location of the Spanish mission, or the content of the site. Since your aim as an active reader is to understand and evaluate what you read, a necessary task of a first reading (besides determining the kind of archaeology and the type of investigation you are reading) is the identification of the issue and the claim (if there is one). In a second or third reading, the claim can (and should) be subjected to close inspection and evaluation.

Chapter 3 has four sections. The first two sections explore ways of identifying issues and claims; the third section illustrates a few of the errors archaeologists make in framing their questions; and the fourth section poses the following question: What is the historical context of the issue and the claim?

What Is the Issue?

In studying the remains of past people and their lifeways, archaeologists ask questions—lots of questions. Were the earliest people hunters or scavengers? How did the bow and arrow spread across North America? What is the most efficient way to discover deeply buried sites? In the critical reading literature, questions like these are called *issues*. Together with the claim and the reasons that support it, the issue is an essential part of the reasoning that runs through many articles and books in archaeology. If a goal of critical reading is to evaluate the reasoning that runs through a text, then the issue must be identified. So how can you identify the issue that structures an article or book?

In many instances the issue is easy to locate, for the author tells us what it is in the introduction to the manuscript. In cases where it is unclear what the issue is, critical readers can search for clues to what it may be in other parts of the manuscript. A place to start is the title. For instance, the titles of the books *Public Benefits of Archaeology* and *Formation Processes of the Archaeological Record* can be recast into the following questions: What are the public benefits of archaeology? How do formation processes affect the structure and content of the archaeological record? Another important clue is the claim or conclusion. Try asking what issue this claim or conclusion could be a response to. You might also check the references cited section to gauge the interests of the author.

It helps, too, to be aware of the kinds of issues that you will most likely come across when reading archaeology. By grouping these issues into categories according to one set of criteria or another, you become attuned early to the kind of claim that would be appropriate for that question. Here are several questions that have proven useful in identifying different kinds of issues in the critical reading literature.[1]

Is It a "W" Question?

If you actually read the articles in the 2000–2010 issues of *American Antiquity*, it will soon become obvious that the most common kind of question in the archaeological literature is a "W" question—that is, a where, when, what, who, or why question.[2] Where is the Spanish mission site located? When was it occupied? What activities took place there? Who lived in the mission? Why was it abandoned?

Is It a "How to" Question?

Manuscripts are also structured by "how to" questions. Here are a few examples: How can rock art be dated? How can the live weight of fish be determined from fish bones? How can the concept "intensive agriculture" be defined in terms of the things found in an archaeological site?

What Is the Question's "Domain of Inquiry"?

A straightforward criterion for grouping like questions is the domain of inquiry. Perhaps the five most frequently investigated domains of inquiry in archaeology are the archaeological record, the past-in-itself, the relationship between the archaeological record and the past-in-itself, the domain of method, and the domain of meta-questions.

Some questions focus on the archaeological record: Do the proportions of pottery sherds from the Black Bear and Grand Mound sites differ? What natural processes (such as rodent burrowing) might have disturbed this site? Where are the village sites located? These kinds of questions are "internal," so to speak, to the archaeological record and are at home in the archaeological context (lower half) of the research cycle.

Other questions focus on the past-in-itself and are "internal" to that context. They are located in the upper half of the cycle. Here are some examples: What were the postmarital residence rules of these villagers? Did Mississippian chiefdoms trade extensively throughout the Upper Midwest? Did Iron Age peoples cluster periodically at hill forts for defense or to carry out seasonal rituals? These kinds of questions are used to build and enrich theories (narratives or interpretations) about past ways of life in the top half of the research cycle.

Still other questions focus on the interrelationship between the archaeological record and past-in-itself contexts, on methodological questions, and on meta-questions. Examples, in order, are the following: What other evidence in the archaeological record besides house size supports the notion that these villagers were matrilocal (which is a pattern of postmarriage settlement location with the wife's kin)? How can the live weight of fish be determined from their remains in sites? Should archaeologists concentrate on questions of function or on questions of meaning?

Is It a Descriptive, Methodological, or Paradigmatic Question?

The five domains of inquiry can be regrouped into another framework that helps us anticipate the nature of claims and arguments when we read archaeology. Questions about the archaeological record, the past-in-itself, and the relationship between the two are questions about the way the world was in the past. By contrast, questions about how to apply a method

and about theoretical orientations are questions about how to do something (date a deposit, for instance) in the first instance and about the nature
of the archaeological enterprise in the second. The first group involves
descriptive questions and the second methodological and paradigmatic
questions, respectively. Since these three basic kinds of questions require
different kinds of answers, the active reader might ask the following when
reading archaeology: Is the question a descriptive question, a methodological question, or a paradigmatic question?

Is It a Cultural Resource Management Question?

Since a large part of the archaeological literature is written by archaeologists engaged in cultural resource management (CRM), the active reader
should learn to recognize the kinds of questions that are typically asked
in that domain. For example: According to federal criteria, are significant
archaeological materials present?

For the sake of simplicity, this section has assumed that only one issue
runs through an article or book. In actuality, archaeologists often address
multiple issues in their writing, especially in longer articles and in books.
Where this is the case, one issue is usually dominant, while the others are
subsidiary. Nonetheless, the process of identifying these issues, both main
and subsidiary, remains the same as described in this section.

What Is the Claim?

As with issues, similar kinds of claims can be grouped together in informative categories. For instance, many claims are straightforward answers to
"W" and "how to" questions and as such do not involve an argument, if
by "an argument" is meant a course of reasoning aimed at demonstrating
the truth or falsehood of something. Consider the typical claims in an excavation report, which are straightforward answers to this question: What
archaeological materials are present in the site? Although there is an issue in
the sense that uncertainty is involved (before excavation, we do not know
what the contents of the site are), there is no argument. Likewise, the answer to the question "Where are Fox Lake archaeological sites located?"
may simply be a distribution map of known Fox Lake sites. Answers to
"how to" questions (how can we date rock art?) typically resolve an uncertainty by telling us how something is done.

These are interesting and important kinds of questions and answers
in archaeology. Nonetheless, we will focus here on identifying a particular kind of claim, a conclusion, which is the end product of an argu-

ment. As critical readers, we most often focus our energies on evaluating arguments—and, as mentioned in the last section, we cannot properly evaluate arguments unless we can identify the argument's issue and conclusion (along with other parts of an argument that are mentioned in chapters 4 and 5).

So how do we identify conclusions? Although finding the conclusion is usually not straightforward or simple, the following clues have proven useful in this task.[3]

Ask What the Issue Is

Try identifying the issue first, for conclusions are intended to be responses (answers, reactions) to issues. To find the issue, follow the clues mentioned above.

Look for Indicator Words

Conclusions are usually—but not always—announced by expressions like "the most obvious explanation is," "the point I'm trying to make is," "points to the conclusion that," and "it should be clear that." Other examples are "therefore," "suggests that," "proves that," "hence," "it follows that," "indicates that," "we may deduce that," "thus," "consequently," "in short," and "shows that."

Look in Likely Locations

Unlike mystery writers, archaeologists try to be transparent about the story line of an article or book. As a consequence, they tend to tell you what the writing is about in the opening paragraphs of the text and summarize their conclusions at the end.

Remember What a Conclusion Is Not

Many statements in the archaeological literature look like conclusions, but they are not. A commonly encountered example is an opinion, which is an unsupported assertion. Since an opinion lacks the essential components of an argument (as described in chapter 4), it is not a conclusion as I am using that word here. Nor is a conclusion a definition or set of definitions, evidence (data), statistics, examples, or any other kind of background information. As a general practice, critical readers should routinely distinguish between these kinds of statements and the conclusions of arguments when they read archaeology.

Ask the Question "So What?"

Given the principle of charity (see chapter 4), we are obligated at least initially to assume that the author has provided us with pages of information for a purpose. If you think there is an argument and still cannot find the conclusion, ask "So what?" The "what" will most likely be the conclusion.

Thinking Critically about Questions

Since the job of the question that structures a manuscript is to announce the issue or claim that is open to debate, you might assume that the questions you encounter in reading archaeology are clearly and fairly presented. However, that is not always the case. Archaeologists occasionally do make errors in framing their questions. Six of the "framing" (or "not framing") questions are mentioned here to illustrate the sort of thing you should look for. Six (or sixteen) more could easily be added.[4]

The *Baconian error* consists of the idea that an archaeologist can conduct research without any preframed questions in mind. This error follows from the now discredited assumption that "an archaeologist should bring no preconceived ideas to her research—not even questions or working hypotheses." Whether or not one thinks that preconceived questions (issues) should structure research, they always do. Therefore, it is better to make them explicit than to pretend that they do not exist.

The *error of many questions* has been variously defined, but in essence it means framing a question in such a way that two or more questions are actually being asked at once—and a single answer is expected.[5] The classic textbook example is "Have you stopped beating your wife?" The question assumes, of course, that you beat your wife. Let's consider the following questions: What part did climate change play in the successful adaptation of the Natufian culture? Why did the Danubian I people decide to migrate up into northwestern Europe? The first assumes that the adaptation of the Natufian was a successful one, and the second assumes that the Danubians made a conscious decision to migrate into Europe. Besides assuming that the Danubians were migrating rather than expanding gradually outward, the latter question accepts (perhaps unwittingly) the assumption that major movements in the past were the result of the conscious decisions of the people involved in the movement.

The *error of false dichotomous questions* is a special form of the error of many questions. It occurs when a question is constructed in such a manner that it requires a choice between two answers that are in fact neither exclusive nor exhaustive. Consider the titles of these fictitious books: *The*

Cause of the Mayan Collapse: Warfare or Environmental Degradation? and *The Origin of Domestication in the Near East: Diffusion or Environmental Response?* These may be false dichotomies for several reasons. For instance, the dichotomies could have coexisted, and a third or fourth possibility might also have existed.

The *error of the metaphysical question* is an attempt to resolve a nonempirical problem by empirical means. Is the following question testable by empirical means: Was the appearance of anatomically modern *Homo sapiens sapiens* inevitable? The question of inevitability is one that archaeologists can never form any but ambivalent opinions about.

The *error of the semantical question* is an attempt to resolve, by empirical investigation of the archaeological record, what is a semantical question about the agreed-upon definition of a word. There is a conflict here between actual happenings in the past and the verbal description of those happenings. An example is this question: Was the subsistence base of the Oneota agriculture or horticulture? The real dispute may not be whether the Oneota were agriculturalists or horticulturalists in some absolute sense, but what the words "agriculture" and "horticulture" are taken to mean.

The *error of tautological questions* is the framing of questions in such a manner that they are true by definition. Tautological questions cannot be empirically contradicted without self-contradiction. An archaeological example is this question: Did the Hopewell culture have an agricultural base? Since the Hopewell built very large mounds, and some archaeologists have assumed that an agricultural base is necessary for people like the Hopewell to have had the time (the social surplus) to build very large mounds, the Hopewell culture (for these archaeologists) must have had an agricultural base. No appeal to the archaeological record is necessary to answer this question except to note that the Hopewell built very large mounds.

Paying attention to the question being asked is important in critical reading, then, for a question may be imperfectly formulated. This is an important issue, for just how a question is asked determines the kind of answer you can expect.

What Is the Historical Context of the Issue and Claim?

Hard-won experience has taught me the value of placing issues and claims in broader historical and intellectual contexts. When I began reading archaeology as a student, I could read the words in a manuscript, but I often could not make sense of the "unresolved matter" or puzzle that structured it. Does it really make a difference, for instance, whether the ancient Maya were maize agriculturalists or harvesters of wild foods? Can anything be duller than asking if the live weight of fish can be determined by measuring their bones?

Eventually I understood that individual articles and books are parts of dialogues that have been going on for decades, if not for centuries. To understand the "unresolved matter" of articles and books, it clearly helps, then, to understand their broader historical and intellectual contexts. It helps to know, for instance, that the question "Were the ancient Maya maize agriculturists?" is part of a larger debate about the subsistence base of the Maya and about the necessary food-energy requirements of all early civilizations. It helps to know, likewise, that the question "Can the live weight of fish be determined by measuring their bones?" is part of a diverse and long-term effort to develop methods for estimating the importance of animal taxa in past diets by examining the contents of the archaeological record.

Even though a grasp of these historical contexts will not turn a poor argument into a good one, it will help critical readers better understand the significance of the issue and the conclusion of an argument. After all, the aim of critical reading in archaeology is not to score debate points against a poorly developed argument but to more adequately understand the way the world was in the past. To double-stress the point, even though I concentrate on short, isolated readings in this book, it is useful to keep in mind that issues and claims are embedded in broader historical and intellectual contexts. This awareness will broaden your comprehension—and thus your understanding—of what you are reading.

What Is the Argument?   **4**

I N CRITICAL READING, a core strategy for evaluating a claim is to determine whether it is the end result—the conclusion—of an argument.
If the claim is not set in an argument or the argument does not support
the claim, then we as readers should not accept the claim. If the claim is
set in an argument and the argument provides convincing reasons for accepting the claim, then we have grounds for accepting it. This approach
to evaluating claims is especially valuable in archaeology when using the
four quadrants approach, for, as critical readers, our primary concern is
whether a claim (in any quadrant) is well supported—and not with the
metaphysical issue of which approach to archaeology is the correct one
(see chapter 15).

In the critical reading literature, the study of arguments involves three
basic questions: How do we know there is an argument in what we are
reading? Why is it necessary to evaluate arguments? How do we evaluate
an argument? The first section of chapter 4 concentrates on identifying an
argument and its parts and on clarifying its structure, the second section
asks why it is necessary to evaluate arguments, and sections three and four
introduce ways of evaluating an argument. The last section introduces
seven ethical or "good faith" principles that, if adopted, ensure that the
arguments we encounter when we read archaeology are evaluated fairly.[1]

Is There an Argument?

An argument consists of one or more statements that are used to provide
support for a conclusion. The visible statements that provide the support
for a conclusion are called the premises of the argument.[2] The premises are

presented in order to persuade us that the conclusion is true or probably true. For this reason, they are known as the "Why should I believe it?" part of the argument. Let's consider an example:

> [P] Since Iron Age assemblages are above Neolithic assemblages in undisturbed cultural deposits, [C] the Iron Age is more recent than the Neolithic.

The first part of the sentence following "Since" is a premise [P], and the last part of the sentence is the conclusion [C]. Since the conclusion is supported by at least one premise (a reason why we should believe it), the sentence contains an argument.

Most of us (in our naivety) probably assume that determining whether a set of statements contains an argument or not should be easy. But arguments are not always easy to recognize. One reason is that archaeologists do not clearly label their premises and conclusions "premise" and "conclusion." Rather, these parts of an argument are usually hidden in an ocean of prose that can be as small as a paragraph, as large as a section or chapter of a book, or even as large as the entire book.

In other works the argument may be incomplete. Sometimes the premises are not stated but implied, and at times the conclusion is not explicitly mentioned. Sometimes, too, though less often in archaeology than in politics, arguments are deliberately disguised (and slippery) so that it appears there is no conclusion, when there really is. In this latter case, the author is hoping that we will unconsciously accept his conclusion.

Although not exhaustive, you should find the following hints useful in identifying the presence (or absence) of an argument.[3]

First, if what you are reading does not contain at least one conclusion and one premise, then there is not an argument. Archaeologists write for a wide variety of reasons. Therefore, not every reading in archaeology necessarily contains an argument. They may be stating preferences ("I find the Iron Age more interesting than . . ."), providing a descriptive list ("The Rainbow site contains scrapers, flakes, and . . ."), offering a simple definition ("A petroglyph is a type of rock art in which . . ."), stating opinions without the support of reasons ("Never trust an archaeologist over thirty"), giving orders ("Sift the dirt!"), asking simple questions ("Does the Rainbow site date to . . . ?"), and providing an explanation (which is a statement about why something happened rather than a statement about whether the something happened; see chapter 16).[4]

Second, conclusions and premises may be scattered throughout a text, making them difficult to recognize. A useful strategy to adopt in situations like this is to look for words that may indicate the presence of a premise or a conclusion. Called premise and conclusion indicators, they often (but not always) signal that what comes after them is a premise or conclusion. Simple examples of premise indicators are the following: "since . . . ," "whereas . . . ," "seeing that . . . ," "the reasons are . . . ," "for . . . ," "it follows from . . . ," "if . . . ," "as shown by . . . ," "because . . . ," "inasmuch . . . ," "given that . . . ," "as indicated by . . . ," "in view of . . . ," and "this is implied by . . ." (a premise would replace the three dots in an actual argument).

Consider the following example:

> [C] The prehistoric Cree were hunters and gatherers rather than farmers, *for* [P] they lived above the 140-day frost-free growing season, which made growing the domestic plants available at the time difficult if not impossible.

Words whose presence often indicates that a conclusion follows include these examples: "therefore . . . ," "so . . . ," "hence . . . ," "consequently . . . ," "thus . . . ," "shows that . . . ," "indicates that . . . ," "suggests that . . . ," "it follows that . . . ," and "points to the conclusion that . . ."

Third, authors may leave out parts of an argument. It is not uncommon when reading archaeology to encounter incompletely formed arguments. The reason is that the training of archaeologists rarely includes exposure to the fundamentals of critical thinking and writing. As a consequence, they may not think to include a critical premise or may assume (incorrectly) that a premise is part of the background knowledge of people who are likely to read the writing. If that is the case, the premise does not have to be included. In some instances even the conclusion will be omitted. In the following argument, the unstated premise must be "The Malone site is a large agricultural village":

> [P] Only large agricultural villages were occupied year-round, *so* [C] the Malone site was occupied year-round.

Likewise, in the following argument, the unstated conclusion is "The Turtle Bay people have the most powerful weapons":

> [P] All other things being equal, the society with the most powerful weapons will control the best hunting grounds, and [P] the Turtle Bay people control the best hunting grounds.

Following the principle of charity (see the last section of this chapter), when critical readers encounter an incompletely presented argument, they should make a good-faith effort to supply the missing premise or conclusion.

Fourth, statements may serve as both a premise and a conclusion in works that include more than one argument. Here is an example in which a premise of one argument is the conclusion of another in the same text:

> [P] Every investigated Sandy Lake site along the shore of a small lake is a wild rice harvesting station. [P] Since the Schroeder Sandy Lake site is also on the shore of a small lake, [C] it is (most likely) a wild rice harvesting station.

> [P] All investigated Sandy Lake wild rice harvesting stations along the shore of small lakes have a thin, scattered midden. [P] The Schroeder site is a Sandy Lake wild rice harvesting station on the shore of a small lake, so [C] it must have a thin, scattered midden.

Here, the claim that the Schroeder site is a wild rice harvesting site is the conclusion in the first argument but a premise in the second.

Fifth, premises for a conclusion may be independent of each other or dependent, or some combination of independent and dependent. Consider the following two arguments:

> [P] Burning the prairie will increase the browse for buffalo. In addition, [P] doing so will increase the forest edge habitat preferred by deer. Therefore, [C] we should burn the prairie.

> [P] By not burning the prairie, we will not attract buffalo. [P] There are too few buffalo on the prairie. Therefore, [C] we should burn the prairie.

In the first example, the two premises (doing so would increase the browse for buffalo; doing so will increase the preferred forest edge habitat for deer) are independent of each other, since one could be true and the other false (there may be no local forests, for example). In contrast, in the second argument the two premises (not burning the prairie will not attract buffalo; there are too few buffalo on the prairie) are dependent on each other, for if one is not true, then the other cannot support the conclusion either (perhaps there are already plenty of buffalo on the prairie, so even though not burning the prairie will not attract more buffalo, we don't need to do it, because there are already enough buffalo).

Even though these differences are of little consequence to the practical task of evaluating arguments, they are relevant to the strength of the arguments, as we will see in the third section below.

Among the very basic questions you should ask of a piece of writing in archaeology, then, are the following: Is there an argument in the writing, and if so, how many are there? What are the premises and conclusion of each argument? Are parts of the argument omitted? Is the conclusion of one argument a premise in another? Are the premises of the argument independent of each other or dependent on each other, or some combination of independent and dependent?

Why Is It Necessary to Evaluate Arguments?

Not all arguments you will encounter when you read archaeology are good. Some may be poorly formulated and others plain bizarre. For instance, you have probably read somewhere that some people think aliens must have directed the construction of the gigantic Nazca figures in the Andean Mountains of Peru, for the figures are on such a scale that they could only have been built following instructions from hovering aircraft—and since there were no human-made airplanes at the time, they must have been operated by aliens! Most of us would agree that this is a pretty nutty conclusion.

Nonetheless, if we think about it a bit, we would probably agree, too, that there must be many other unacceptable (if less bizarre) arguments in the archaeological literature. In fact, after further thought, we would likely conclude that the arguments produced by archaeologists (like those we hear every day at the local coffee house) must run the scale from really strong to pretty weak. If we can agree on this, then it is an easy step to grasp why we must develop skills that will help us distinguish between acceptable and unacceptable arguments.

Is It a Good Argument?

Even if an argument contains a conclusion and one or more premises in its support, it may or may not be a good argument. It may in fact be a very poor argument that, if uncritically accepted, will fill our head with misinformation. Consequently, critical readers of archaeology must develop a repertoire of skills for evaluating the arguments they encounter when they read archaeology. Through experience, I have found that a straightforward procedure for doing this is to ask two questions: Are the premises reasonable? Do the premises support the conclusion?[5] Familiarity with the dichotomies good-bad, valid-invalid, and strong-weak will help clarify the intent of these questions.

Arguments vary along a spectrum from very good to very bad, depending on the strength of the grounds given in support of the conclusion. But what does "strength of the grounds" mean? In what ways can the grounds given in support of a conclusion vary from very good to very bad? One way is whether the argument is valid, where "a valid argument" means that the conclusion must follow from the premises.[6] This is a useful manner of evaluating an argument, for if the premises are true, then the conclusion must be true, too. Nonetheless, an argument can also be valid but not true. Here's an example:

> [P] Every chiefdom has an intensive agricultural subsistence base and [P] many late prehistoric Northwest Coast archaeological cultures were chiefdoms. So, [C] late prehistoric Northwest Coast chiefdoms had an intensive agricultural subsistence base.

This is a valid argument, for if every chiefdom has an intensive agricultural base and many Northwest Coast archaeological cultures were chiefdoms, then late prehistoric Northwest Coast chiefdoms would also have had an intensive agricultural subsistence base.

Although the argument about these late prehistoric Northwest Coast archaeological cultures is valid—that is, the conclusion does follow from the premises—one of the premises is not true. Not every chiefdom has an intensive agricultural subsistence base, and while many late prehistoric Northwest Coast archaeological cultures were chiefdoms, they did not have an intensive agricultural subsistence base. So the argument, while valid, is undermined by the false premise that every chiefdom has an intensive agricultural subsistence base. Still, the concept of a valid argument remains useful in determining whether an argument is good, for if the premises of the argument are true, then the conclusion must be true, too.

An argument that has both true premises and a valid form is called a sound argument. Consider this example:

> [P] Every chiefdom is a socially ranked society, and [P] Tikopia was a Polynesian chiefdom. Therefore, [C] Tikopia was a socially ranked society.

The argument is sound because it has both a valid form and true premises—and, since the conclusion follows logically from the premises, the conclusion is also true.

Familiarity with these four concepts—valid, invalid, strong, and weak—will help you decide whether an argument is good or bad, or somewhere along the spectrum between good and bad.

However, be warned: An argument that is not sound may still be a useful argument. Consider this example. An archaeologist working in the American Southwest notes that some Pueblo people moved to other areas of the Southwest following a long period of very dry years. She proposes the following argument:

> [P] There was a long period of very dry years in the American Southwest, and [P] some Pueblo people moved to other areas of the Southwest during this period. Therefore, [C] some Pueblo people moved to other areas of the Southwest because of the long period of very dry years.

This argument is neither sound nor valid, because even though the premises are true, the conclusion could still be false. Perhaps the Pueblo people moved because of increased warfare or some other reason other than the long period of very dry years. Nonetheless, even though it is neither sound nor valid, it is still a useful argument. In fact, it is this kind of "what if" thinking that is often encountered in theory building in archaeology.[7]

A Checklist for Evaluating Arguments

As we will see in later chapters, arguments can be evaluated along many dimensions.[8] For starters, however, ask yourself the following questions when evaluating the arguments you encounter in your reading:

Is the Argument Internally Self-Contradictory?

A self-contradictory argument is an argument in which one or more premises contradict the conclusion or each other. Contradictory statements like these cannot both be true. For instance, in the first chapter of a book you are reading the author claims that societies in the region are warlike, yet in another chapter the Nquag people, who also lived in the region, are called peaceful horticulturalists. All societies living in the region cannot be both peaceful horticulturalists and warlike. The book contains contradictory claims. Perhaps there is a reason for this discrepancy. Regardless, the author can still be faulted for the presence of ambiguity in his writing (see chapter 6 for the problem of ambiguity in the evaluation of an argument).

Is the Argument Consistent with
What Is Considered Objective Fact?

If either the premises offered in support of an argument or the conclusion of the argument itself are false, the argument is considered inconsistent with objective fact. An example of the latter would be an argument that begins with information about the disturbing activities of some anthropologists on

Indian reservations and then concludes that all of anthropology is a harmful, exploitative enterprise. The false implication of this position is apparent in that a great deal of our understanding of human culture is the result of the activities of anthropologists. Although the disturbing activities of those anthropologists should be condemned, the conclusion of the argument is not consistent with objective fact.

Are Any Premises False or Unacceptable?

In some arguments the premises given in support of the argument may be simply false, while in others they may be true but unacceptable because the conclusion does not follow from them. In the critical thinking literature, the latter instance is called a non sequitur, for the conclusion does not follow from the premises given in support of it.[9] Stated more tersely, the premises are unconnected to the conclusion. For example, an argument may reach the conclusion that plants were first domesticated at the end of the Pleistocene because of a change in climate. However, even though the premise (the climate changed at the end of the Pleistocene) is true, it may be irrelevant to the conclusion. There is no necessary direct connection between the beginnings of plant domestication and the end of the Pleistocene. People in some areas of the world may have begun domesticating plants thousands of years before or after the end of the Pleistocene.

Is There an Exception to the Generalization?

If there are any exceptions to a generalization, then the generalization is false. As a consequence, the generalization should not be used as a premise or assumption in an argument. For instance, the presence of hunter-gatherer chiefdoms along the early historic Northwest Coast of North America falsifies (or at least weakens) the generalization that "chiefdom societies have agricultural subsistence systems." The generalization as stated should not be used as a premise or assumption in an argument.

Evaluating Arguments Fairly

As critical readers, how do we go about evaluating arguments fairly? After all, we are more intent on learning about the past-in-itself than in scoring debate points. The following seven principles are frequently mentioned in codes of conduct for effective rational discussion and are oriented toward readers.[10]

The Fallibility Principle

A necessary first principle for critical readers of archaeology is the assumption that not all positions on a disputed issue can be true. If there are alternative positions, some must be false. In fact, it is possible that none deserve acceptance, at least as currently worded. Consequently, critical readers always maintain some degree of wariness toward what they read.

The Truth-Seeking Principle

Critical readers are committed to seeking the truth or at least the best available answer to an issue, rather than to the amassing of "one-upmanship" points.

The Principle of Charity

A goal of clear writing is the presentation of arguments free of linguistic confusion and not overly intertwined with other positions and issues (this is the *principle of clarity* for writers). Since this is not always the case, the writer's argument, if unclear, should be reworded as clearly as possible (as you understand it).

The Burden of Proof Principle

The burden of proof rests with the author of the piece you are reading. It is not your fault if you still fail to make sense of an argument after a fair-minded attempt to reformulate it. Don't feel guilty or inadequate, for it is not your burden.

The Resolution Principle

If an argument is both valid and sound, then, according to the resolution principle, you as a reader should consider the issue settled—at least for the moment (see the reconsideration principle below). To ensure that the issue is settled, a good argument also reviews alternative positions on the issue and shows why they should be dismissed or at least are weaker than the argument advanced by the author.

The Suspension of Judgment Principle

Suspend judgment on the issue (or at least on this author's take on the issue) if the claim is not successfully supported.

The Reconsideration Principle

Be willing to reconsider a claim if what appeared to be a good argument for it is found to be flawed (perhaps a critical unstated assumption has been shown to lack merit).[11] According to our code of conduct for effective and positive argumentation, we should always be open to the reconsideration of issues whenever doubts about previously accepted resolutions to the issue have been raised (this principle is intertwined with the fallibility principle discussed above).

While somewhat abstract and dense, chapter 4 provides some insight into what is involved in recognizing and evaluating an argument. I elaborate on this introductory discussion throughout the book.

What Are the Assumptions?   **5**

I N CHAPTER 4 WE LEARNED how to identify a conclusion and the premise or premises that support it when reading archaeology. Although an essential task in outlining an argument, it is not the only task a critical reader must engage in when trying to understand an argument. In the critical thinking literature, an argument is compared to an iceberg, with the conclusion and supporting premise or premises being the visible, above-water part of the iceberg. Hidden below the water is a vast mass of thoughts and evidence that also provides support for the visible parts of the argument. Referred to as (background) assumptions, they often provide clues as to why a premise supports a conclusion.[1] Consider the following brief argument:

> [C] The federal government must increase its commitment to saving our cultural heritage through stricter legislation and increased funding, for [P] more and more archaeological and historic sites are being destroyed each year by construction activities.

The premise appears to support the conclusion: if our cultural heritage is being destroyed at an alarming rate, it makes sense that the federal government should increase its efforts to protect it. At least, that is the assumption. Perhaps surprisingly, your neighbor down the street may believe instead that the federal government should not impinge on the rights and obligations of local communities where local issues are involved. In her view, it is the responsibility of the local community to protect local cultural heritage properties. Therefore, even though the premise in the argument is true, the argument as stated is unconvincing for those people who agree with the unstated assumption that it is not the responsibility of the federal government to protect local cultural heritage properties.

As human beings we grow up in a context of cultural beliefs and world-views. When we form an argument, these ideas are typically not stated and usually do not enter our consciousness. Nonetheless, these ideas are important invisible links in the reasoning process, for they make an argument more (or less) convincing. To fully understand and evaluate an argument, the critical reader must make an effort, then, to recognize these invisible links.

This chapter will help you identify assumptions and understand their role in understanding both arguments and the more general views about the past that characterize schools of archaeology. The first section in chapter 5 reviews types of assumptions and their function in arguments; the second lists clues for locating assumptions; and the third applies these hints to several examples. The fourth and final section introduces the notion of a research program. In archaeology, as in other systems of thought, sets of assumptions reoccur from one argument to another. It is these sets of assumptions or schools of thought that I refer to as a research program, for they are programs (or agendas or blueprints) for doing archaeology.

Types of Assumptions and Their Function in Arguments

To summarize the point made above, whether a conclusion is supported by the visible premises given in its support depends upon the reasonable-ness of the connection between the two parts of the argument. In reading archaeology you may wonder at times what the logical connection between a premise and a conclusion is. Perhaps the connection isn't obvious or just doesn't make sense to you. It is the supporting cast of assumptions that provides relevance to—that makes sense of—the structure of an argument. Phrased more tersely, all arguments require assumptions.

Granted. But this understanding leaves critical readers with two additional tasks: to identify key supporting but implicit assumptions and to evaluate the relevance of their support to the argument. If you are satisfied that the linkage seems reasonable, then the premise provides logical support for the conclusion. If you are not satisfied (as in the example in the first paragraph of this chapter), then you reject the linkage between premise and conclusion. Note that in the latter case, while you reject the argument as given, you should suspend judgment on the conclusion. The reason: you have not been given convincing enough evidence to either support or reject the conclusion as stated.

In archaeology, assumptions are generally rooted in an archaeologist's vision of proper procedure and of what is considered worth doing when doing archaeology, and in her understanding of the nature of the sociocultural and natural world around her—that is, in notions about methodology, value, and reality. Some assumptions concern the nature of being human or the fundamental structure of human societies and the natural world. The following four statements are examples of this type of reality assumption: people act more or less rationally (the assumption of rationality); social facts must be explained in social terms; the laws of the natural world remain constant; and culture is a hodgepodge of disparate and unrelated traits.

Other assumptions are methodological in that they are concerned with proper procedure in the research process. The following four statements are examples of this type of assumption: fact collecting in itself is insufficient scientific procedure; when accounting for phenomena, do not multiply entities beyond necessity (Occam's razor); theoretical statements should be capable of falsification; and the history of anything constitutes a sufficient explanation of it.

Some underlying assumptions in archaeology are so basic that they are rarely debated or even thought about. Many archaeologists and readers would assume that they are self-evident truths about the world rather than tacit beliefs that they have unconsciously adopted. Examples are "The study of history matters" and "The past is knowable." Consider the root assumption "Social relics exist." This assumption refers to the belief that artifacts and features retain social and cultural information about past ways of life—and the fact that they do makes an understanding of the past through the medium of archaeology possible. If they did not, then understanding the past through its material remains would be an impossible task.

Three other root assumptions that are widely shared and rarely debated in archaeology are as follows: material culture, the physical, human-made remains surviving from the past, can be used as evidence about the past; the processes at work in the past were the same as those in operation at the present (the principle of uniformitarianism); and people did things in the past for the same reasons they do things today.

Still other assumptions once widely held within the archaeological community—such as "The patterning of material remains in an archaeological site is a direct reflection of the patterned behavior of the members of extinct societies"—have been vigorously challenged within the discipline itself (the challenge is based upon the likely action of natural and cultural formation processes that result in a disjunction between the two kinds of pattern).

To repeat, a reality assumption is a belief (again, often unstated) about how the world is, or was, or will become. While value and methodological assumptions are needed in order to link premises to conclusions, reality assumptions are necessary for a premise to be true. We will return to this difference later in the book when we discuss the evaluation of arguments.

Hints for Locating Assumptions

Finding the invisible assumptions that illuminate an argument is more often than not a difficult task that requires imagination, hard work, and, in archaeology, a great deal of background information. Nonetheless, it is an essential task in reading archaeology, for determining the strengths and weaknesses of a visible argument will depend in many instances on understanding these hidden assumptions. The following hints, which are adapted from Browne and Keeley's *Asking the Right Questions: A Guide to Critical Thinking*, will prove helpful in your search for assumptions when you read archaeology.

Look for Ideas That Support Premises

In our reading we can often think of one or more assumptions that we believe support the link between a premise and a conclusion. Since we take these assumptions for granted or at least think they are reasonable, we accept that the premise supports the conclusion. The following argument illustrates such a case:

> [C] The federal government must increase the money it spends each year on saving historical properties. [P] Too many historical properties are lost each year because sufficient effort to save them is not being made.

Here it is being assumed that (A1) it is the responsibility of the federal government to save historical properties, and (A2) increased funding, if dedicated to reducing the number of historic properties that are lost each year, will be effective in attaining that goal (since most U.S. antiquities laws lack enforcement "teeth," money spent on increased education may have little impact on the annual rate of destruction).

If we accept both assumptions, we have confidence in the link between the premise and the conclusion. In this case we are relying on our own background, taken-for-granted assumptions in supporting the link.

Identify with the Writer

Another approach is to look at the argument from the point of view of the author. What was the author's thought process? In this case you might ask:

What would the writer have had to take for granted to link the premise and conclusion? You might also look into the writer's background and read the titles of her other articles. You can also ask what assumptions a person with the interests and background of the writer is likely to make.

Identify with the Opposition

Try reversing roles. Ask yourself what kind of assumptions people who reject the argument might make. Understanding these assumptions will give you a fresh perspective on the assumptions that supporters of the argument make.

Learn More about the Issues

In many instances in our reading, we will not be familiar enough with an issue to determine what assumptions a writer might have made. In cases like this we are better off learning more about the issue before we begin evaluating the truthfulness of the argument.

Avoid Wasting Time on Trivial Assumptions

Archaeologists generally agree that a line must be drawn somewhere in constructing arguments between trivial and important assumptions; otherwise arguments can become unwieldy and lack closure. For instance, they are likely to assume in their reading that an author believes that his premises are true, and that the premises and conclusion are logically related (that the author is not intentionally trying to trick us with a false argument). Likewise, it is a pretty good bet that archaeologists assume that the past existed and that the world (and all our memories) was not created by a mischievous imp only five minutes ago.

Look in the Right Places

There are two places to start looking for critical assumptions that underlie and support arguments. The first is for those unstated thoughts and evidence in the underwater portion of the iceberg that lend support to the truthfulness of the visible premises. The second is for those unstated thoughts and evidence that link premises to the conclusion (these are called linkage assumptions).

Look for Patterns in the Arguments of Archaeologists

It is also helpful to be able to recognize patterns in the arguments of archaeologists. Many arguments in archaeology share similar assumptions, because the writers are adherents of one school of archaeology or another. By learning about these schools of archaeology (what are called research programs in the last section of this chapter), you attune yourself to common, shared sets of assumptions.

Avoid Mistaking Incompletely Established Premises for Assumptions

A problem that critical readers will encounter when they read archaeology is the confusion in poorly constructed arguments between assumptions and inadequately supported premises. Since the premise lacks adequate support, it can be mistaken for an assumption. Rather than an assumption, you have most likely come across an argument whose premises need more robust support. Consider the following example in which a poorly established premise is mistaken for an assumption:

> [Somewhere in an article is the statement] Professors are so busy doing research that they do not have time to teach well. [Elsewhere in the article] The pressure on professors to publish has resulted in poorly trained students.

In outlining the structure of the argument, you identify as an assumption the belief that "pressure on professors to publish really does result in poor teaching." In actuality, you have identified a premise ("Professors are so busy doing research that they do not have time to teach well") that has been incompletely established.

Research Programs: An Introduction

When archaeologists take a position on a methodological issue, they are preferring one way of doing archaeology to another.[2] Stated another way, they are displaying methodological priorities based on value and reality assumptions. The rest of this chapter is devoted to increasing your awareness of the role played by methodological conflicts and priorities within archaeology in determining archaeologists' opinions and conclusions. This awareness will help you better understand what you are reading.

Although reality, value, and methodological assumptions are isolated separately when analyzing arguments, they most often occur in recurring clusters in the thought structure of archaeologists. An archaeologist who believes, for instance, that "culture is meaningfully constituted" is more likely to also believe that "the relationship between material culture and human organization is dependent in part on a set of cultural attitudes that cannot be predicted from or reduced to an environment" than an archaeologist who believes that "cultures are systems of thought whose primary function is to adapt people to their surroundings." In archaeology these clusters of assumptions form schools of thought that have been given names like cultural historical archaeology, processual archaeology, and postprocessual archaeology. Following the lead of philosopher of science Imre Lakatos, I call these clusters of assumptions research programs, for they provide a program of research (that is, a procedure for solving a problem, including the conceptualization of the problem, data collection and processing, and presentation of results), as we will see below and throughout the remainder of the book.

Since the underlying assumptions of research programs differ, archaeologists who adopt different programs will necessarily differ in what research questions they ask, in the procedures they follow, in what are considered acceptable solutions to research puzzles, and in what they think an acceptable product of the research, such as an article or the structure of an argument, should look like. Methodology is the logic of working within and developing a research program. Methodological debate is about the appropriateness of various methods, techniques, and goals in this process. Understanding how research programs affect the arguments archaeologists construct is an essential task in learning to read archaeology critically.

The foundational assumptions of research programs have a significant impact on the research process itself, for they result in admonitions about what are acceptable procedures, arguments, and results and what are not. These admonitions are methodological rules that direct archaeologists to proceed in one way and not in another. Examples are "Focus on the subsistence adaptation of an archaeological culture" and "Gather facts without any preconception of what they may mean." Methodological rules are simply methodological assumptions and other kinds of assumptions rephrased as declarative sentences. For instance, the methodological principle "Knowledge evolves through the amassing of facts" implies the methodological rule "Amass facts!"

Here are four additional examples of methodological rules: "State everything as clearly as possible," "Search for regularities and causalities," "Build systems rather than make detailed studies of particulars," and "Do not use analogies as a source of proof."

The clusters of assumptions and rules that form schools of thought in archaeology form the broad intellectual context within which research is carried out and within which arguments are formulated. A part of understanding what an archaeologist is "up to," then, involves not only being able to identify the assumptions that support an argument but also being familiar with these broad intellectual contexts—the research programs—within which the argument is formulated.

As stressed throughout this chapter, identifying the assumptions that lie behind what you are reading is not always an easy, straightforward process. The same is true for "excavating" out the rules that governed the procedures that an archaeologist followed as she conducted her research. Likewise, there is often confusion between assumptions, which are metaphysical entities that are not true or false (but preferred or not preferred), and hypotheses, which are in principle true or false.

Transforming Methodological Assumptions into Methodological Rules

Assumptions are transformed into methodological rules by making them declarative statements. Here are three examples: "Culture is meaningfully constituted" becomes "Read cultural meanings"; "The relationship between material culture and human organization is dependent in part on a set of cultural attitudes that cannot be predicted from or reduced to an environment" becomes "Identify that part of the relationship between material culture and human organization that is dependent on cultural attitudes"; "Cultural relationships are not caused by anything else outside themselves (they just are)" becomes "Assume that cultural relationships are not caused by anything else outside themselves."

As with assumptions, recognizing and understanding methodological rules are not always straightforward tasks. Since they are often implied or implicit in the literature, the reader has to work at formulating and reformulating them to capture the intent of the author.

Distinguishing between Assumptions and Hypotheses

The difference between methodological and value assumptions, which are metaphysical and not subject in principle to scientific verification, and hypotheses, which in principle are, is not always clear. Rather than a sharp gradient between these two kinds of statement, they tend to grade into one another. The following paragraph from Ian Hodder's *Reading the Past* is packed with hypotheses.

> For example, it had earlier been suggested that the stylistic similarity between objects increased as interaction between people increased. In fact, at the borders between ethnic groups in Baringo, the more interaction between people, the less the stylistic similarity. But, again, such findings

can be incorporated within New Archaeology because it is possible to generalize and state the "law" that material culture distinctiveness is correlated with the degree of negative reciprocity between groups. So the more competition between groups the more marked the material culture boundaries between them.

In this study, the opposing hypotheses, "At the borders between ethnic groups in Baringo, the stylistic similarity between objects increased as interaction between people increased" and "At the borders between ethnic groups in Baringo, the more interaction between people, the less the stylistic similarity," were evaluated by field research and the latter hypothesis supported. From this study, one could go on and state the following regularity: the more competition between groups, the more marked the material culture boundaries between them. Unlike a metaphysical statement, this is a testable proposition about the nature of the world and the relationships of the things in it.

It is useful to think of schools of archaeology as research programs, programs for research that are founded on a core of essentially unchallenged (at least within the program) methodological, value, and reality assumptions. The research programs archaeologists adopt are thus theoretical-methodological stances—stances that inevitably influence the theoretical and operational definitions of basic concepts, problem orientations, and other aspects of the archaeological enterprise. However, research programs in archaeology are not equivalent to well-thought-out paradigms in physics and other natural sciences for a number of reasons. First, archaeology is characterized by multiple research programs rather than a single, accepted research program (paradigm). Second, research programs in archaeology tend to be so loosely developed conceptually that they include logical inconsistencies. And third, archaeologists tend to merge elements of different research programs in their research projects, even if the methodological principles of these different research programs are logically incompatible. Chapter 15 lays out in more detail the focus and assumptions of four of the main research programs in archaeology.

In chapters 3, 4, and 5, I have concentrated on the visible and invisible structure of an argument. The next three chapters introduce some of the many problems in writing and reasoning that can mask or distort an argument. Recognizing and dealing with these problems are further tasks for the critical reader.

Is the Writing Clear?   **6**

C HAPTERS 3, 4, AND 5 of this book introduce the fundamentals—the visible and invisible structural components—of an argument. By now, you should be able to identify an archaeologist's
conclusion, premises, and (at least some) assumptions. These are necessary
skills in evaluating what you read when you read archaeology critically. In
this chapter I focus on the details of the language used in an argument. If
you do not understand the intended meaning of a writer's argument, you
may misunderstand what you are deciding to accept or believe when you
evaluate the argument. In many instances this means examining the exact
meaning of key words and phrases in an article or book.

Consider the following example:

> Some Midwest archaeologists have maintained that the northern expansion
> of late prehistoric agricultural societies halted at the 120-degree frost-free
> season isotherm, because corn and other domesticated crops at the time
> required at least this many frost-free days to produce a useable crop. Pro-
> fessor Smith has challenged this conclusion, for he has found corn and a
> hoe on a site in Manitoba above this line.

The force of this argument rests on the meaning of "agricultural society," for this term has different possible meanings. For some archaeologists,
it refers to a society that relied for much of its food supply on domesticated
plants or animals, or both; for others, it merely means that the members
of a society planted gardens and grew some domesticated plants. Perhaps
Professor Smith is using this second meaning of agricultural society, and
those whose conclusion he opposes are using the first. If so, then they are
not talking about the same kind of society. How can you evaluate this

argument unless you know how key terms like "agricultural society" are being used? This example illustrates an important point: while the meaning of key terms and phrases may seem obvious, it often is not.[1]

When you cannot figure out what a writer is claiming or arguing, any number of concerns may be causing the problem. Examples are an unorganized and unfocused writing style, ill-defined terms, poorly chosen words (that is, incorrect usage), unintended ambiguity, vagueness, and poorly crafted comparisons. This chapter examines these problems as they apply to the evaluation of an argument.

Organization and Style

Some arguments in archaeology are difficult to understand because the text within which they appear is jumbled and difficult to follow. A good piece of writing, then, should at the very least be well organized. Among the characteristics of good organization that you should look for—especially during a first reading—are an introductory statement of intent that makes it clear at the outset what the issue is and what the author's claim about that issue will be; a focus on the issue and claim throughout the essay, either in the form of the development of an argument supporting the claim or in the development of responses to possible objections to that claim and argument; a well-thought-out and understandable sequence of development of the argument, once the issue and claim are clearly stated; and completeness (that is, the presence of all of the structural components of the argument or position).

Experienced critical readers ask as a matter of routine questions such as the following: Does the author stick to the issue or does he spiral off into irrelevancies (as far as the issue is concerned)? Are points made before they are clarified? Are thoughts expressed completely throughout the argument, or are some thoughts left dangling? Most basically, if you cannot outline what you are reading with ease, the author has not properly sequenced his material.

The critical reader is also alert to the presence of violations of good style, for the presence of these violations may make an argument difficult to identify, understand, and evaluate. Common examples are the use of clichés, the failure to be specific, the use of excessive jargon, inappropriate generalization, use of the passive voice, and unwarranted exaggeration.

Ambiguous Words and Phrases

As indicated in the last section, a well-organized argument must also be written clearly. So after asking "Is the argument well organized?" you must ask "Is the writing clear?" Said more forcefully, from a reader's perspective, before you accept what someone else writes, you must clearly understand what the argument is. Consider this familiar example in the critical thinking literature as altered to fit a focus on archaeology:

> When I worked as an archaeologist in the forest service, I was told that many good men and women wore the uniform that was issued to me.

Does the writer really mean that many good men and women wore *the* uniform that was issued to her?

If more than one meaning can be assigned to a claim and you cannot decide which meaning was intended in what you are reading, then the claim is ambiguous. There are a number of reasons why you may find a word or phrase ambiguous. For instance, a word or phrase may be ambiguous because of the ambiguity of the word or phrase itself. The word "culture," with its dozens of different meanings, is an example. A conclusion or a reason may also be ambiguous because of the structure of a sentence. Consider the sentence "They were excavating the site next to me." Were they excavating the same site as you (and next to you) or were they excavating the next site over?

Let's begin by identifying several different kinds of ambiguity with the idea that if you know what you are looking for, it is easier to find. We will then list several ways you can spot ambiguities and end by asking "Once you have spotted an ambiguity, what should you do about it?"

The Natural Plasticity of Words

We have already mentioned that individual words themselves may be ambiguous. Let's look at this source of ambiguity in more detail. As a glance through a dictionary will confirm, many words have multiple definitions. Take the word "point," which seems like an innocent enough word. However, according to *Webster's New College Dictionary*, it can mean "a sharp or tapered end," "something that has a sharp or tapered end," "a mark formed by the sharp end of something," "a decimal point," "a crucial situation," "a purpose, goal, advantage, or reason," "a significant or outstanding idea," or "a separate or individual item," among other meanings. This flexibility is true as well of many words used by archaeologists. Consider the multiple meanings of such words as "culture," "society," "artifact," and "archaeological culture." In their classic review of the meanings of the word "culture," Albert Kroeber and Clyde Kluckhohn identified dozens of different definitions of this word.[2]

Since archaeologists seldom define their terms (but take the meaning for granted), these multiple meanings can create problems in determining the worth of an argument. In the earlier argument about the northern limits of agricultural societies in the late prehistoric Midwest, it is easy to find the conclusion and the supporting premises. Nonetheless, the quality of the reasoning is difficult to judge because of the ambiguous use of the expression "agricultural society." Thus, even when you can identify the fundamental components of an argument, you may still have to grapple with the meaning of key words in that structure. A warning, then: Because of the natural plasticity of words, do not assume that you and the author whose work you are reading share the same meaning of words and expressions.

Grouping Ambiguity

Grouping ambiguity occurs when an author refers to a collection of items without clearly specifying whether the reference is to the collection as a group or to the items as individual items. Consider the sentence "Blackduck pottery weighs more than Sandy Lake pottery." Is this claim true or false? We really can't say, for we don't know what the claim is—and that is because we don't know what "Blackduck pottery" and "Sandy Lake pottery" refer to. Is the claim that all of the Blackduck pottery in the museum's collections weighs more en masse than does all of the Sandy Lake pottery in the collections—or that as a rule individual Blackduck sherds or pots weight more than individual Sandy Lake sherds or pots?

The Fallacies of Composition and Division

Another common problem that can lead to a misunderstanding of an argument is confusion over the relation of parts and wholes.[3] Can we assume that what is true of the parts is necessarily true of the whole? To make this assumption is to commit the fallacy of composition ("from each to all"). Here is an example of this fallacy:

> The agency [your choice] doesn't spend much money on salaries for heritage preservation specialists. After all, who ever heard of anyone getting rich in the agency? (In other words, the agency doesn't spend that much money on heritage preservation specialists *individually*; therefore, it doesn't spend much on them as a *group*.)

The fallacy of division is the reverse of this situation. In this fallacy we assume that what is true of a whole is necessarily true of its parts as well. Here is an example:

The Department of Archaeology at the University of Wiswell has an outstanding international reputation; therefore, Professor Capaldi, who is on the faculty of the department, must have an outstanding international reputation.

Spotting Ambiguities

To review: a word or phrase is ambiguous when its meaning is so uncertain in the context of the argument that you are reading that you need further clarification before you can judge the adequacy of the reasoning. Given this definition, how can you spot ambiguities? The following hints will get you started.[4]

Consciously Search for Ambiguities

The first hint is obvious: whenever you read archaeology, make it a habit to consciously search for ambiguity. Passive readers are more likely than not to assume that they understand what the author means by a word, phrase, or claim, but that is an error in reading. Unless you deliberately search for ambiguity, you may be missing the author's point.

Consider Alternative Meanings

Here is a test for identifying an unclear term: substitute two or more alternative meanings for the term into the reasoning structure and note whether it has an effect on the meaning and strength of the argument. For example, an alternative meaning of a term in a premise may affect the strength of the support of the premise for the conclusion. If the extent to which a reason would support a conclusion is affected by which meaning is assumed, then you have located a significant ambiguity. You can safely conclude that the reasoning needs more work before you can decide whether to agree with it.

Look at the Context

Another tactic for determining the meaning of a term or phrase is to look at the context within which it occurs. Here the word "context" is defined quite broadly. It may refer to traditional uses of the term or phrase within that particular issue in archaeology, to how the word or phrase tends to be used within the research program that the writer appears to be associated with, to the apparent meaning of other words and phrases in the reading in which you encounter the ambiguity, and to other articles and books written by the author.

Look at the Issue

The issue that is the focus of something you are reading can also provide clues to the possible meaning of key terms, for archaeologists working in different research programs frequently concentrate on different issues. Processual archaeologists, for example, are commonly interested in how human societies at different levels of sociocultural complexity adapt to their natural environment. This focus is apparent in their definition of the word "culture" as "human beings' mode of adaptation to the natural environment." If the issue involves the investigation of a human society's adaptation to its natural environment and the writer is a processualist, then check to see whether this meaning of the word "culture" is being used too.

Look at the Conclusion and the Premises

You do not have to concern yourself with all ambiguities in what you are reading, of course. As a critical reader, only the ambiguity in the reasoning is crucial. Focus your search for ambiguities, then, on the key terms and phrases in the reasoning structure—and resist the temptation to grapple with the unclear meaning of any and all words or phrases in what you are reading. Experience shows that the latter is generally a waste of mental effort.

Focus on Abstract Words and Phrases

As a rule, abstract words and phrases tend to have multiple meanings—and the more abstract they are, the greater the variety of associated meanings. Here the term "abstract" refers to meanings that are more conceptual or theoretical and less tangible or concrete. It is in this sense that "artifact," "archaeological culture," and "aggression" are more abstract than "Clovis projectile point," "Sandy Lake culture," and "doing deliberate physical harm to another person." Since words and phrases like "Clovis projectile point" and "Sandy Lake culture" are more concrete than "artifact" and "archaeological culture," they tend to be less ambiguous when encountered in your reading.

Reverse Role-Play

Another interesting method of detecting words and phrases that may be ambiguous is to deliberately take a position on what an author is writing about from the perspective of another research program. In the critical thinking literature, this method of spotting ambiguities in its many guises is called reverse role-playing. Take the word "adaptation." An archaeologist who believes that the natural environment is an active agent in culture change is likely to define adaptation quite differently from someone who regards the environment as a passive backdrop to the play of human emotions and intentions. Is the intent of the use of the term clear in what you are reading? If not, you have identified a possible ambiguity.

Use Common Sense

Finally, if all else fails, try common sense. It may occasionally indicate which of two possible meanings is intended. If you see the story caption "Enraged Cow Injures Archaeologist with Shovel," it is safe to assume that "Shovel" refers to something held by the archaeologist rather than the cow.

Clarifying Ambiguity

Learning to identify ambiguities in what you are reading is only a first step in understanding what you are reading. As an active reader, you must also make an attempt to clarify the ambiguities you encounter in your reading when you read archaeology. In this process it helps to be aware of obstacles that get in the way of clarifying the ambiguities you encounter.

A frequent obstacle to understanding an argument in archaeology is the assumption that you and the author share the meaning of key words and phrases, perhaps because the argument is written in English and you have encountered the words and phrases before in the archaeological literature. On the contrary, since most words have multiple meanings, it is better to begin your examination of an argument by assuming that you do not share meanings until proven otherwise. Instead of "mind reading," train yourself to ask "How can I determine what she means by that?"

Another obstacle is the assumption that terms and phrases have only a limited number of meanings. Since different disciplines and research programs often give words different meanings, it is wiser to ask "Am I aware of the range of meanings of this term, at least within archaeology?"

It also helps to be aware of the strengths and weaknesses of dictionary definitions when checking the possible meanings of words. A good dictionary generally illuminates the meaning of a term by providing a list of synonyms, a few examples, and what are known as "definitions by specific criteria." Consider the word "adapt":

1. To adapt is to adjust (synonym).
2. To adapt is to adjust to fit new or different conditions, such as changes in a society in adjustment to a severe drought (example).

3. To adapt is the modification of something or its parts that makes it more fit for existence under the conditions of its current environment (specific criteria).

If you are unfamiliar with a term, associating it with a more familiar term (a synonym) or hearing it used in an example can be very helpful. In other cases terms are inadequate, for they fail to tell you the specific properties that are crucial for an unambiguous understanding. If you are already familiar with a term, the most useful definition will be the one that specifies criteria for usage—and the more specific, the better. Chapter 19 looks at the adequacy of definitions in archaeology from another perspective.

Before moving on to the next point, the obvious should be repeated: in many instances you will not find any of the definitions in a dictionary helpful (if it even lists the word), for, as stressed above, archaeologists, like the members of other professions, tend to give even everyday terms—like "culture"—special meanings.

Finally, it is important to determine, if possible, whether the ambiguities you discover are intended, for the presence of ambiguity is not always an accident or mistake. Some writers intentionally try to persuade you to adopt a position by playing on the strong emotions that surround certain words and phrases such as "justice," "burial," "doing what is right," and "acting ethically." Phrases such as "doing what is right" and "acting ethically" have multiple meanings, and some of those meanings are loaded with emotion. After all, who wants to do what is not right or to act unethically? At least some of these writers will try to bully you into accepting their position by playing on these emotions (by tugging on your heart, so to speak). A wary eye on words and phrases that tug at your emotions will often expose this kind of duplicity.

In summary, learning to ask "Which words or phrases are ambiguous?" "What could the author have intended?" and "What did the author mean?" gives you a fair-minded procedure for understanding an author's argument as far as ambiguity is concerned.

Vague Claims and Puzzling Comparisons

The presence of ambiguous terms and phrases in what you are reading when you read archaeology is not the only or even the most common obstacle to clearly understanding what you are reading. In contrast to an ambiguity, which is distinguished by the presence of two or more possible meanings, the meaning of a vague claim is hazy or unclear.[5] In archaeology, claims generally vary in degree of vagueness. As a consequence, you should be aware of the implications of the degrees of vagueness included in what you are reading. Consider the following examples: "The site is old" is vaguer than "The site is at least 700 years old," and "The site is at least 700 years old" is vaguer than "The site is 850 years old."

Note that there is nothing wrong with the presence of vagueness in some contexts, for greater precision may be unnecessary. For example, if you are trying to determine whether a site is too recent to be eligible for nomination to the National Register of Historic Places, the statement "The site is old enough" is less precise than possible, but it is not less precise than is desirable for your purpose. But if you are trying to nominate the site based in part on its great age (say, "more than 10,000 years old"), the same statement is not precise enough.

Claims that make comparisons like the following can be puzzling too.

"More thoroughly efficient" (field techniques)
"More than 20 percent greater" (number of field projects)
"More user-friendly by far" (a new computer program)
"More comprehensive than ever" (a journal)

Presented as isolated phrases, we are left asking what the "by fars," "greater thans," and so on mean. More thoroughly than what? Twenty percent larger than what? More user-friendly by far than what? Since the amount of vagueness you can ignore in a comparative claim depends on its importance within the structure of an argument, it is important to ask probing questions about comparisons like these. Here are some examples:

Is the Amount of Vagueness in the Comparison Tolerable?
Knowing that the agency funds more than 20 percent more field projects now than it did five years ago may be all it takes for you to understand the increase in the agency's funding during the last five years.

Does the Comparison Omit Important Information?
An angry recent letter to the editor of a major newspaper claims that funding for the office of the state archaeologist is out of control, for its funding has increased more than 20 percent in the last five years. The implication is that the state archaeologist has been inefficient and is wasting taxpayer money. In her reply, the state archaeologist points out that while her workload has increased by 30 percent, she has efficiently managed that

increase with only a 20 percent increase in funds. In that case, she seems to be doing her job in an exemplary manner. The first writer failed to mention this important information in his letter.

Are the Comparisons Being Used Based on Equivalent Information and Reporting Practices?

Be alert to the presence of this source of misleading comparison. In the last example, part of the funding increase may have been to cover inflation; perhaps that apparent 30 percent increase in workload is simply due to a change in the way workload is calculated. In comparing the samples of animal bone from two different archaeological sites, a report might fail to mention that water flotation was used to retrieve bone from one site but not the other. How valuable, then, is this comparison?

Are Unlike Things Being Compared?

The unwary reader may assume that what is being compared in an article is legitimately comparable when it is not. Consider this example: A comparison between the subsistence practices of Middle Archaic societies and those of Late Woodland Blackduck people may be deceiving, for the comparison is between an archaeological tradition and an archaeological culture. What you really need to know is the annual subsistence practices of (say) a typical Middle Archaic residential group and a typical Blackduck residential group—and that may be difficult to determine because of the vagueness and ambiguity of the terms "typical" and "society."

Is Sufficient Information Included to Assess Comparisons between Averages?

An important example in archaeology is the comparison of the average amount of rain that falls each year in different regions, since the annual amount of rainfall a region receives affects the prehistoric agricultural potential of that region. Nonetheless, as important as the amount of rain that falls each year is when it falls. In making comparisons like this, it is important to remember to ask just when during the year the rain falls. Likewise, to say that the average number of potsherds found on Friedman culture sites is seventy-two masks the fact that the actual number of sherds found ranges from three to two hundred—a fact that may point to important differences among these sites. It is important to remember, then, that by their very nature averages omit details that could be significant to an argument—and that there are different kinds of averages, as we will see in chapter 11. As a general rule, be insistent in asking questions about comparisons between averages. For instance, is sufficient information provided to assess the value of the comparison?

Unfamiliar Words and Phrases

In archaeology, it is not unusual to encounter words and phrases that are unclear, not because they are vague or ambiguous, but because they are unfamiliar. Unless you have some experience reading archaeology, what are you to make of terms like "half-life," "phytolith," "archaeological culture," "transformation process," and "thick description"? As you may have already found out, discovering the meaning of these terms is not always easy. Because they are specialized terms ("half-life," "phytolith," "Z-twist," "unidirectional core," and "Mohs scale") or ordinary terms ("culture," "isolate," "element," "feature," and "flake") used in special ways, you are unlikely to find useful definitions in your dictionary. Sources of useful definitions include glossaries in textbooks, knowledgeable experts, and occasionally the context of the term or phrase.

Part of becoming an accomplished reader in archaeology is becoming familiar with the specialized terms used in the field. I usually circle words or phrases whose meaning I am unfamiliar with in pencil (or write them in a notebook, if I'm reading a library book). When I have the time, I look them up and write out their definition. Until you are familiar with how these terms and phrases are generally used in archaeology, you may find it difficult to distinguish between ambiguous terms and unfamiliar ones.

This chapter has focused on four important skills in judging the clarity of the arguments you will encounter when reading archaeology. These are the ability to identify the key terms and phrases in an argument; establish whether the meaning of these key terms or phrases is clear; determine whether an alternative definition, if substituted into the argument, significantly changes the meaning or strength of the argument; and decide where, if present, ambiguity still remains within the structure of the argument.

What are your options if you are still uncertain about the meaning of a key term or phrase after going through this process? An increasingly feasible possibility today is to contact the writer through e-mail and ask her what she meant. If this is not possible (the writer has died, say) or you get no response, it is better to suspend judgment about the soundness of claims associated with ambiguous or vague statements than to accept them too readily. As a critical reader who accepts the principle of charity in assessing arguments, you are committed to try to clarify that uncertainty, but not to read minds! This does not mean, of course, that when a reason is unclear you should completely disregard the entire argument itself. Other reasons offered by the writer may be sufficient to support the conclusion of the argument. It does mean, however, that the argument must be evaluated without reference to those reasons that remain unclear.

Are (Deceptive) Rhetorical   7
Devices Used?

WRITERS CAN ALSO INFLUENCE readers through the use of rhetorical gimmickry or "spin." When we read archaeology, we assume (perhaps naively) that the writer is relating in an objective manner the conclusion of her research or the point of an article. But can we be sure? Is the archaeologist whose book is being reviewed in a major journal *self-assured* or *arrogant*? Were the New Archaeologists of the 1960s *passionately devoted* to improving archaeology or *fanatical*? Since words like "self-assured" and "arrogant," and "passionately devoted" and "fanatical," have different emotive force, our evaluation of what we read when we read archaeology may be manipulated.

Rhetoric, then, involves using words or phrases to give a statement a positive or negative spin. Since rhetoric is often used as a substitute for an argument—or at least a sound argument—it is natural to discount arguments that contain obvious spin. But that is a mistake. The use of rhetorically charged language often improves the readability of what may otherwise be a very dry argument. Of course, the danger lies in accepting or rejecting an argument solely on the basis of the rhetorical gimmickry used in its presentation.

Critical readers should, then, be familiar with the most common rhetorical techniques.[1] Because the intent of their use is to give what we read a negative or positive slant, the techniques are commonly called slanters.

Euphemisms and Dysphemisms

It is a fairly common and understandable practice for writers to attempt to affect readers' opinions by using the flexibility of language. By substituting one word for another, the content of a sentence can be given a positive or negative slant. A euphemism gives a positive slant to something that has negative connotations or is overly harsh.[2] A rather dim student is now "a few sandwiches short of a picnic," my bald colleague is "a little thin on the top," and our fired assistant state archaeologist was "downsized." Voters are more likely to support additional funding for "heritage preservation" than they are for "site survey in construction zones." A training track in a department of anthropology had the same curriculum when called "a training track for professional archaeologists" as it does now under the name "a training track for public archaeology." The current name is more likely to attract outside funds for development than is the old name, which suggests a fascinating but perhaps frivolous career choice.

A dysphemism has roughly the opposite intent of a euphemism. Rather than a positive slant, the use of a dysphemism gives a statement an intentionally negative or harsh slant. Whereas "public archaeologist" is a euphemism for one kind of archaeologist, "pot hunter" is a dysphemism for another kind. While dysphemisms are intentionally used to give something a negative slant, the use of euphemisms is more varied. For instance, a wise writer will avoid the use of terms that some readers would find insensitive or otherwise offensive. "Skeletal parts" is certainly a more neutral phrase than is "dead body parts." Try your hand at "feces" and "intestinal contents"! A critical reader must be attentive, then, to how a dysphemism is being used.

Persuasive Comparisons, Definitions, and Explanations

Comparisons, definitions, and explanations can also be used to slant.

Persuasive Comparisons

A skillful writer can easily give a comparison a positive or negative slant. Consider these two examples: A note in an association's bulletin might make the point that the well-regarded winner of the association's book award is of large build by comparing him with an offensive lineman in football; calling him tubby, obese, or fat would be a negative slant. While paging through a nineteenth-century newspaper, you run across an ad that compares the red of some colonial ceramics with the red of roses; the ad would be less effective if the comparison was with the red of blood.

Persuasive Definitions

An opportunity for slanting is present, too, when terms are defined.[3] Cannibalism and other practices described in anthropology textbooks provide instructive examples. According to the principle of cultural relativism, the practices of other cultures are to be judged according to their own understandings. However, some of these practices stir emotions in the West. While some might define cannibalism as "the murder and eating of human beings," people who practice cannibalism might understand it as a practice intended "to endow them with some of the characteristics of the deceased." Likewise, the practice of bride price can be defined as "a means of degrading women by implying that they are property to be bought" or as "payment made in exchange for the bride's family's loss of her labor and fertility within her kin group." When reading archaeology, many of us accept without question definitions given in the reading. But be alert: the definitions chosen may be intended to influence our attitude toward the writer's point of view.

Persuasive Explanations

Explanations can be favorable or unfavorable as well. Consider these alternative explanations: The Dunlop culture deteriorated through time, since its material culture became simpler following the onset of harsher climatic conditions. According to a more favorable explanation, the material culture of the Dunlop people became simpler through time as it adjusted to harsher climatic conditions. Although the material culture did become simpler through time, it was simply a sign of the adaptability of the culture, not of its deterioration.

Stereotypes, Innuendo, and Loaded Questions

It seems to be a habit of human beings to label people and things with a single word, a word that usually begins with "the." Examples in archaeology are the postprocessualist, the academic archaeologist, and the Neolithic. The habit makes sense, for a single expansive label eases thinking about a complex world. But the habit results in stereotyping when items are included in a category based on little or no evidence, or at least skewed evidence.

Thinking that postprocessualists are nothing but spinners of webs of gossamer (with the end result having no more substance than a spider's web), that processualists are naive measurers whose results (though full of sound and fury) signify nothing, and that Mesolithic cultures are drab are all examples of stereotyping. As critical thinkers, yet another of our many tasks is to be aware of the presence of potential stereotypes that, either intentionally used or not, work to bias our understanding of a group of people, things, or notions.

Dysphemisms and euphemisms frequently involve stereotypes whose presence can tug at our emotions. Here is a commonly encountered negative stereotype (a dysphemism) in archaeology: processual archaeologists are naive measurers—sure, their measurements are precise, but they neglect the meaning of artifacts to the people who made them. A positive stereotype (a euphemism) found in a book review might associate the author with the image of the trained scientist. Thus, the reviewer writes, "Professor Stuart analyzed the artifact collection with care and precision."

Another slanter intended to manipulate our understanding of what we read when we read archaeology is innuendo. For instance, if a reviewer in a book review states that "George Klimp has written a thorough site report this time," the suggestion is that Klimp doesn't usually produce thorough site reports. Or a reviewer of my book *Archaeology of Minnesota* might state that it is "a good start in summarizing the archaeology of Minnesota." Both of these reviewers are insinuating something deprecating about a publication.

A classic example of innuendo in the critical thinking literature, as adapted for archaeology, are these two sentences in an e-mail sent to members of an archaeological association:

> Vote for George Klimp. We need to elect a candidate for this position who does not have a drinking problem.

This example shows how subtle an innuendo can be. No mention is made of Klimp's opponents. Nonetheless, a seed has been planted—one or more, if not all, of his opponents in the election have a drinking problem.

If a writer wants to criticize an opponent's book without seeming completely obnoxious, another strategy is to refer to the book with faint praise. A reviewer of Klimp's most recent book is practicing this strategy when he writes that "Klimp has written a good book, at least according to some reviewers." The hint is that the book does not measure up. This is an innuendo.

Most readers of archaeology in North America are familiar with common, taken-for-granted assumptions in English-language literature, so these assumptions are rarely overtly stated. For instance, a statement in a site report that "all of the artifacts were washed" is referring to the artifacts examined in writing the report, not all the artifacts in the laboratory (or some other universe). An article claiming that a study of Sandy Lake pottery identified three decorative patterns is referring, of course, to the Sandy Lake pottery used in the study, not to all Sandy Lake pottery ever made. To spell out these unstated, taken-for-granted assumptions would make a report unwieldy and tedious—and archaeologists who normally write in English are likely unaware of the gamut of taken-for-granted assumptions they make and therefore could not identify them anyway.

Unlike a taken-for-granted assumption (as in "all of the artifacts were washed"), a loaded question is intended to slant, for it presupposes an answer to an implicit question.[4] Since this fallacy involves a complex of questions, it is also known as the *complex question fallacy* and the *many questions fallacy*. The implicit assumption in the most widely used example—"Have you stopped beating your wife?"—is that you did beat your wife. If the implicit assumption (which is a form of innuendo because implied) is unwarranted, then the question is a loaded one.

Weaselers, Downplayers, and Sarcasm

A weaseler is a substitute word or expression that softens or hedges a claim.[5] Archaeologists use weaselers when they do not want to make an outright assertion. Examples are "perhaps," "maybe," "probably," "often," and "it has been claimed that." Some weaselers like "maybe," "perhaps," and "possibly" may be a source of innuendo if their purpose is to interject a hint of doubt about something. The writer of a popular book on North American archaeology who claims that "the Hopewell Mound-Builders may have been cannibals" is not claiming that they *were* cannibals. Nonetheless, the idea has been planted in the reader's mind that they were indeed cannibals.

Of course, words intended to soften or hedge a claim may be perfectly legitimate if the intent is to convey uncertainty. For instance, an archaeologist might conclude after considering all of the evidence that the Hopewell Mound-Builders may have been cannibals. That is, there is evidence that suggests that they were cannibals, but the evidence is not conclusive. In this case, the archaeologist is being cautious in presenting the claim. The critical reader will have to assess, then, the writer, the context, and the issue—and any other available information—to decide whether the use of a weaseler like "may have been" is intended to produce innuendo or to convey uncertainty.

Many of the slanters that we have already considered can be used to downplay. For example:

> Don't pay attention to what Professor Robinson wrote; he is an out-of-date cultural historical archaeologist.

In this example, a stereotype of a cultural historical archaeologist—here an archaeologist who concentrates on "describing" the archaeological record rather than explaining it—is being used to downplay the significance of Professor Robinson's views about the peopling of the New World.

Words commonly used to downplay the significance of something or someone's opinion include "still," "but," "however," "only," "nevertheless," "mere," and "merely." Example: If in a review of a report the reviewer implies that the writer has a mere BS degree, you might be tempted to assume that had an archaeologist with a master's or PhD degree written the report, it would have been better. Whether the report has merit, of course, should depend on its own qualities and not on the degree or degrees its author holds. Still another standard downplayer is the use of quotation marks, as in "He got his 'MA degree' from one of those one-year British archaeology programs."

Downplaying can be quite subtle as in these two versions of what is the same claim:

> Important archaeological materials were destroyed during construction, because the random sampling survey employed missed them; however, we must remember that random sampling strategies allow the investigation of many large project areas and save many sites from destruction every year.

> Although random sampling strategies allow the investigation of many large project areas and save many sites from destruction every year, it was just such a strategy that allowed the destruction of important archaeological materials during construction.

Even though a "however" occurs in the first version, it is the chosen mix of words in the second that downplays the significance of random sampling survey strategies.

In general, a critical reader must be aware of background information to determine whether an author intended to downplay a claim. Consider this statement overheard at a meeting of a local archaeological society: "Charlie is a loyal member of our society, but he has only been collecting artifacts for six years and is unfamiliar with many local artifact types." Is the use of the term "only" intended to downplay Charlie's competence in properly identifying local artifact types?

Downplayers, like weaselers, innuendo, loaded questions, and other slanters, can be used intentionally to make something less significant or worthy than it is. In other situations their use adds spark and perhaps a bit of humor to what is otherwise a dull piece of academic writing. In my experience, the most effective strategy for determining the intent of a slanter is to become intimately familiar with major types of slanters and numerous examples of their use.

Another slanter that can be used either to downgrade an opinion or accomplishment or to inject a bit of humor into an article is sarcasm. None of us like to have our opinions ridiculed. Here is a use of sarcasm heard in conversation: "Do archaeology north of Mexico? You have to be kidding. Ha, ha."

Remember, though, that the wittiest who slings the sharpest barbs has not offered a meaningful argument against her opponent's position—she has just let her readers know that she doesn't agree with that position.

Hyperbole and Proof Surrogates

An extravagant overstatement is hyperbole. A reviewer of an ordinary site report who claims that the report is "a future classic in archaeology" is engaging in hyperbole. Often the use of hyperbole is more subtle than that. An example is when an archaeologist refers to another as a "scientist" because he excavates in a careful and deliberate manner. You don't have to be a scientist to carry out your work in a careful and deliberate manner. In many instances there is a fuzzy line between hyperbole and strong language like "brilliant," "outstanding," and "one of the best young archaeologists." To refer to someone as "the best taphonomist in the history of archaeology" is likely hyperbole. To refer to the same person as "an extremely competent taphonomist" is a strong claim.

Some of the other slanters mentioned in this chapter—such as persuasive comparisons, explanations, and definitions; sarcasm; and dysphemism—can contain hyperbole. If a writer refers to archaeologists who helped enact legislation that led to the reburial of Native American artifacts as "traitors to the discipline," that is a dysphemism used as hyperbole. To say that the state archaeologist knows less about the archaeology of the state than a beet is to engage in hyperbole using a persuasive comparison.[6]

The last slanter considered in this chapter is proof surrogate. A proof surrogate cites an authority or the existence of evidence in support of a claim, though neither the authority nor the evidence is named or given in detail. By hinting that support exists, an archaeologist who cannot prove a claim plants the notion that the claim is true without having to produce the proof. Phrases like "as experts in the field know," "I have heard lab workers say," and "a professor I know" are familiar ways of offering surrogate proof for a claim. But which experts, which lab workers, and which professor?

Many readers of archaeology will recognize this proof surrogate:

> After reviewing the relevant literature and talking with authorities, it seems obvious that the subsistence base of the [your choice] culture was corn agriculture.

What literature? Which authorities? Obvious to whom? In other words, where is the evidence? As critical readers, our best option is to simply conclude that the writer believes that the subsistence base of the (your choice) culture was corn agriculture. Without evidence, such assertions tell you something about the author's beliefs but nothing about the (your choice) culture.

A surrogate is something that takes the place of another—and a proof surrogate is just that, a substitute for real evidence or proof. As charitable readers, we accept that the writer believes or presumes that the evidence or proof exists. However, we suspend judgment on a claim until the evidence or proof in support of it is presented. Of course, as we learned in chapter 5, the evidence or proof may be part of taken-for-granted knowledge in that realm of archaeology. Thus the importance of becoming intimately familiar with the literature in the area of archaeology you are most interested in.

In summary, writers may intentionally or unintentionally influence our opinion of a claim when we read archaeology by using a rhetorical device. In this chapter, thirteen of the most commonly encountered devices are introduced. They are as follows: euphemisms and dysphemisms; persuasive comparisons, definitions, and explanations; stereotypes, innuendo, and loaded questions; weaselers, downplayers, and sarcasm; and hyperbole and proof surrogates. The use of these devices may impart positive or negative emotional connotations or otherwise manipulate our perceptions as readers. As has been emphasized throughout the chapter, not all uses of these common rhetorical devices are intended to deceive. Some uses are intended to enliven what would otherwise be a rather dull piece of writing. Other uses result from careless writing. The task for critical readers is to distinguish among these various uses of rhetorical devices when they read archaeology.

Is There a Fallacy in the Reasoning?   **8**

U P TO THIS POINT in our review of background issues in critical
reading, we have learned ways to identify the key components
of an argument and the underlying assumptions that help them
hang together. We have also learned to clarify the argument by "excavating out" the meaning of key terms, phrases, and claims from their context
and from other sources of information. We have learned to do this by asking the following questions: What are the issue and the claim? What is the
argument? What are the assumptions? Is the argument masked by poor or
deliberately deceptive writing?

With these tools in our critical reading toolkit, we should by now
have some insight into the writer's reasoning, as clouded as it occasionally
can be. In this chapter, we begin to examine the reasoning structure to
determine whether it contains deceptive or faulty reasoning of one kind
or another that might mask the argument. This chapter gives you practice
in identifying fallacies. The chapter is divided into five sections. The first
section introduces the idea of a fallacy; the following sections present thirteen of the more common fallacies. These common fallacies are arranged
by four types of violation of the principles of a good argument, which are
described below.

Errors in Reasoning

Formal logic concentrates exclusively on the form of an argument—that is,
on whether the argument is valid or invalid. In a valid argument the conclusion necessarily follows from the premises, even if the premises are false;

in an invalid argument, the conclusion does not follow from the premises, even if the premises are true. Consider the following two arguments:

> Since [P1] all whales are huge and [P2] all humans are whales, [C] all humans are huge.

> Since [P1] all archaeologists work for the Park Service and [P2] Justin works for the Park Service, [C] Justin must be an archaeologist.

In the first argument, the conclusion does necessarily follow from the premises. If all whales are huge and all humans are whales, then all humans must be huge. Since the conclusion necessarily follows from the premises, the argument is valid, even though one of the premises (P2) is obviously false.

The second argument exhibits a different category of error. Even though both premises are true, the argument is invalid, for the conclusion does not follow necessarily from the premises (Justin could, for example, be a freshwater biologist).

In contrast to formal logic with its concentration on the validity of an argument, informal logic and critical reading in archaeology are concerned as well with the soundness of an argument. Sound arguments have both a valid form and true premises. Arguments like the "all whales are huge" example that have a valid form and one or more false premises are said to be unsound.

Flawed errors like this—either formal or informal—are called fallacies.[1] Unlike unclear writing (chapter 6) and deceptive rhetorical devices (chapter 7) that can obscure reasoning, fallacies are true errors in reasoning *sensu stricto* (that is, in a "strict sense"). The fallacies reviewed here are organized into categories, depending on whether they stem from the irrelevance of a premise, from the unacceptability of a premise, from the insufficiency of the combined premises to support a conclusion, or from the failure of an argument to give an effective rebuttal to the most serious challenges to its conclusion or to the argument itself.[2] Other fallacies besides those presented in this chapter are scattered throughout the book.

Fallacies That Violate the Relevance Criterion

The three patterns of faulty reasoning in this section are fallacies that violate the relevance criterion for a good argument, for the premises used to support a conclusion are logically irrelevant to that task. A premise is irrelevant to the truth of a conclusion if it does not provide grounds for determining whether the conclusion is true or false. In other words, it is inconsequential in the evaluation of the argument.

Appeal to Common Opinion

As history reminds us, the truth or falseness of a conclusion is logically independent of how many people believe that it is true or false. The earth is flat and the sun revolves around the earth. Need more be said? Nonetheless, the appeal to common opinion fallacy makes just this assertion. Consider the following argument:

> [C] Human beings cannot have been in the Americas before 15,000 B.C.
> [P] According to a leading journal, more than 80 percent of the archaeologists polled in a recent survey believe that humans did not enter the Americas before that date.

Whether human beings were in the Americas before 15,000 B.C. cannot be determined by taking a poll. Polls may indicate what many archaeologists are thinking, but very little regarding the truth or merit of the claim. As individuals interested in archaeology, we should be interested in what polls show archaeologists believe about an issue like the date of the earliest peopling of the Americas. However, opinion is a poor source of evidence (see chapter 10). If the appeal is the only or main reason in support of the conclusion, we conclude that it provides no real evidence in support of the truth or falseness of the conclusion. This fallacy is also known as the bandwagon fallacy, an appeal to popularity, *ad populum*, and *consensus gentium*.

The Genetic Fallacy

It is a mistake to reject a position or procedure just because it was formerly adopted, say, by a 1960s processual archaeologist or a 1950s cultural historical archaeologist. The position or procedure may have been widely held or used throughout the social sciences, after all, and thus was not uniquely held by either of these research programs. These arguments typically overlook, too, changes that may have altered the character of the position or procedure in the interim. Consider the following argument:

> [C] We were urged not to make detailed, formal typological analyses of our artifact assemblages, for our adviser said [P] those types of analysis are characteristic of 1960s processual archaeology and [P] that sort of archaeology is now passé.

To meet the relevance criterion of a good argument, the premise or premises given in support of the conclusion must aid in determining the truth or falsity of the conclusion. Like the appeal to common opinion and the irrelevant proof, the genetic fallacy fails to meet this criterion. Rather, the position or procedure is being rejected merely because of its origin or genesis.

Appeal to Pedantry

In the last chapter, we met the fallacy of *argumentum ad verecundiam*, which is an appeal to authority. The crudest form of an *argumentum ad verecundiam* in archaeological writing is an appeal to professional status.

For example, the views of amateur archaeologists are often dismissed out of hand by professional archaeologists with PhDs. While it is reasonable to assume that amateur archaeologists are not as knowledgeable as professionals as a whole, that assumption does not imply that all views of amateur archaeologists are false and should be dismissed. The contributions of amateur archaeologists to our understanding of the past are legend.

Reliance on the trappings of pedantry to promote one's views is fairly common in archaeology, as it is in the other social sciences. Common examples are the use of jargon (never use a little word when a big one will do!), attempts to convince through the length or density of an exposition, and a reliance on the use of mathematical symbols to impress.[3] Of course, mathematical symbols, technical terms, and so on have a valuable role to play in scholarship. The complaint is their use merely for effect.

Fallacies That Violate the Acceptability Criterion

Each of the four fallacies discussed in this section uses a premise that fails to meet standard conditions of acceptability for a good argument. These conditions include criteria of acceptability, such as "A premise is acceptable if it is the conclusion of another good argument," and conditions of unacceptability, such as "A premise (or conclusion) is unacceptable if it is linguistically confusing."

Appeal to Recentness

The appeal to recentness (also called the fallacy of novelty and an "*argumentum ad novitatem*") appears in several different forms, but the basic idea is that an idea, position, or procedure is better simply because it is new and modern. A common example in archaeology is the excessive weight that is given to the most recent interpretation of any given subject.

An appeal to recentness is an attractive form of argument, for it is based on the notion that the tools of archaeological reasoning have steadily improved over time. Indeed, that may be the case. However, that line of reasoning is a fallacy if the strength of an argument rests solely on the appeal to newness. Do we really want to support the claim that all novelty is good? We have to be shown why a new idea, position, or procedure is better. Critical readers will occasionally, but more rarely in archaeology, come across an *appeal to tradition*, which is the opposite of an appeal to recentness. In appeals to tradition the claim is that the "old ways" were superior to the new ideas of today.

Begging the Question

This informal fallacy is present in arguments in which the conclusion is in one of the premises or reasons (the fallacy is also called a circular argument, a vicious circle, and *petitio principii* ["assuming the answer"], among other terms). Begging the question can be difficult to spot in an argument, for it is usually associated with lengthy arguments with many premises, and the offending premise may be somewhat disguised. Here's a simple example of begging the question that, say, you might run across in a book review:

> [C] Programmed-learning texts are clearly superior to traditional texts in learning effectiveness because [P] it is highly advantageous for learning to have materials presented in a step-by-step fashion.

Here the premise and the conclusion are using different words to restate the definition of programmed learning, which is learning using a step-by-step procedure. The reviewer is arguing that programmed learning is better because programmed learning is better. Here the structure of the reasoning assumes, rather than proves, the conclusion—in this instance the question has been "begged." Although the question has been "begged," the presence of the fallacy does not mean that the conclusion is necessarily incorrect; it is just inadequately supported.

False Alternatives

When a complex situation is oversimplified by limiting the position being considered to only two alternatives, the fallacy of false alternatives may be present. Of course, there may be only two alternatives, but that has to be shown rather than assumed. The risk in prematurely limiting the alternatives considered is that neither of the two alternatives may be true. This fallacy is also called the either-or fallacy and the false dilemma fallacy, or, when extreme alternatives are involved, the black-and-white fallacy. Consider this example:

> In a lengthy argument whose conclusion is "The federal government's National Register of Historic Places program should be scrapped," you spot the following premise: "Local communities, not the federal government, should have the right to decide what local cultural heritage properties should be recognized and preserved."

Although this may seem like a reasonable statement, it is actually deceptive, for it implies that there are only two choices. This may not be the case, as in this example. An alternative, third possibility is for the federal government's National Register of Historic Places program to exist in close interaction with the wishes and concerns of local communities (which is the case).

Be on the lookout, then, for phrases like "either . . . or . . . ," "the only alternative is . . . ," "the two choices are . . . ," and "because they were not As, they must be Bs," for still other alternatives may exist. Of course, the presence of these and similar phrases should cause you to pause and ask, "Are there really only two choices?"

Fallacy of Equivocation

The fallacy of equivocation occurs when a term or phrase is used in an argument as if it has the same meaning throughout the argument, when it is actually being used in two or more senses. Equivocation may be the result of purposeful deception or, more likely in archaeology, unfamiliarity with the construction of a good argument. So, when reading an argument, ask yourself if the words or phrases in the argument retain the same meaning all through the argument. For writers, this is an easy error to make, especially in long arguments that course through a book or lengthy article. The underlying message is that the words or phrases used in an argument must retain the same meaning all through the argument. Consider this example:

> State-run gambling should be legalized, for a portion of the profit could be used to fund historic preservation activities. The reasoning is simple: gambling is something we can't avoid. It is an integral part of the human experience; people gamble every time they get in their car or decide to get married. Why not use gambling, then, to fund historic preservation activities?

Two meanings of the word "gambling" are being used here. In the first use the word refers to games of chance in which money (or some other valuable like the family farm) is involved, while in the second it refers to the chances—the risks—that we all face in making decisions in everyday life. Since the word "gambling" shifts meaning in the argument, it violates the acceptability criterion of a good argument.

Fallacies That Violate the Sufficiency Criterion

Even though one or more premises are presented in an argument in support of the conclusion, the support provided may be insufficient for several reasons. Some premises may provide no direct support at all, others biased support, and still others very weak support. In some instances critical evidence is not mentioned at all. To provide sufficient support for a conclusion, the premises provided must, then, be of sufficient number, kind, and weight. Arguments that do not meet this level of support violate the sufficiency criterion of a good argument. The following two fallacies violate this sufficiency criterion.

Appeal to Ignorance

Appeals to ignorance take either a negative or a positive form. Using its negative form, an author maintains that because a conclusion has not been proven, it must be false. For example, since we cannot prove that the Oneota moved southward in response to increasingly cold weather, that conclusion must be false. In its positive form, an author maintains that since his conclusion has not been disproven, it must be true. For example, since no one has disproved that the Oneota moved southward in response to increasingly cold weather, that conclusion must be true. But just because no convincing counterevidence is presently known does not make this conclusion true. The fallacy is called an appeal to ignorance because conclusions are based on an absence of evidence—that is, on ignorance.

Here is another example of this appeal. What is the hidden assumption in the argument?

> [Read in a CRM report] While surveying for sites, I did not see any "No Trespassing" signs, so I assumed that it was all right to walk through the farmer's field.

Post Hoc Fallacy

In a post hoc fallacy the assumption is made that just because one event preceded another, the first event is the cause of the second.[4] But temporal succession is not a sufficient reason in itself for claiming a causal relationship (see chapter 17, where the fallacy is given its longer name of "post hoc, ergo propter hoc"; the fallacy is also known as the false cause fallacy and the false cause-and-effect fallacy). Consider these two examples:

> It was only two months after Jason came back from the archaeological field school that he started smoking pot. Those archaeologists in the field school must have got him started on the stuff.

The only evidence presented in support of the conclusion that "those archaeologists in the field school must have got him started on the stuff" is the temporal priority of Jason's field school visit. No causal link between the two events has been established.

> Late prehistoric Oneota peoples moved southward after the onset of the Little Ice Age. They must have moved southward because of the onset of colder weather conditions.

Again, since temporal priority fails to provide sufficient evidence for a causal claim, the argument fails the sufficiency criterion of a good argument. Note that this does not mean that the Oneota did not move southward because of the onset of colder weather; it merely means that the causal connection has not been sufficiently demonstrated.

Fallacies That Violate the Rebuttal Criterion

Fallacies that violate the rebuttal criterion fail to present a strong rebuttal of criticism of the author's argument, as well as other compelling arguments against the position supported by the author. Arguments generally fail to meet this criterion for one of two reasons. The first reason, which follows from the definition of the rebuttal criterion, is a failure to provide a response to counterevidence. Here the writer simply does not mention or minimizes the counterevidence. The second reason is the adoption of a diversionary tactic. A classic example is an attack on a writer rather than on the writer's position (the fallacies in this category are called *ad hominem* fallacies). The danger here is becoming ensnared in the emotion of a personal attack at the expense of a rational evaluation of the argument itself. Less emotionally charged fallacies of diversion include the red herring and straw person fallacies, both of which are described in this section.

Denying the Counterevidence

This fallacy is a straightforward example of the first reason for failing to satisfy the rebuttal criterion. The fallacy occurs in both a strong and a weak sense. In the strong sense a writer simply ignores the counterevidence, pretending that it does not exist. In the weak sense the writer minimizes or downplays the counterevidence. For readers who are not specialists on an issue, it can be difficult to determine whether the fallacy of denying the counterevidence is in play. To make that determination, one has to be familiar with the relevant literature.

Ad Hominem Argument

The fallacy of *argumentum ad hominem* occurs in many different forms, all of which serve to shift attention from the argument to the arguer. Among its more common varieties are the abusive ad hominem, which directly denounces an opponent; the circumstantial ad hominem, which suggests that an opponent's argument is merely a reflection of her (biased) interests; and the associative ad hominem, which attempts to undercut an opponent by reference to the (bad) company he keeps. For example:

> A scholar studying the Kensington rune stone is derisively attacked because (1) he must be nutty, (2) he only supports the authenticity of the rune stone because he is of Scandinavian descent, and (3) there are a lot of kooks who believe in the authenticity of the rune stone, so he must be a kook too.

Red Herring Fallacy

The red herring fallacy is a classic diversion fallacy, for it switches the focus of discussion from one topic to an unrelated issue by using a "red herring." It is generally adopted to divert attention away from a weak position.

> Academic archaeologist to a CRM archaeologist: "Why don't you concentrate on explaining what happened in the prehistoric past? You spend all of your time writing sterile descriptive reports." The CRM archaeologist replies, "Why are you always picking on CRM archaeology?"

The "you're picking on me" charge is a good way to divert attention from CRM reports if one feels uneasy about those reports. However, claiming that they are being picked on by academic archaeologists is obviously not an adequate defense of the types of reports they write (and CRM archaeologists do have good reasons for the content of the reports they write). For good reason, this fallacy is also called the smoke screen fallacy and the ignoring the question fallacy.

Straw Person Fallacy

In this fallacy a counterargument is written in such a manner as to make the original argument more vulnerable to counterattack. Since the writer is deliberately misrepresenting someone's position in order to more easily refute it, the rebuttal criterion is not satisfied.

A very clear case of misrepresentation that involves drawing unwarranted inferences can be seen in this short exchange between a proponent and an opponent of a plan to increase funding for historic preservation activities.

> PROPONENT: Unless we increase funding for historic preservation activities soon, we will not be able to save significant historic properties from destruction through urban sprawl.

> OPPONENT: What you're saying is that you couldn't care less about the rights of property owners to make decisions about what happens to things on their property.

The opponent to increased funding for historic preservation activities has drawn an inference from the proponent's argument that is clearly unwarranted. In no way could one conclude from the argument that the proponent was unconcerned about the rights of individual property owners. Indeed, it is possible that every consideration was given to ensure that property owners have the right to decide what happens to historic structures on their property.

Critical readers will not learn how to identify the range of fallacies that might occur in what they read in a chapter or two in an introductory-level book like this. At best, they will become aware of what the issues are.

Are There Skeptical Postmodern Themes in the Argument?

9

THE IDEA OF A RESEARCH CYCLE that proceeds by logically rigorous argumentation—as used to structure this book—has been
challenged as "nothing but a dream." In fact, modern thought re-
sulting from the Enlightenment, which is based on notions such as reason,
rationality, truth, method, and science, is under attack in many disciplines.
Today, "modern" thought is increasingly being viewed as enslaving, eth-
nocentric, male centered, and suppressive of the culturally varied views of
the world. Defenses of traditional Western understandings of science and
epistemology or a modernist perspective—a perspective based on reason,
rationality, truth, method, and so on—is now viewed by many to be, at
best, narrow or overly structured, and at worst bigoted, racist, sexist, or insensitive to and intolerant of other cultures with different ideas and world
visions. The banner of reason and method has clearly fallen—at least in
many people's opinion. Postmodernism in either a weak (moderate postmodernism) or a strong (skeptical postmodernism) form has been all the
rage since the 1980s, especially in the humanities but also among a vocal
minority in archaeology and the social sciences more generally.[1]

In this chapter, our objective is simply to get a feel for what these views
look like in the archaeological literature and for how other archaeologists
have reacted to these views in print. We summarize what is at stake in the
first two sections by asking the following questions: What is at the root
of these arguments? What gives them their force? How have these themes
influenced notions like history, time, space, theory, truth, and method,
which seem basic to the (traditional) archaeological enterprise? The third
section examines one expression of these themes in archaeology. The last

section reviews a few of the ways in which other archaeologists and other individuals have responded to this critique.

Unmasking the Foundations of Science

At the very root of the postmodern critique of modern thought and science are severe challenges to the notion that science and modern thought in general rest on an objective observational base. According to skeptical postmodernists, once that base is cut away, the fundamental notions of a fact, objectivity, and a test lose their force. Like superstition and revelation, science and modern thought are set adrift from the factual world and must find their justification elsewhere. Two of these challenges are reviewed here. One concerns the nature of observation and the other the indeterminacy of language.

The Nature of Observation

The first claim is that observation by its very nature involves interpretation—that is, that by definition an observation is no more or less than an interpreted sense impression. Empiricism, a view of science still popular today, requires that theories be tested by comparing their predictions (test implications) to (rock hard) observations. For the empiricist, it is this appeal to theory-free observation data that guarantees the objectivity of science. Stated another way, the notion that science is anchored in facts or has a solid foundation in facts allows scientists to adjudicate between true and false hypotheses and between better and worse models of the workings of the world. This view is based on the naive realist belief that observation provides a picture of the world around us as it really is—that is, that perception provides us with pure facts.

Research projects in psychology and the natural sciences since the 1960s have shown that this is an untenable position—that observation is inescapably theory laden.[2] This conclusion has been demonstrated in a number of ways, only two of which are mentioned here. Studies by psychologists and anthropologists have conclusively demonstrated that people see things in different ways—even the same "thing." There is a significant difference, then, between simply "seeing" and "seeing as"—between seeing something as a piece of rock, for example, and seeing it as a Neolithic projectile point. "Seeing as" requires a great deal of highly specialized knowledge. In the process of gaining that knowledge, we are also learning to see the object (interaction, process, etc.)—we are becoming enculturated (some would say predisposed) into seeing in a certain way. Think, for instance, of all those artifacts in archaeological sites that are called "ceremonial objects" because archaeologists have not learned to "see" them properly. In sum, as the philosopher of science Norwood Russell Hanson once put it, "There is more to seeing than meets the eye."[3]

Neurophysiologists have approached the study of observation from another direction. They have demonstrated through the close study of neurons, axons, neural networks, receptor chemistry, and so on that perception involves the construction of a description. In fact, they have demonstrated that there is a very wide difference between how we see and what we see and how and what a cat or a housefly sees—that is, they have demonstrated that what we see and how we see it are both species-specific adaptations.

Studies like these—that demonstrate that observation is a physiological, psychological, and cultural process—raise questions about the role observation legitimately plays in science and in the construction of scientific knowledge. For instance, if observation is species specific and theory laden, it is difficult to argue that observations *qua* observations can be used without interpretation to deduce the falsity of a theory.

Scholars have responded to critiques like this by adopting one of two alternative positions. Representationalism maintains that while "seeing" necessarily distorts the outer world, it does nonetheless provide reliable news of that outer world. Phenomenalism (or idealism) dispenses with the external world altogether. Only the mind and its images exist. It is this latter position that provides a basis for the more skeptical forms of postmodernism. Skeptical postmodernists would say that they have "unmasked" (or exposed) the false claims scientists make about the objectivity of observation.

Linguistic Indeterminacy

The second, and more common, unmasking of the objective base of science and modern thought has to do with the indeterminacy of language, with what is called linguistic indeterminacy. As human beings, we characteristically represent the external world through the symbols and signs of language. As members of a more or less homogeneous culture, most of us assume that our representations have a fixed meaning—that is, that they are natural. We assume that there really *are* rabbits, elm trees, and aunts and uncles in the world. We also assume that everyone else understands them in more or less the same way we do. If they do not, this is a sign that they are "primitive," from an "underdeveloped" part of the world, or just plain strange.

Anthropologists and other kinds of scholars have argued, however, that diverse meanings are possible for any symbol, gesture, and word—and that this diversity is to be explored (is a proper subject of study) rather than dismissed as a sure sign of weirdness. More extreme positions hold that language has no direct relationship to the real world; it is, rather, only symbolic. Stated another way, symbols by themselves do not represent anything—they have no equivalent in reality. Once this conclusion is accepted, it seems that there is no choice but to adopt a skeptical postmodern position.

The Influence of Postmodernism in Scholarly Research

How have these notions influenced modern concepts like history, time, space, theory, truth, epistemology, and methodology? Before reviewing these issues, readers should review the definition of two terms and review once again our earlier procedure for ferreting out the basic presuppositions of theoretical stances. The two terms are "ontology" and "epistemology." Ontology is about what exists. For instance, is a social group a thing? What about a cloud? Epistemology is about the proper study of the things that are thought to exist. For example, if a social group is assumed to be "a thing" that is greater than the sum of its parts (individual people), how should that "something greater than" be properly studied?

Using the terms introduced above, the basic presuppositions of theoretical stances provide an ontological and epistemological framework for research strategies, strategies that are called research programs in chapters 5 and 15. They do this by defining what exists in the world, by identifying which of these "things" is most worth studying, and by laying out rules for the proper study of these "things." Since these presuppositions are assumptions about the nature of the world and the research process, they are properly called the metaphysical content of research strategies. Following are examples of presuppositions that underlie approaches to archaeology and anthropology more generally that are germane to this chapter's topic:

- Observation provides a picture of the world around us as it really is (and therefore there are cold, hard facts that can adjudicate between the truthfulness of competing theories).
- Only the mind and its images exist (therefore, be suspicious of anyone who claims to have "the facts," for they are either up to no good [e.g., they have strong-male biases] or they are not very bright).

- Human concepts are not reflections of the world as it really is but are the creations of idealized cognitive models that we know are inaccurate (and so, as a methodological rule, "study the cognitive structures of the human mind/brain!").

Skeptical postmodernists question almost everything that we normally take for granted about the concepts of history, time, and space. They would reject, for example, the following presuppositions:

- There is a real knowable past.
- Knowledge of history is essential for comprehending the present.
- Archaeologists (and historians) must be objective.
- Time is linear.
- Time exists outside language.
- Space is fixed, constant, and measurable.

They would also contend that:

- History is logocentric (a source of myth, ideology, and prejudice).
- History is the creation of modern Western nations. Its purpose is to oppress Third World peoples and those from other cultures by privileging one or another cultural tradition (Greek, Western) as the ultimate origin or register of truth and meaning (in whose terms all else must be interpreted).
- History is not (cannot be) a truth-seeking activity so much as a storytelling activity—and there are many different "stories" to tell.
- History should (must be radically revised to) concentrate on the daily experience of ordinary people (in contrast to the pyramids, palaces, and other remains of oppressive elites).

Presuppositions like these have led to reassessments of the purpose (if any) of history and, by implication, archaeology. Examples are the end of history movement, a skeptical postmodern project that calls for an end to the writing of history, and the new history movement, a moderate postmodern project that calls for a shift in the focus of history from elites to ordinary people and processes.[4]

Skeptical postmodernists also reject any understanding of time as chronological or linear. They call (pejoratively) this traditional conception of time chronophonism. Since most archaeologists are chronophonists, some attention should be paid to the core presuppositions of this perspective. The following are examples:

- The modern conception of time is oppressive, for it measures and controls our activities. (Can you think of a popular metaphor that illustrates this idea?)
- As a human creation—a function of language—time is arbitrary or indeterminate.
- Things are never either entirely present or entirely absent.

Skeptical postmodernists claim (ironically?) that these views receive support from science. For instance, they cite the following statement from Stephen Hawking's *A Brief History of Time* as an example: "Imaginary time is really the real time, and what we call real time is just a figment of our imaginations" (though they and Hawking would disagree about what is intended here).[5]

A few additional presuppositions of skeptical postmodernism provide a fuller sense of this critique of modernism and science—and by implication traditional archaeology:

- Because all knowledge is language based, truth is forever arbitrary or meaningless.
- Truth claims are the product of power games, manipulated into position by those whose interests they serve.
- No single interpretation of any phenomenon can be claimed superior to any other.
- Modern science is a cultural artifact (on a par, for example, with magic).
- The goal of seeking truth should be abandoned (for it is futile).
- Archaeology/anthropology is at best persuasive fiction or poetry.
- There is no (true) reality out there to be discovered.
- No cultural tradition can analytically encompass the discourse of another cultural tradition.
- As far as method is concerned, "anything goes!"

Six Responses to Skeptical Postmodernism

Before we examine possible responses to the postmodern critique, let's briefly summarize what is at stake if we take this critique seriously. Skeptical postmodernists claim that "modern" concepts like truth, method, theory, history, space, time, and reason are cultural fabrications of Western society. According to these skeptics, their use tends to subordinate, oppress, regulate, demean, and so on some cultures rather than others. A consequence of skeptical postmodernism—if accepted—is that there are no criteria to adjudicate between alternative views of the past. Anything goes! Postmodernism has become so pervasive in contemporary scholarship that some scholars refer to the second half of the twentieth century as the Age of Relativism or the Age of Postmodernism.

Critical readers of archaeology should be able to recognize skeptical postmodern themes in what they read and, equally, should be alert to responses to these themes. This section reviews six of these possible responses.

Observations Can Be Objective

Lewis Binford, the founding father of processual ("new") archaeology in the 1960s, has actively engaged the postmodern critique in many articles. At the core of his defense of processualism is his belief that observation can be objective if it is part of a pattern of observations that reoccur and are agreed upon by multiple observers.[6] For Binford, this is not a methodological stance, but a statement of fact about the ability of human beings to "see" the natural world in a non-theory-laden manner.

Scholars who study observation would respond by restating their research conclusions that observation—and patterns of observations—are interpreted sense impressions—that is, that people learn to "see" as members of a culture or a discipline like archaeology. Even though many of Binford's fellow archaeologists might agree with him that they "see" the same things (more or less), they have learned to "see" as members of their cultural subgroup. To convince skeptics, Binford must do more than merely voice his opinion. He must demonstrate that all peoples in all cultures "see" the same things he sees. Nonetheless, he has at least engaged the critique.

Adopt a Worldview

A pragmatic option is to explicitly adopt a worldview that addresses some of the concerns of postmodernists. Of course, skeptical postmodernists would find the assumptions that underlie the worldview beside the point, for (in their view) they remain impossible-to-justify assertions. Still, it is a compromise position that makes a fact-based archaeology within the confines of a research program possible. As an example, consider the following presuppositions taken from John Searle's *The Construction of Social Reality* (1995):

- Reality (the world) exists independently of our representations of it (a position called external realism).
- Human beings have a variety of interconnected ways of having access to and of representing features of the world to themselves. These include perception, thought, language, beliefs, pictures, maps, and so on. Collectively, these interconnected ways are called representations. According to this view, there is a brute reality that human beings comprehend through representations.
- Some of these representations, such as beliefs and statements, are intended to represent how things are in reality. To the extent that they succeed or fail, they are said to be true or false, respectively. They are true if and only if they correspond to the facts in reality. This is a version of the correspondence theory of truth.

    (As an aside, science is successful primarily because it insists that ideas about the world must be continually confronted by brute reality. From this perspective, some hypotheses are true and others are not.)
- Systems of representation, such as vocabularies and conceptual schemes (worldviews), are human creations and to that extent are arbitrary. It is possible to have any number of different systems of representation for representing the same reality. This latter notion is called conceptual relativity.
- Actual human efforts to get true representations of reality are influenced by all sorts of factors—cultural, economic, psychological, and so on. Complete objectivity is difficult, sometimes impossible, because actual representations are always from a point of view, are motivated by all sorts of personal factors, and are made within a cultural, historical, and linguistic context.
- Having knowledge involves having true representations for which we can give certain sorts of justification or evidence. Knowledge is thus objective, because the criteria for knowledge are not arbitrary, and they are impersonal.

Unlike Binford, who accepts his view as fact, Searle is deliberately constructing a worldview based on a set of explicit presuppositions that address many of the fundamental ontological and epistemological issues that underlie the skeptical postmodern critique. Since this is a deliberately constructed research program, the nature and implications of the presuppositions can be tinkered with a bit as our understanding of the observation process and science develop.

Become Sensitive to Postmodern Issues

Even if you as a critical reader do not have the time to delve into the contentious world of the postmodern debate, an effort should be made to become sensitive to postmodern issues, especially the ways in which the reconstructions of the past by archaeologists may subordinate, oppress, regulate, and so on the cultures and peoples of the past. Pauline Rosenau's *Post-modernism and the Social Sciences* (1992) provides an excellent review of these issues.

Accept That the Practice of Archaeology Cannot Be Detached from Metaphysical Assumptions about Nature, Society, People, Culture, and So Forth

This suggestion follows from the problems of observation and linguistic indeterminacy mentioned in the first section of this chapter. Most archaeologists are probably unaware that they have "adopted" a set of presuppositions and therefore remain unreflective about those presuppositions. Because they consider themselves scientists or humanists, they do not think that their activities are (necessarily) cultural in the same way that they assume ritual in a hunter-gatherer community is cultural. Such an acceptance should be the indisputable starting point of all archaeological projects—and is a necessary assumption for the active reader. To conduct research without being aware that that research is based on a set of adopted presuppositions is to commit the epistemic fallacy, which is an error in reasoning to knowledge.

Explicitly Adopt a Research Program for Doing Archaeology

Most archaeologists would probably agree that they should know something about the postmodern critique. But they would also argue that they have no interest in engaging in the debate. A reasonable way to proceed is to explicitly adopt a research program and then tinker with it to accommodate a changing understanding of the enterprise of archaeology (see chapter 15).

Pay Attention to the Presuppositions That Underlie Research Programs in Archaeology

Regardless of how you respond to the skeptical postmodern critique, critical readers should pay attention to the presuppositions that underlie what they read. Remember, research programs in archaeology are general worldviews for doing archaeology—they are sets of presuppositions about the nature of the archaeological record, artifacts, culture, reality, and so on. Examples of research programs in archaeology include the trait-centered approach, system-centered approach, agency-centered approach, and integral approach (if we accept the principle of conceptual relativity, these contrasting research programs can be thought of as different ways of "knowing" or "engaging" reality, whether perceived in right-side or left-side quadrants). By "excavating" out their presuppositions, the critical reader will have a better understanding of an author's position on the fundamental ontological and epistemological issues that are central to the skeptical postmodern critique.

Of course, skeptical postmodernists challenge the very idea of our commonsense understanding of archaeology, as well as our received concepts of history, time, space, theory, truth, and method. If these claims are correct, archaeology as a discipline that tells us something real (truthful) about past peoples and cultures is "nothing but a dream." From a moderate postmodern perspective, however, the practice of archaeology as a social science remains a possible, if uncertain, enterprise.[7] This chapter has briefly reviewed what is at stake and how these arguments might affect what we read when we read archaeology.

FROM OBSERVATIONS TO POPULATION ESTIMATES

II

ART II FOCUSES ON STATISTICAL IDEAS and their use in archaeology. A useful definition of statistics is "a collection of procedures and principles for gaining and processing information in order to make decisions when faced with uncertainty."[1] Although the invention of statistical methods is one of the most important developments of modern times, many otherwise competent readers experience instant mental paralysis (mathphobia) when they encounter statistics, for they may have an inadequate background in the discipline. Consequently, the goal of the material in this part is to increase your awareness of the usefulness of data and to help you interpret and critically evaluate the data sections of the reports you read. If it eases any anxiety you may have, you should know that these chapters are written for readers with little or no statistical knowledge. Furthermore, the chapters only brush lightly through this section of the research cycle.

Within the bottom left quadrant of the research cycle, statistical methods serve two indispensable research objectives: they transform sets of observations made on some part of the archaeological record into descriptive summaries of those observations, and they transform statements about observations into statements about the usually incompletely known populations of which the observations are samples. Chapter 11 concentrates on the first of these two transformations, and chapter 13 focuses on the second transformation.

Since the methodological controls of the first transformation are descriptive statistics and the methodological controls of the second are inferential statistics, these two sequential information transformations can be considered the descriptive phase and the inferential phase, respectively, of empirical research in archaeology. They are empirical because they are about the material content—the artifacts, ecofacts, features, sites, and other constituents—of the archaeological record. The transformation to statements about people and sociocultural systems has not yet been made.

Chapter 10, the introductory chapter, explores the basic differences between facts, opinions, and other types of evidence, such as testimonials, that might be presented to support a claim. Since the transformation of statements about observations to statements about the populations of which they are samples involves an inductive argument, chapter 12 explores some of the issues involved in making an inductive argument.

Are Facts Clearly Distinguished from Opinions and Other Claims? **10**

I N PART I, "FOUNDATIONS," we began the process of evaluating what we read when we read archaeology by learning how to detect the kind of archaeology we are reading, the basic components of an argument, and the presence of fallacies and other errors in the reasoning structure of an argument. In this chapter, we look at another piece of the reasoning structure: the diversity and quality of claims and the reasons given in their support—in short, the facts. Here are three typical factual claims:

- Sandy Lake sites are larger than Blackduck sites.
- Hide working became more important in the Rochester culture, for stone scrapers now made up 37 percent of formal chipped stone tools.
- Our cultural heritage is safer than ever; cultural resource management archaeologists have increased the total amount of land they survey each year by 15 percent in the last five years.

Can these factual statements be accepted at face value? What evidence supports the claim that Sandy Lake sites are larger than Blackduck sites? Is this an opinion or a fact—and what is the difference between an opinion and a fact? In their own way, each of these questions is asking how good the evidence is.

How Factual Are Factual Claims?

When we read archaeology, the arguments we generally encounter contain claims about the way the world was in the past. We can assume that the writer wants us to accept these claims as facts. Following common practice, I refer to claims about the way the world was in the past as factual claims or, less cautiously, facts.[1]

When reading archaeology, we feel more certain about some factual claims than others. For example, we probably feel quite certain that the claim "the inhabitants of precontact America were (with a few possible exceptions) American Indians" is true. We are probably less certain that the assertion "Scandinavian voyageurs traveled through the present state of Minnesota in the fourteenth century" is true. Whether we feel more or less certain about the truthfulness of a claim is less important than the quality of the evidence provided in its support. So how do we go about evaluating the quality of evidence provided in support of a factual claim?

First, a caution: A lesson drawn from years of evaluating evidence in support of a factual claim is that it is generally difficult to prove that a claim is absolutely true or false. A strategy I adopt is to ask how true or false a claim is on a scale from zero (absolutely false) to ten (absolutely true).[2] As the quality and quantity of evidence supporting a factual claim approaches ten, the more confidence we have in the "factualness" of the claim. When the indicator falls between eight and ten on the scale, I call the claim a "fact," though people differ widely in what they are willing to call a fact. For some, a six or seven is good enough, while for others anything that falls below nine is either false or a mere assertion. Some (unreasonable) folks even maintain that a fact is a ten and only a ten.

A factual claim that falls in a reader's opinion in the lower half of the zero-to-ten scale is not necessarily valueless. In the early phases of a project, claims are more likely to be hunches. The more Sandy Lake sites are shown to be larger than Blackduck sites, the more factual the claim "Sandy Lake sites are larger than Blackduck sites" becomes. Therefore, before we judge the persuasiveness of a piece of writing, we need to know how credible the factual claims are—and to know that involves a complex of new thinking skills. As critical readers, we have to be able to locate factual claims, to distinguish between different kinds of evidence backing the claims, and to determine the credibility of that evidence.

The Credibility of Evidence

How do we determine the credibility of evidence? The remaining three chapters in part II and the chapters in part IV are concerned with this question. Here I stress that critical readers ask questions like the following: What is the proof? Where is the evidence? Why should I believe that?

Did the writer prove it? In archaeology, the process is not as difficult as evaluating the claims that we hear daily on television. Most archaeologists know that they have to substantiate their claims—and are even eager to share their evidence in the hope that you the reader will share their conclusions. But before we can answer those questions, we have to locate a writer's factual claims.

Recognizing Factual Claims in Your Reading

One strategy for locating factual claims is to become aware of the different functions they serve. Some factual claims function as descriptive conclusions, as in this example:

> *During the early Late Woodland period, people in the northern part of the region captured bears in large-scale drives.* Zooarchaeologists studying animal remains from these sites have found caches of dozens and even hundreds of bear skulls of both sexes and all ages.

The sentence "During the early Late Woodland . . ." is a descriptive conclusion because it makes a claim about how the world is, was, or will be. Its justification is the discovery of "dozens and even hundreds of bear skulls of both sexes and all ages" in sites in the area.

The following factual claim (in italics) functions as a reason offered in support of a descriptive (or prescriptive) conclusion:

> The size of introductory archaeology classes at universities should be decreased. *Large classes are leading to greater student apathy,* according to recent statistics gathered in a survey by a national archaeological association.

The factual claim, "Large classes are leading to greater student apathy," is a reason offered in support of the prescriptive conclusion, "The size of introductory archaeology classes at universities should be decreased."

Factual claims can also function as descriptive assumptions, as in this example:

> Colleges should warn students who are interested in training for positions in cultural resource management that there are already more professionals looking for positions than the number of available positions. [Unstated assumption linking the reason to the conclusion: *If the students knew that the market was already saturated, they would not want to compete for these positions.*]

This factual claim is a descriptive assumption, for it is unstated.

Major Kinds of Evidence

As readers of archaeology, we are most concerned with the kinds of evidence archaeologists offer in their written arguments. By evidence is generally meant "specific information that can be used to support the dependability of factual claims."[3] Major kinds of evidence include intuition, authorities and their testimonials, personal observations, case studies and examples, analogies, and research studies.[4] Although each of these kinds of evidence has its uses in discussions about a factual claim, they vary widely in the strength of their support for the claim.

Although this section reviews each of the major kinds of evidence mentioned above, it concentrates on research studies, for that is the type of evidence critical readers most often have to evaluate when they read archaeology.

Intuition, Authority, and Testimonials

After years of working in a region, archaeologists tend to intuit where sites are located. But is their intuition reliable enough to base a large-scale and expensive regional survey for sites on it? Should surveyors limit their search for sites to places where someone thinks sites are located? Do other archaeologists share the same intuition? The history of archaeology suggests that such intuitions are best regarded as an important source of hypotheses, but not of proof.

A similar caution exists when authorities' testimonials are offered as evidence in support of a claim. Initially, at least, it seems reasonable to accept their testimonials, for they are, after all, experts in their field of study. Typical examples of appeals to authorities in archaeology are "One of the best books of the year" (in a book review), "Studies of historical ceramics show . . ." (researchers), and "The appropriate way to excavate a site is . . ." (college professors).

But like the intuitions of experienced archaeologists, the testimonials of authorities can differ sharply from one another. Think of the heated debates that swirl around topics like the early peopling of the New World. When encountering testimonials by authorities in archaeology, it remains useful to ask questions like the following: Is there any reason why the authority might be biased in this instance? Has the authority actually worked on and written about this particular research topic? Is the authority's knowledge about the topic up to date?

The use of personal testimonials as evidence is rarer in archaeology than it is in daily life ("Smoothest ride I have ever had in a car. You should consider buying one."). Nonetheless, you will occasionally run into testimonials, especially in book cover blurbs and newsletters, and you should be familiar with some of their problems. Common problems are bias in the testimonial (written by a good friend), sparseness of information (due to the short length of a testimonial), and what is, after all, just one person's opinion. For this reason, it is always best to read as many reviews of a book as you can find.

Personal Observation, Case Studies, and Analogies

One might think that personal observations of the archaeological record would be the most secure type of evidence in archaeology. But consider this situation. In describing a sample of projectile points, attributes like raw material type, type of point, color, and basic dimensions of length, width, and thickness are measured. Sounds straightforward, doesn't it? However, archaeologists disagree, more often than one might think, on raw material, color, and point type. Furthermore, since basic dimensions can be measured in different ways, even these basic measures can differ from one person to another. Thus, as critical readers we must develop a "wait and see" attitude toward observations made by the author of an article until they are verified (repeated, confirmed) by other observers.

Archaeologists often rely for their claims on the study of a single artifact assemblage or a single site. Called case studies, such studies are a kind of observational evidence that, like personal observations, can be alluring, for they will be consistent with the conclusion that the study draws. However, on the zero-to-ten scale of factuality, they cannot fall into the blue "it's a fact" zone, for they provide an argument from a sample of one. So again, be cautious in accepting the results of case studies.

Errors occur, too, when archaeologists use analogy to determine the past function of an artifact or feature. Since an artifact made nine thousand years ago may look like better-studied artifacts made in the early historic period, they must have had the same function. The reasoning is based on the similarity in form of the artifacts. But how reliable is resemblance as a source of evidence? Experience suggests caution. So, once again, analogy is best used as a source of hypothesis, but not of proof.

So how does one go about evaluating reasoning by analogy in archaeology? Several strategies have been suggested.[5] Three are mentioned here. The first strategy is simply to recognize the use of an analogy in what you are reading. Besides recognizing the presence of an analogy, remember that the use of analogy does not mean that it will be a persuasive one. A similarity in form in a sample of artifacts does not mean that they were used or thought about in the same way. A second strategy is to concentrate on the relevance of the similarities and differences of the things compared. Do use-wear marks and chemical residues support the claim of a similar function? As a general rule, the greater the ratio of relevant similarities to relevant differences among forms, the stronger the analogy.

Finally, try to think of an alternative analogy or two. What other analogy might account for what is present in the archaeological record? Does the alternative analogy contradict or support the reasoning of the initial analogy? For example, when processual archaeologists argue that a culture is like an adaptive system, they are using a particular analogy to infer conclusions about cultures. Postprocessual archaeologists, however, are more apt to think of a culture as a dysfunctional mishmash of contested meanings and understandings. Whatever one thinks of this analogy, it does create doubts about the persuasiveness of the original "culture as an adaptive system" analogy.

Research Studies as Evidence

In archaeology, the results of research studies are considered the strongest source of evidence for the claims archaeologists make. Since methods of making and recording observations have been established over many decades, it seems reasonable to conclude that the evidence produced in a research study is more reliable than intuition, testimonials, and other kinds of evidence. But ever the inquisitive skeptics, critical readers will still ask a lot of questions. This section of the chapter raises some of the most basic of these questions.[6]

It helps in evaluating research studies to be aware of some of the characteristics of the scientific method and of some of the problems that may crop up with research findings based on this method. To repeat the view of scientific inquiry that was presented in chapter 1, there are three strands of all valid knowledge. These strands are (1) instrumental injunction: a research program, practice, or experiment of the form "If you want to know this, do this"; (2) direct apprehension: a direct experience or apprehension of data brought forth by the injunction; and (3) communal confirmation (or rejection): a checking of the results—the data, the evidence—with others who have the appropriate skills to carry out the injunction.

Note that scientific inquiry as defined here applies to all four quadrants and that "data" refers to direct and immediate experience in any quadrant, not just to the sensory empirical in the upper right quadrant as advocated by flatland modernists. Although each quadrant has its own distinctive kind of reality, type of valid knowledge, mode of study, and means of validation, each is subject to scientific inquiry, since each makes truth claims that are falsifiable through its own kind of experiential evidence.

When reading a piece of literature in archaeology that relies on scientific inquiry as a source of evidence, ask questions like the following:

What Is the Quality of the Source of the Report?

There is well-done research and there is poorly done research. Just because the research has been published does not guarantee that the study is not flawed in important ways. As a general rule, if the results of scholarly research are published in a peer-reviewed journal or book, they are more reliable. Of course, this rule does not mean that research published in a local archaeological journal or other nonreviewed publication outlet is unreliable. Nonetheless, the rule is a place to begin in evaluating research results in a publication.

Have Other Archaeologists Reached a More or Less Similar Conclusion?

As mentioned earlier in the chapter, case studies can be aberrant because of either an aberrant sample of artifacts or unsystematic research procedures. Thus, single research studies presented out of the context of the family of research studies that have investigated this issue can often be misleading. Research findings that are in line with those of other groups of researchers deserve our confidence more than findings that are at odds with them. This does not mean, of course, that the dissident view is necessarily wrong— only that extraordinary claims require extraordinary evidence. We should be open to but wary of claims like these.

Is There Evidence of Strong-Sense Critical Thinking?

Does the writer take into consideration all other relevant research in the area of study? For instance, are studies with contradictory results mentioned? Are there seemingly deliberate deceptive rhetorical flourishes or fallacies in the reasoning? Furthermore, since most conclusions from research have limitations, such as in sample size or representativeness, it is always fair to ask if the writer has adequately qualified (guarded) his conclusions.

Could the Research Be Distorted for One Reason or Another?

This caution covers a number of potential problems, only some of which are mentioned here. One source of bias is the expectations, values, attitudes, and so forth of the researcher himself. As critical readers, we cannot forget that science is not a neutral, value-free, totally objective enterprise. Since important subjective (metaphysical) elements are always involved, we should ask, "Has the author made public his procedures and results so that I and others can judge the merit of his research?" Pressures to get tenure and promotion, to obtain large grants, and to become famous may also influence the objectivity of research findings. Other sources of bias are errors in measurement and sampling.

Was the Research Situation Confusing?

In science, this question generally refers to the relationship between the conditions under which a research study is conducted and the situation the researcher is generalizing about. To what extent can we generalize from mice to humans, for instance? As a general rule, the more unlike two situations are, the more unreliable it is to generalize from one to the other. In archaeology, distortion of this kind is introduced—as we will see—by the disjunction between the archaeological record, the focus of our field and laboratory work, and past human societies, the focus of our conclusions. Both natural and cultural transformation processes also distort the archaeological record. The nature of these distortions is a major defining characteristic of archaeology as a way of knowing the past.

Has the Research Conclusion Been Overgeneralized or Oversimplified?

It is not uncommon for a writer to overgeneralize or oversimplify a research conclusion. Archaeologists often overgeneralize from inadequate samples (for example, they will say something about all Bronze Age spears after studying a sample of thirty of them). They also tend to oversimplify complex situations in search of single causes of culture change (for example, "The culture changed because of climatic change"). In this regard, we should remember that most conclusions from research need to be qualified because of research limitations. A warning buzzer should go off when we encounter a universal conclusion or an overly simple and pat conclusion.

An important characteristic of research findings that has not been stressed is that they do not prove conclusions. At best, they support conclusions. Unlike potsherds, research findings do not speak for themselves. Researchers must always interpret the meaning of their findings—and all findings can be interpreted in more than one way. Thus, researchers' conclusions should not be treated as demonstrated "truths." When you encounter statements like "research shows . . . ," you should retranslate them into "researchers interpret their research findings as showing . . ."

This chapter has shifted our focus to the evaluation of evidence. We have discussed the following kinds of evidence: intuition, appeal to authority, personal observation and testimonial, case studies, analogies, and research studies. Each source has its strengths and weaknesses. Regardless, when we encounter any evidence, we should try to determine its quality by asking, "How good is the evidence?"

How Are the Observations Summarized?

11

ARCHAEOLOGISTS SUMMARIZE the observations they make on some part of the archaeological record through the methodological control of descriptive statistics.[1] The purpose of descriptive statistics is to condense and describe large bodies of data in a precise manner. By reducing an unwieldy mass of observations (data) to manageable proportions, archaeologists are able to ask questions like the following: What is the average volume of the pottery vessels in my site sample? How many have a greater or lesser volume than the average-sized vessel? Do smaller vessels occur more regularly with burials than do larger vessels?

Of course, a summary of a sample of observations is not a transformation from one kind of information to another. Rather, observations are reorganized in order to display their characteristics as a set of data in a more comprehensible and digestible manner. How samples are reorganized and summarized is determined by the objectives (the design) of a research project or, more commonly, by local conventions in the practice of archaeology. For example, descriptions of projectile points typically include measures of length, width, thickness, and weight regardless of the purpose of the project. Sample summaries like these usually form the bulk of the artifact portion of archaeological reports. Chapter 11 provides an overview of the use of these kinds of descriptive statistics in archaeology.

What Are Data?

In archaeological analysis, observations on the archaeological record are generally called data (singular, "datum") and the set of observations together a data set (or database). Each type of observation, such as length, width, and weight, is called a variable or attribute. By convention, variables are measured on one of four scales. In reading a study, it is important to recognize the scale on which variables are measured, for individual statistical techniques are normally restricted to certain scales of measurement.

In ascending order, the four scales are the nominal, ordinal, interval, and ratio scale. An example of a nominal scale variable (in name only) is the presence or absence of beveling along the edge of the blade of a projectile point. Beveling is either absent (0 in the "Bevel." column in table 11.1) or present (1). An ordinal scale variable (forming a sequence) has inherent ordering or ranking but no fixed distance between categories. An example is the extent of grinding around the base of a projectile point. In table 11.1, it can be light (1) or heavy (2) when present. An interval scale variable is a sequence with a fixed distance between measures but an arbitrary zero point, such as C.E. (common era) and B.C.E. (before the common era) dates. The highest level of measurement is a ratio scale variable. A ratio scale variable has the properties of an interval scale variable plus a fixed zero point. An example is a metric measure that has a natural zero point like ten centimeters in length and five grams in weight. It is common to refer to nominal and ordinal variables as categorical (or qualitative) variables and to interval and ratio variables as continuous (or quantitative) variables. Many qualitative variables are dichotomous nominal variables, for they have only two categories, such as present and absent.

When you encounter data in the archaeological literature, ask yourself these questions: Are the units used for measurement (millimeters, grams, pounds) stated clearly? Is a consistent set of measurement units used, or are the measurement units mixed, such as inches and centimeters? What is the scale of the measure (nominal, ordinal, interval, or ratio)?

Tabular and Pictorial Methods of Displaying Data

Descriptive statistics are concerned with the display and summary of data, for tables, diagrams, and individual summary statistics enable a rapid understanding of the characteristics of a raw database. The parameters of individual variables, different relationships between two variables, and trends and peaks within the data set can all be recognized and quantified with these simple techniques. This section describes simple examples of tabular and pictorial statistics.

Since a database in archaeology usually consists of a large number of items, archaeologists normally transform individual measures to frequen-

Table 11.1. Database for Side-Notched Projectile Points

No.	Length	Width	Thick.	Stem Length	Stem Width	Notch Width	Notch Depth	Wt.	Basal Grind	Serra.	Bevel.	Age B.C.E.
1	93	37	10	14	32	7	8	33	1	0	0	8000
2	68	34	8	12	27	5	7	17	0	0	0	7200
3	48	28	6	8	30	4	2	14	0	0	0	7500
4	59	33	7	11	26	4	3	16	0	0	0	6100
5	45	26	6	8	19	3	4	11	0	0	0	6500
6	62	35	8	12	27	5	8	18	0	0	0	7000
7	87	36	8	13	31	6	7	31	0	0	0	7300
8	35	24	6	8	20	3	2	5	0	0	0	6200
9	91	35	8	14	32	7	8	32	0	0	0	6000
10	63	34	8	11	26	5	6	8	0	0	0	6600
11	38	28	7	10	23	4	3	6	0	0	0	7000
12	82	35	8	13	32	6	7	30	0	0	0	7300
13	64	36	9	10	28	5	7	14	0	0	0	7900
14	44	28	7	9	19	4	4	9	0	0	0	6100
15	61	33	7	11	26	5	6	13	0	0	0	6900
16	57	31	6	8	20	4	6	11	0	0	0	6300
17	84	35	8	13	31	7	7	31	0	0	0	7600
18	32	23	6	8	19	3	4	5	0	0	0	6600

(continued)

Table 11.1. (continued)

No.	Length	Width	Thick.	Stem Length	Stem Width	Notch Width	Notch Depth	Wt.	Basal Grind	Serra.	Bevel.	Age B.C.E.
19	55	30	7	10	22	4	5	12	0	0	0	7600
20	59	33	7	11	25	4	6	13	0	0	0	6800
21	57	37	9	19	33	6	8	16	0	0	0	7500
22	45	30	9	17	27	5	6	14	0	0	0	7400
23	90	53	11	25	39	9	11	38	2	1	1	7800
24	51	31	7	16	27	3	6	14	1	0	1	7200
25	77	42	11	22	36	7	9	28	0	2	1	7100
26	58	38	10	20	34	6	9	17	0	0	0	7500
27	94	55	12	26	41	10	12	43	2	1	1	7000
28	66	42	11	22	37	8	9	19	0	0	1	7500
29	46	33	8	17	29	5	7	14	0	0	1	7200
30	72	45	10	22	35	7	10	28	0	2	1	7700
31	91	52	11	25	40	9	11	40	1	1	0	7300
32	69	43	11	23	38	8	9	29	0	0	0	6800
33	81	49	9	22	35	8	9	35	1	0	1	7100
34	48	30	9	16	25	5	6	12	0	0	1	7000
35	88	51	10	24	39	9	10	37	2	1	1	7000
36	40	28	8	15	23	4	5	9	0	0	0	7300
37	85	50	10	23	38	8	10	35	2	1	1	6900
38	41	28	8	16	24	5	6	11	0	0	1	7500
39	93	54	12	26	33	6	9	32	1	1	1	7400
40	78	42	11	21	36	7	9	29	1	2	1	7000

cies when preparing pictorial displays of the database. A frequency (usually abbreviated as f) is the number of times a particular value (measure or attribute) occurs in a database. The result is a frequency count, such as the breakdown of the forty projectile points in table 11.1 into five that have light basal grinding (1 in the basal grind column), four that have very heavy grinding (2), and thirty-one that lack basal grinding altogether (0).

Archaeologists often mention the percentages of certain items in a sample in their reports in addition to counts. Frequencies are converted to percentages by dividing each frequency by the total number of items or measures and multiplying by one hundred. Thus, the percentage of points that have light basal grinding in the sample of forty points in table 11.1 is obtained by dividing 5 by 40 and multiplying by 100 ($5/40 \times 100 = 12.5$ percent). Percentages are a useful transformation, for they normalize differences in size among samples. Table 11.1 is a simple, if typical, frequency table with percentages.

A bar chart is a graphic version of a frequency table. The vertical scale can be in frequencies or percentages (in which case it is a percentage bar chart). If percentages are used, the frequency for each bar is normally also shown. The bars should be of the same width, with each bar separated by a gap to show that the variable is categorical and not continuous. A histogram is the pictorial equivalent of the grouped frequency table; it displays a continuous variable that has been divided into classes. As with bar charts, histograms can be horizontal or vertical, although you will not encounter many horizontal histograms in the archaeological literature. Other approaches to the pictorial display of continuous data include stem-and-leaf plots, the ogive (or cumulative frequency graph), pictograms (a bar chart that uses pictures for bars), and scatterplots (which allow the plotting of the values of one variable against another variable). Figures 11.1 and 11.2 contain examples of several of these pictorial methods of displaying data.

When you encounter statistical pictures in your reading, ask yourself the following questions: Does the picture include a title that adequately summarizes the purpose of the picture? Is the purpose of the picture within the context of the study clear? Are all units of measurement clearly stated? If percentages are used, are actual counts included so that the percentages can be checked or the actual counts studied? Is everything clearly labeled, leaving no ambiguity? Is a source given for the data, either with the picture or in the accompanying report? Is there information cluttering the picture or misleading the eye? Is the picture sufficiently large so that detail is clear? Is the number of decimal places in ratio variables standardized, certainly within the measurements of one variable, and preferably within the whole picture?

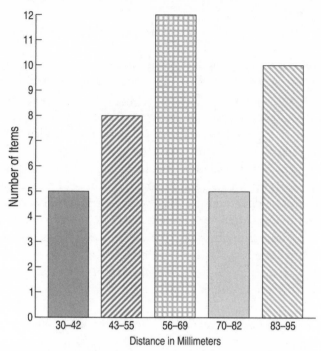

Figure 11.1. Histogram of the length measurements of forty stone projectile points in millimeters.

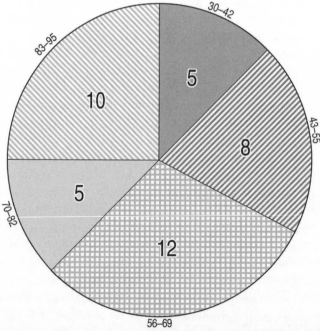

Figure 11.2. Pie chart of the length measurements of forty stone projectile points in millimeters (mm). Values inside the circle refer to number of items; numbers outside the circle refer to distances in mm.

Measures of Position: The Average

If you were to encounter table 11.1 in your reading, it would be difficult, at a glance, to get at some information about the projectile points in the sample because there is too much raw detail. Take point length ("Length" in column 2), for example. As far as length is concerned, what is an average length of a point in the data set? How many points are larger or smaller than that average? The tabular and pictorial displays of the last section go some way toward summarizing and making sense of this data set, but it is possible to be even more precise (see table 11.2).

Table 11.2.   Univariate (one variable) Frequency Table Comparing the Length Measurements of Forty Stone Projectile Points (mm)

Point Length	Frequency	Percentage
Long	9	22.5
Medium	20	50.0
Short	11	27.5
Total	40	100.0

Although the term "average" is regularly encountered in the archaeological literature, it is frequently used in an imprecise manner. When most people talk of the average (add up all the values and divide by the total number of values), they are referring to the mean. But there are two other common measures of position or average that are useful in archaeology: the mode and the median. In your reading, it is important to recognize the particular type of "average" being used, for all three measures have different advantages and disadvantages. Usually, the most suitable measure of position depends on the scale of the variable being measured.

The *mode* of a frequency distribution is that measure (or set of measures) that is present most often. That is, it is the most popular measure or the measure that has the highest frequency count. While the mode can be used for variables measured at any level, it is the only measure of position that can be used for nominal data. When used with interval and ratio scale variables, measures must be grouped into discrete sets, with the set with the greatest number of measures being the mode. For the nominal variable "presence or absence of beveling" ("Bevel.") in table 11.1, fourteen projectile points were found with beveling along the edges of the blade (1) and twenty-six without beveling (2). Since attribute 2 (no beveling) is the most common (frequent or popular), it is the mode or modal measure for this variable.

Because the mode is a relatively simple statistic, readers should be aware that problems can occur when it is used. To begin with, it is an unstable measure, for it can change wildly by the alteration of only a few measures. For example, a histogram of point length values in table 11.1 would indicate that the span 50 to 70 mm, which has a frequency of fourteen, is the modal class. It would only take the addition of four more values to the 30 to 50 mm length span, however, to change the mode. Despite these problems, it is still occasionally useful to know the "typical" or "most popular" value in a distribution. If the variable is nominal, then there is no alternative when speaking of the "average" but to use the mode.

The *median* of a distribution is that value that cuts the distribution in half. One half of the values will be larger than the median and the other half smaller. While the median can be calculated for variables that are ordinal or higher, it is most suitable for ordinal variables. The median cannot be used with nominal variables. The median is calculated by listing the values in order and determining the central value. In the sequence 3, 5, 8, 9, 10, the median is 8 (the middle number). If the number of values is even, the median (often abbreviated "Md." in reports) is halfway between the middle two (add the two values and divide by 2). For example, there are forty measures for the variable age ("Age BCE") that range from 6000 to 8000 B.C.E. If they are listed in order, the middle two values would be 7100 and 7200. The median, then, would be $(7100 + 7200)/2 = 7150$ B.C.E.

As with the mode, changes in just one or two values can affect the median. In the "date" example above, changing the twentieth measure to 7100 B.C.E. would cause the median to also change to 7100 B.C.E. (you might want to work this out yourself). However, the median has the advantage of not being sensitive to occasional extreme values (outliers) that can seriously influence the mean (see below).

The statistical *mean* is the most common form of average and can be used on interval or ratio data but not on nominal or ordinal data. The usual notation for the mean of a variable x is an "x" with a bar over it. The mean is calculated by summing the measures and dividing by the total number of measures. For example, the mean of the length measures in table 11.1 is calculated by adding up all of the measures (the total is 2,597) and dividing by the total number of measures (40); in this case, the mean is 64.9 mm. Note that calculating a mean usually produces an answer to several decimal places, especially when using a calculator (in this case 64.925). In your reading, means are generally rounded down to a level of accuracy that makes sense archaeologically. In most instances, rounding to a tenth (64.9 in the above example) is a sufficient degree of accuracy.

The mean is only truly representative of the center of a set of measures if the measures are grouped closely around a central measure. However, since it is sensitive to all measures in the distribution, it can be a very misleading measure of position. If the distribution is widely spread, unevenly distributed, has groups toward the extremes, or even has just one or two outliers, the mean will not be a good measure of position or average.

It is important for you to understand that the mode, median, and mean are three quite different measures of position, for they measure different qualities of the same distribution. This is why researchers often give three different values when applied to the same data set. Consequently, you should be wary when only one of these measures is cited as the "average." So, when you encounter measures of central tendency in the archaeological literature, ask yourself the following questions: Is it clear which "average" is being used? If the mode is the measure of central tendency, are the problems associated with the use of the mode present? If the median is the measure of central tendency, are the problems associated with the use of the median present? If the mean is the measure of central tendency, are the problems associated with the use of the mean present?

Measures of Variability: The Spread

By using methods like those described in the last section, archaeologists are able to display the distribution of a variable and give a measure of its "average" value. However, these statistics alone are not enough to adequately describe a distribution, as shown in figure 11.3.

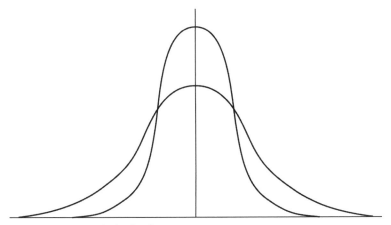

Figure 11.3.   Spread of a distribution.

The two hypothetical distributions in figure 11.3 have the same mean (and median and mode), but they are obviously very different. One has widespread values, and the other has values that are clustered around the mean. This section describes several ways archaeologists quantify the spread or variation within a distribution. These statistics, which only apply to interval and ratio data, are called measures of variability or dispersion.

The *range* measures the total spread of the distribution. It is a simple measure and is of limited use. The range is calculated by subtracting the minimum value from the maximum value. For example, the variable length in table 11.1 has a maximum value of 94, a minimum value of 32, and thus a range of 62 (94 − 32 = 62).

Because the range is such a simple measure, there are problems with its use. Like the mean, it is seriously affected by outliers (single extreme values). If the maximum length variable in table 11.1 had a value of 130 rather than 94, the range for the sample of lengths would be 130 − 32 = 98. The addition of this one value alters the range from 62 to 98, an addition of thirty-six points. The range can only be used as a sensible measure of dispersion when all the values are clustered together, for it gives the reader the impression that a distribution is evenly spread, when in reality there may be extreme outliers.

The standard deviation (usually shortened to "S.D." in reports) is the most common measure of dispersion in archaeology. A straightforward definition of the standard deviation is the average distance of the observed values from their mean. Like the mean, the standard deviation is also important because it forms the basis of further statistical tests.

Here are the steps necessary to compute the standard deviation (most calculators and computer programs now handle this task for you):

1. Find the mean.
2. Find the deviation of each value from the mean (that is, subtract the value from the mean).
3. Square the deviations.
4. Sum the squared deviations.
5. Divide the sum of the squares by the total number of values less one, which gives a number called the variance.
6. Take the square root of the variance. The result is the standard deviation.

As an example, consider the length of projectile points in table 11.1. How variable is this sample of lengths of points? Let's follow the steps above for calculating the standard deviation.

Step 1. Calculate the different between each value and the mean (64.9): starting at the top we would get 64.9 − 93 = −28.1, 64.9 − 68 = −3.1, 64.9 − 48 = 16.9, and so on for all forty values.

Step 2. Square each difference: −28.1 squared = 789.6, −3.1 squared = 9.6, 16.9 squared = 285.6, and so on.

Step 3. Add the squared differences, which equals 13,766.9.

Step 4. Divide the sum of the squares by the total number of values less one (13,766.9/40 − 1), which equals 353.0.

Step 5. Take the square root of the last number (353.0) to find the standard deviation, which is 18.8.

If we calculate the standard deviation of the maximum length of the set of projectile points in rows 1 through 20 and the set of points in rows 21 through 40 (these are two early Archaic point types in the Eastern Woodlands of North America), we obtain a standard deviation (S.D.) of 18.3 for the points in the first point type and 18.9 for the points in the second point type. At least in this sample, the standard deviation or dispersion of the two point types is roughly the same; the two types cannot be distinguished on the basis of the standard deviation or pattern of dispersion of the lengths of their points.

Without a proper investigation of the dispersion or variability of a distribution, no meaningful comparisons or inferences can be made. Of all the different measures of variation, the standard deviation is certainly the most used in archaeology. Other measures of variability not considered here include the interquartile range and quartile deviation, the mean deviation, the coefficient of variation, and boxplots, which are sometimes also called box-and-whisker plots.

The summary statistics introduced in this chapter are best used in an exploratory manner. No one statistic, such as the mean, for example, provides "the measure" of a data set. Consequently, the reader will notice that archaeologists tend to explore the characteristics of the data sets they are working with in their reports. They do this by using different techniques, including graphical representations whenever possible, and then comparing the results. It is a worthwhile exercise to compare sample summaries in different reports to gauge how archaeologists vary in their degree of "playfulness" in applying descriptive statistics to their databases.

Is There an Inductive Argument?   **12**

S INCE THE TRANSFORMATION of a sample summary to an empirical generalization—the next phase in the research cycle—involves an inductive argument, this seems an appropriate place to review inductive reasoning in general. Although the examples of inductive reasoning included in that transformation are still confined to statements about the archaeological record (the leap to statements about past real-world contexts has not yet been made), the same kind of reasoning is often involved in developing interpretations of the past from archaeological evidence, a process that is reviewed in part III of this book.

In books on critical thinking, three core kinds of inductive argument are identified: inductive generalizations, analogical arguments, and arguments for causation in populations.[1] The second and third sections of this chapter look at the first two of these kinds of inductive argument; arguments for causation in populations are considered in the general review of causal arguments in chapter 17. The first section differentiates between deductive and inductive arguments, and the last section considers some of the fallacies (errors in reasoning) associated with inductive reasoning.

Deductive and Inductive Arguments

In a valid deductive argument, the conclusion follows with logical necessity from the reasons provided in support of it. Said another way, the conclusion must be true if the argument is correctly formed and the reasons given in support of it are true. For example:

> [P] Since all Sandy Lake village sites contain evidence of intensive wild rice harvesting, and [P] the Upper Rice Lake site is a Sandy Lake village

site, therefore [C] the Upper Rice Lake site contains evidence of intensive
wild rice harvesting.

As in this example the conclusion of a valid deductive argument is
contained in the reasons given for it. Since the Upper Rice Lake site is a
Sandy Lake village site and all Sandy Lake village sites contain evidence
of intensive wild rice harvesting, it follows with logical certainty that the
Upper Rice Lake site contains evidence of intensive wild rice harvesting.
The conclusion has been drawn out of the premises.

An inductive argument is one in which the premises are intended to
provide some evidence in support of the truth of the conclusion. In contrast to a correctly formed deductive argument with true premises, the
conclusion of an inductive argument does not follow with logical necessity
or certainty from the premises. This is so even if all the premises are true.
The reason is that the conclusion is not already contained in any of the
premises. Consider this example:

> [P] Since all Sandy Lake village sites studied contain evidence of intensive
> wild rice harvesting, and [P] the Upper Rice Lake site is a Sandy Lake vil-
> lage site, therefore [C] the Upper Rice Lake site will contain evidence of
> intensive wild rice harvesting too.

In inductive arguments like this one, the conclusion is a probable, but
not a certain, outcome of the argument. For this reason, deductive and inductive arguments use different terms to indicate the presence of a good or
bad argument. Deductive arguments are either valid or invalid (and sound
or unsound; see chapter 18), while inductive arguments run the spectrum
from weak to strong.

Inductive Generalizations

A form of reasoning that draws an inference (a conjecture or supposition)
from specific instances to a conclusion is called an inductive generalization.
Archaeologists make inductive generalizations all the time. Let's say that
in a flint-chipping replication study a stone is struck in a particular way
with a certain amount of force. After dozens of replications of the same
experiment, the archaeologist conducting the study is ready to conclude
from a sample of strikes that the result (the conclusion) will be the same if
the stone is struck in the same way with the same amount of force. The
principle in inductive thinking is that if all or most of the results of a sample
of tests (or excavation situations) have a certain outcome, then many, if not
all, future tests will have the same result. Consider the following example:

[P] Most Sandy Lake village sites I have excavated contain evidence of intensive wild rice harvesting. [C] Most Sandy Lake village sites contain evidence of intensive wild rice harvesting.

The members of the sample in the premise have a property, evidence of intensive wild rice harvesting. It is this property that the conclusion claims is a likely property of most Sandy Lake sites. In inductive arguments, properties like this are called the property in question, and the overall population that supposedly has this property as well is called the target population (or simply the population). Here the sample is those Sandy Lake sites I have excavated, the property in question is containing evidence of intensive wild rice harvesting, and the target population is most Sandy Lake sites.

Representativeness and Bias

In the above example, I have reasoned inductively that if a sample has a property, then the target population of which it is assumed to be a part will (or is likely to) have the property too. But note the "of which it is assumed to be a part." Are all of the Sandy Lake sites that I have excavated really village sites? Since most archaeological sites are multicomponent (contain two or more occupations from different time periods or archaeological cultures), perhaps the extensive spread of lithic debris, animal bone, and subsurface storage pits that I assumed was associated with the Sandy Lake component is actually associated with an earlier or later component at one or more of these sites.

A crucial criterion, then, of an inductive argument is that a sample must be representative of the target population. Furthermore, the assumption is being made in the Sandy Lake example that all of the village sites are similar. What if only late summer–early fall village sites contain evidence of intensive wild rice harvesting and late spring–early summer sites do not? Thus, a sample represents a target population only if the members of the sample and the population are similar (or nearly so) regarding the property in question. If they are not, then the sample is biased.

In inductive generalizations, a sample that is not representative of its target population will not provide strong (if any) support for the conclusion of the generalization. Since it is a biased sample, the inductive generalization is very weak or possibly false. A crucial task for you as a critical reader, then, is to determine whether the sample used in something you are reading is representative of the target population of the study.

How do archaeologists go about selecting samples that are representative of a target population? One way is to determine whether a population of things is most likely homogeneous. If it is, then a researcher can be confident in the representativeness of the sample. Consider the situation in which a historical archaeologist finds five metal bolts at a site that are embossed with the same manufacturer name and model number. In this situation, we as readers can be confident that this sample accurately represents the entire population of bolts of this model. However, this is a rare situation, for most populations that archaeologists work with are not homogeneous.

How, then, should populations that are heterogeneous or diverse in character be sampled in order to achieve a representative sample? Statistical experiments show that the best way to do this is to select a sample at random from the population. For our purposes, a random sample of a population can be defined as one in which every item in a population has an equal or known chance of being selected. Whether this ideal is always practical or achievable in archaeology is another matter. For example, are archaeologists aware of the location of every Sandy Lake village site? What if some Sandy Lake village sites have been destroyed? And so on.

Random Variation

Errors in drawing inductive generalizations are frequently the result, too, of random differences from one sample to another. For instance, even if you know that there are fifty black and fifty white marbles in a bowl, you would not expect to get five black and five white marbles each time you draw ten marbles. On some draws you might get four and six, and on others eight and two.

As illustrative as this example is of the problem of random variation in samples, it does not come close to representing archaeological reality. Let's say than an archaeologist is interested in the average length of Waubesa projectile points, a common point type in the Upper Mississippi River region. Two hundred Waubesa points are available for measurement. As an exercise in teaching his students the meaning of random variation in samples, he measures the length of all points in his population of two hundred points and determines that their average length is 5.6 cm. He then has each member of the class measure the length of fifteen points that they pick out of the population of two hundred points. Since stone points like the Waubesa point were made by a variety of different knappers and not stamped out by a machine, they vary somewhat in length. In addition, their length became shorter when they were resharpened, and some points were resharpened more often than others. What is the likelihood that the calculated length of each sample of points would be exactly 5.6 cm? It is more likely that some calculated averages would be less than and others greater than 5.6 cm. The spread of these calculated averages around the true mean is called the error margin. In this example it may be 5.6 ± 1.2 cm.

Critical readers should know that the margin of error around a known value of a target population is related to sample size. As a rule, the error margin around a value becomes smaller as sample size becomes larger (think about it). Conversely, the wider the error margin, the more likely it is that the value of an inductive generalization to an unknown population will fall somewhere within the range of the error margin. In the marble example, suppose we find that 30 percent of a handful of marbles from the bowl are black. We can be more confident that 30 ± 10 percent of all the marbles in the bowl are black than we can that 30 ± 2 percent of the marbles have the property of being black.

Evaluations of the strength of inductive generalizations depend, then, on both the size of the randomly generated sample and on the width of the error margin (called the level of confidence). The strength of a generalization increases the larger the sample and the wider the error margin. But is this a completely satisfying result? Wouldn't an inductive generalization that has a smaller margin of error be preferred? In statistical reasoning, there are trade-offs. Although a smaller error margin seems more precise, the probability of a true value falling within a wider margin of error is greater.

When you encounter an inductive generalization in your readings of archaeology, ask yourself the following questions: Is the sample homogeneous or heterogeneous? If it is a heterogeneous sample, was it collected using a random sampling technique? Did the writer take sample size, width of error margin, and the degree of heterogeneity of the sample into consideration when making an inductive generalization?

Analogical Arguments

Analogical arguments are another kind of inductive argument. Consider the following:

> Blackduck and Kathio culture Lake Woodland sites are alike in many ways. They share the same environmental setting, although in adjacent regions. They contain similar-appearing pottery, evidence for a hunter-gatherer lifeway, and a scattering of different kinds of functional sites in similar niches. Given these similarities, we would expect there to be other similarities. For

example, if we learn through excavation that Kathio sites lack deep storage pits, we might predict that Blackduck sites lack deep storage pits too.

Underlying an analogical argument is the assumption that if two or more things share some traits together, they are likely to share others—and if they share many traits together, they are likely to share many more traits together. The pattern of an analogical argument is based on this assumption.[2] When expressed formally, the argument runs as follows:

X, Y, and Z have properties a, b, c, etc.
Furthermore, X and Y have the additional property f.
Therefore, Z has feature f, too.

In this line of reasoning, f is the property (or attribute) in question (that is, is Z likely to have f?), a property known to be present in the sample, X and Y. Since X, Y, and Z have a number of other properties in common (a, b, c, etc.), the case can be made that Z has (or is likely to have) the property in question, f. In the literature, Z is often called the target item.

In contrast to an inductive generalization, which generalizes from a sample of an unknown total population to that population, an analogical argument extends its claim from a sample of a population to another member of that population. Nonetheless, the two forms of inductive argument share an important feature in common: in both forms of argument, the sample and the target item belong to the same population. Of course, the problem is determining just what that shared population is. Since it remains to be established, it is commonly referred to as the implied target population.

As with inductive generalizations, when you encounter an analogical argument in your reading, ask this question: Is there some reason why the sample is not representative of the implied target population (perhaps the members of the population are quite heterogeneous and the sample was not selected using random sampling techniques, or perhaps the sample is made up of apples and oranges—that is, of members that actually belong to different populations)? Is the conclusion appropriate to the nature of the sample (that is, does the writer overstate the evidence)?

Fallacies of Inductive Reasoning

Fallacies of inductive reasoning commonly do not satisfy the sufficiency criterion of a good argument. That is, the premises provided in their support are not sufficient in number or quality to justify accepting the conclusion. There are many fallacies of inductive reasoning.[3] Six that you are likely to encounter when you read archaeology are mentioned here.

Hasty Generalization

In their enthusiasm, archaeologists will occasionally (and more likely often) overextend the conclusion of an inductive argument, whether an inductive generalization or an analogical argument. The reason is frequently a sample that either is too small or has an integrity that has not been established. The word "integrity" refers here to a sample whose members are all part of the same implied target population. When an archaeologist overextends a generalization or is unguarded in drawing a conclusion, he has committed the fallacy of hasty generalization. If you think that all assemblages of Blackduck pottery sherds have an average thickness of 6.2 mm on the grounds that an assemblage of sherds from the site you recently excavated has that average thickness, you commit this fallacy. This is one of the more pervasive errors in archaeological reasoning.

Appeal to Anecdotal Evidence

A common form of hasty generalization is to base an inductive generalization or the conclusion of an analogical argument on an anecdote. Let's say that two friends of Tim, a friend of yours, attended an archaeological field school in (let's assume) the northern Great Plains. Both told tales of how the field school instructor and his visiting northern Great Plains fellow archaeologists drank and caroused at the local bar every evening. Tim concluded that archaeologists on the northern Great Plains drank and caroused too much. He decided to apply to a field school in Ireland. Do all northern Great Plains archaeologists drink and carouse too much? Rollicking tales about a few northern Great Plains archaeologists do not support the conclusion that all northern Great Plains archaeologists drink and carouse too much.

Biased Generalization

A third common fallacy of inductive reasoning is biased generalization. A biased generalization occurs when the sample is not representative of a population, as in this example:

> Suppose you examine the large Late Woodland sample of pottery from one county and that this sample is larger than all of the samples put together that exist for the ten lesser investigated counties near it. Without additional

information, you cannot assume that your large sample is representative of Late Woodland pottery in all eleven counties. Your county may, for example, border the Great Plains and have, therefore, a greater amount of Plains ceramic traits than is characteristic of the Late Woodland pottery in the other ten counties, which are (let's say) further away from the Great Plains.

The data are not representative because they were not proportionately drawn from all relevant subpopulations and the target population itself is not homogeneous. The problem here is not sample size but representativeness.[4]

Gambler's Fallacy

It is also worth mentioning a famous error in inductive reasoning that on the surface seems intuitively correct. This fallacy is called the gambler's fallacy because it refers to the probability of something occurring, which is the very heart of gambling. The usual example is a flip of a coin that has come up heads four times in a row. Shouldn't the next flip be tails to make up for the previous heads? In this example, because the two choices remain heads or tails, the probability of getting another head remains 50 percent. An archaeological example is whether a Type A or a Type B projectile point will show up next when four Type A points in a row have been selected at random from a list of two hundred points, half of which are Type As and half of which are Type Bs.

Availability Bias

This is a common fallacy in archaeology. Let's say an archaeologist bases his measurements of the average length of a type of projectile point on the readily available sample in her laboratory. What are the chances that the points in the laboratory collection are a representative sample of all points of that type? Perhaps only the most evenly shaped of that type of point were added to the collection. This fallacy, which also violates the sufficiency criterion of a good argument, may occur when the only reason a sample is used in a study is its ready availability.

Confirmation Bias

Archaeologists commit the confirmation bias when they purposely choose (either consciously or not) data that strengthen support for a hypothesis and disregard data that are less supportive. A principle of the scientific method is that data chosen to test a hypothesis should be chosen in an unbiased manner. According to Karl Popper's falsifiability criterion, every effort should be made to falsify a hypothesis rather than to confirm it.[5] The reasoning is that while the recording of the presence of hundreds of white swans adds confirmation to the conclusion that "All swans are white," it takes only one black swan (present in Australia, for example) to disprove the conclusion. Likewise, it takes only one Raddatz projectile point 1.7 cm long to disprove the generalization that all Raddatz points are between 2.1 and 5.4 cm in length.

It is important for you as a critical reader to understand the nature and purpose of inductive reasoning, for most of the arguments you encounter when reading archaeology will be inductive arguments. However, it is not sufficient to know only something in general about inductive reasoning; it is as important to understand the function of inductive reasoning in the research cycle. In chapter 13, we look at its use in transforming sample summaries into empirical generalizations.

Is There a Population Estimate from a Sample?

13

S AMPLE SUMMARIES ANSWER certain kinds of questions in archaeology and generate new research puzzles. However, if the conclusions of most studies of artifacts are a guide, archaeologists are more interested in the populations from which these samples were drawn. For instance, after measuring the attributes of ten projectile points of a certain kind, they will generalize their conclusions to all projectile points of that type. There is a shift in focus in these reports from the information content of sample summaries to the information content of empirical generalizations. Because of this focus on populations, the transformation of sample summaries to empirical generalizations is generally the more important of the two transformations in the bottom left quadrant of the research cycle.

As we saw in the last chapter, empirical generalizations are made through the process of induction from a smaller, often randomly selected sample to a usually unknown, larger set called a population. The process expands sample descriptions to generalizations. That is, it expands statements about the characteristics of samples to statements about the characteristics of the populations of which the samples are subsets. Some empirical generalizations are inferences (reasoned guesses) about single properties of classes or types of artifacts or features, such as the average weight, the range in length, and the number of a class or type of artifact in an incompletely known universe. Examples of incompletely known universes are the full contents of a partially excavated site, all of the axes made in a region during the Bronze Age, and all of the habitation sites in an area that were in existence at a certain time in the past.

Another kind of empirical generalization is a statement about associations between properties of artifacts, features, sites, and ecofacts. An example is a statement that claims that there is a high correlation between the presence of stone scraping tools and the presence of fish bones in a series of sites. Although these statements began as claims about associations among a series of samples, they have been transformed through inferential statistics to claims about the relationships between the populations of which the samples are subsets.

Since this second kind of transformation involves a conceptual leap from statements about the known (samples) to references to something incompletely known (populations), an uncertainty enters the research process—no matter how rigorously the transformation has been made. This kind of uncertainty, which accumulates as one moves around the research cycle, makes the evaluation of interpretations of the past in archaeology difficult, as we will see in part IV.

Readers should notice that these statements, like sample summaries, are still about the material patterns that exist or may exist in the archaeological record. They are empirical generalizations because they are about the material (empirical) stuff of archaeology. Nonetheless, they generalize beyond the samples studied to the populations of which they are a subset.

Chapter 13 has three sections. The first introduces the concept of statistical inference, the second the formal process of hypothesis testing, and the third a case study that illustrates these notions in some detail. Though necessarily brief, the chapter introduces the use of statistical inference in archaeology.

Statistical Inference

All sciences grapple with the problem of drawing reasonable conclusions about finite universes (populations) when only samples are available for study. While archaeologists often make inspired guesses about the characteristics of universes based on a familiarity with samples, the most reliable method available for making accurate inferences from samples to populations is statistical inference. Statistical inference is a process of reasoning from a sample description (a statistic) to a population description (a parameter) using the principles of probability. This inferential leap to a new kind of information is controlled by the process of probability sampling, a process designed to determine the chance of error occurring in making inferences of this kind once a set of observations has been made.

In easy summary, the core concepts of inferential statistics are natural variability, probability, independence, distribution, sample size, and statistical significance.

Natural Variability

When archaeologists measure the same variable across several samples, such as the length of projectile points from two sites, they are bound to get some variability. Although some of this may be due to differences in measuring instruments or procedures, most is simply due to the fact that every point is somewhat different. Variability is simply inherent in artifact samples and in the world in general. Therefore, if archaeologists want to determine whether the two samples could have come from the same population, they first need to know how much variability to expect in the population. The more variability there is within a population, the more difficult it is to determine whether the two samples are members of the same population. This basic idea, comparing natural variability to the variability induced by different behaviors or cultural ideals, forms the heart of modern statistics.

Probability

The probability of something is simply the likelihood of its occurring given the variability within a population. An example is the likelihood (probability) of choosing at random a projectile point in table 11.1 that has serrations along the blade edge (it is 0.225 or 22.5 percent). Here, "random" simply means that every spearhead was given an equal chance of being chosen.

Independence

This concept refers to situations in which the probability of one variable being present or absent makes no difference to the probability that another variable will be present or absent. If that is the case, then the variables are independent; otherwise they are dependent. In our data set, corner notches and quality of material are dependent, because if a projectile point has corner notches, it is more likely to be made of high-quality stone than of low-quality stone. In testing models, archaeologists are intensely interested in whether the relationship among two or more variables is independent or dependent.

Distribution

Distribution refers to the shape of the population from which a sample is drawn. Since different shapes have different mathematical properties, archaeologists are able to make inferences about a population from a sample if they are able to accurately infer the shape of the population from the sample. For variables that are measured on a ratio, interval, or ordinal scale, the most important shape is the normal distribution (the familiar bell-shaped curve), because many naturally occurring distributions are very similar to it, and its mathematical properties have been worked out in detail.

Sample Size

Given the range of natural and culturally induced variability within a population, it is common sense that larger samples will more often than not be more like the populations from which they are drawn than will smaller samples. The classic example of this principle is a flipped coin. While a series of one hundred flips may begin with five straight heads, the proportion of heads to tails generally evens out as one hundred flips are approached. You can try this experiment yourself with the projectile point data set. Choose a variable and then sample the values using different-size samples. What results did you get?

Statistical Significance

Since archaeologists normally work with samples, they are naturally interested in whether the characteristics (statistics) of their samples differ from the characteristics (parameters) of the presumed populations from which they are drawn. Phrased another way, since most populations are variable, they are interested in this question: How often would we expect to get the results at hand by grabbing a sample of the variable population at random? By using appropriate statistical models, they try to determine what the likelihood of that result is given certain assumptions about the population and a predetermined probability standard. If the likelihood is very small, then they have grounds to assume that the sample was not drawn from that population. However, if the likelihood is high, then they have grounds to assume that the sample was drawn from the population.

If you are somewhat confused because of the abstractness of this discussion, do not despair, for these concepts weave throughout the remainder of the chapter.

Statistical inference is for three main uses in the lower left quadrant of the research cycle. The first use is the comparison of sample summaries. These comparisons allow archaeologists to answer questions like the following: Do the bronze spearheads in a cemetery tend to occur more often with male rather than female burials? Are the larger, richer burials around an Iron Age settlement closer to the settlement than are the smaller, poorer burials? Is the proportion of pottery Type A the same at two sites, even though the sample numbers obtained are somewhat different? In all of these examples, the question being asked is the same: Is the difference between two numbers significant (in a statistical sense), or is the difference the result of chance alone?

A second use of statistical inference in the lower left quadrant of the research cycle is to determine whether a sample is representative of a hypothetical (modeled) population. For example, an optimal foraging model might predict that 67 percent of the large- and medium-sized animal bones recovered from a particular fall hunting camp should be deer bone. The actual percentage of deer bone recovered during a partial excavation of the site is only 53 percent. Is the difference between the two numbers significant or could the difference be the result of chance alone?

The third use of statistical inference in this quadrant is in the estimation of the parameters (the characteristics) of populations. Let's assume that an archaeologist has test excavated fifteen of the thirty known sites of an archaeological complex and has found that the sample of Walser projectile points recovered during these test excavations range in length from four to six inches. What is the likelihood (the probability) that this is the actual range in length of all Walser points ever made? What is the most accurate way of portraying this parameter (the length of all Walser points ever made)?

The first two uses of statistical inference in the research cycle are commonly used in the testing of deductions derived from interpretations of the past (the top of the research cycle) that have been given archaeological interpretations (the upper right quadrant of the research cycle). In statistical hypothesis testing, archaeologists are interested in how well new data support an interpretation of the past and its logical implications (its hypotheses) when transformed into statements about the archaeological record. The question being asked is whether the interpretation of the past and its implications are strongly supported, weakly supported, or not at all supported by these new data.

The third use is in the construction of interpretations of the past. This use involves the process of estimation. Here the question is as follows: What are the properties of the population of archaeological things (artifacts, features, etc.) that we are going to build our interpretation (theory) on?

Hypothesis Testing

Each of the three uses of statistical inference mentioned above involves the formal process of statistical hypothesis testing. To get the idea, imagine an opaque plastic bowl that contains seventy black and thirty white marbles. Two people each reach into the bowl and, without looking, take out ten marbles. One person's sample has eight black and two white marbles. The other person's sample has five black and five white marbles. Now, if we did not know that there were one hundred marbles in the bowl, that seventy were black and thirty white, and that both samples were drawn from the same bowl, how could we go about determining whether the two samples could have come from the same bowl?

Archaeologists grapple with this same kind of uncertainty constantly because of situations like site destruction, incompletely excavated sites, destroyed or lost artifacts, and unwritten reports. All of these situations mask the nature of the populations that are being studied. Consequently, they find themselves having to reason from possibly unrelated samples to unknown populations. The following example illustrates the severity of this problem:

> With the aid of a grant, a team of archaeologists has counted (as best they can) the numbers of bronze spearheads from different regions of Europe. In reviewing their numbers, they find that the proportions of types of spearheads vary from one region to another. Can they assume that the differences are a result of sampling variability (and therefore that the samples were drawn from the same population), or must they conclude that the spearheads represent different populations of spearheads? A statistical estimation study using their largest sample concluded that 80 percent of all bronze spearheads in the hypothetical population were Type As and that the other 20 percent were Type Bs. What is the likelihood that these percentages are the real parameters for this variable in the population from which the study sample was drawn?

Even a brief exposure to statistical inference will demonstrate that the answer to questions like the one above is not intuitively obvious. It is for this reason that probability theory, which estimates the likelihood of something happening or being the case if certain conditions are met, is the best (the most rigorous) means we have of answering these kinds of questions.

In statistical hypothesis testing, archaeologists proceed by testing the null hypothesis (H_0), the hypothesis that there is no difference between two samples or between a sample and a population. In the latter case, they are maintaining that the sample is a sample of that population and not of another. They compare the null hypothesis to the alternative hypothesis (H_1), which claims that there is a significant difference between the two samples or the sample and population. Here they are maintaining that the two samples most likely come from different populations or, in the second instance, that the sample was probably drawn from some other population.

The null hypothesis is rejected or accepted on the basis of a level of significance, which is usually set at .05 or .01 in archaeology (and in the social sciences in general). This means that the probability of the outcome occurring by chance is only five (or one) times or less in one hundred trials. If a test obtains a probability this low or lower, the research team has statistical support for the conclusion that there is a difference in the case in question—that is, that they have sufficient support to accept the alternative hypothesis. We will examine an example of this kind of formal argument in the following section.

In this process of decision-making, you should be aware that two types of error can be made. The first kind of error, called a Type 1 error, occurs when the null hypothesis is rejected when it is true. The second type of error, a Type 2 error, occurs when the null hypothesis is accepted when it is false. Since it is more serious to claim a relationship when none exists (that is, to make a Type 1 error), it is better to err on the side of caution and risk making a Type 2 error.

As presented in the above sections, these ideas are too abstract to be of practical use in reading archaeology. However, the example in the next section provides some idea of how these abstract ideas are used in archaeology.

An Example of Formal Hypothesis Testing

The following case study illustrates the steps discussed in the last section:

Wealth and Gender in a Bronze Age Cemetery

Let's assume that a research team has obtained a grant to study a Bronze Age cemetery in Germany.[1] During their study, they conclude that female burials can be divided into two groups, "rich" and "poor," based on the abundance and quality of grave goods associated with them. They are less certain, however, whether the age at death of the women in these two groups differed. While only fifty-one "rich" women were "Adultus" or older compared to sixty-seven "poor" women, there are many more adult "rich" women when these numbers are expressed in terms of percent of the total number of "rich" and "poor" women (67 percent versus 50 percent). It seems that rich women lived longer than poor women. Did they?

Expressed another way, given that the percentages are not exactly the same, is the difference big enough (statistically) to say that they really are different? Is there "a case to answer"? The result is obviously important, for it will have considerable bearing on how the cemetery and Bronze Age society in this part of Germany are interpreted.

In answering this question, the team followed the steps used by statisticians in testing a hypothesis. Those steps are followed here to illustrate and clarify the process.

1. Set up a null hypothesis and its alternative:

    H_0: There is no difference between the "rich" and "poor" female burials in their distribution of ages at death.

    H_1: There is a difference between the "rich" and "poor" female burials in their distribution of ages at death.

2. Select a level of significance: .05. In this test, the H_0 will be rejected if the results observed would only occur by chance five times or less out of one hundred.

3. Select a test suitable to the level of measurement of the data. Since the age categories represent ordinal scales (that is, the exact number of years in each category is not specified), the Kolmogorov-Smirnov test is selected.

4. Convert the original counts into proportions of their category total. For instance, there are seventy-six "rich" burials. Six of the seventy-six belong in the "Infans I" age category, which proportionally is $6/76 = 0.079$ on a scale from 0 to 1 (table 13.1).

Table 13.1.   Proportions of Wealth by Age Category at Death in a Bronze Age Cemetery

Age Category at Death	Wealth Category			
	Rich		Poor	
Infans I	6	0.079	23	0.169
Infans II	8	0.105	21	0.154
Juvenilis	11	0.145	25	0.184
Adultus	29	0.382	36	0.265
Maturus	19	0.250	27	0.199
Senilis	3	0.039	4	0.029
Total	76	1.000	136	1.000

5. In the fifth step of this statistical procedure, the proportions for each age category within each "wealth" class are first added up to produce a cumulative distribution. The difference between the numbers on each line is then determined. Finally, the largest difference is highlighted, regardless of whether the difference is positive or negative (table 13.2).

Table 13.2. Differences between the Cumulative Distributions of Wealth by Age Categories in a Bronze Age Cemetery

Age Category at Death	Wealth Category		
	Rich	Poor	Difference
Infans I	0.079	0.169	0.090
Infans II	0.184	0.323	0.139
Juvenilis	0.329	0.507	**0.178**
Adultus	0.711	0.772	0.061
Maturus	0.961	0.971	0.010
Senilis	1.000	1.000	1.000

6. The largest difference lies in the "Juvenilis" category and is 0.178. By the end of the Juvenilis age category, 50.7 percent of the "poor" individuals are dead, but only 32.9 percent of the "rich" ones are. Should we regard this as an unusually large difference between the two distributions on the null hypothesis assumption? In the Kolmogorov-Smirnov test, the following formula can be used to determine the appropriate significance level at .05. If the observed maximum difference is equal to or greater than this, it is statistically significant at the set level. That is, the null hypothesis would be rejected.

$$1.36 \ \frac{n_1 + n_2}{n_1 \, n_2} \quad = \quad 1.36 \ \frac{76 + 136}{(76)(136)} \quad = \quad 0.195$$

7. We see that the observed maximum difference of 0.178 is not as great as the minimum required difference to reject the null hypothesis at the .05 level, which is 0.195. Since the observed difference is less than the minimum required, we cannot reject the null hypothesis. There is not a significant difference in the distribution of ages at death between the "rich" and "poor" categories.

Note that this conclusion does not mean that the distributions are the same. It simply means that there is insufficient evidence to suggest that they are different. That is, there does not appear to be "a case to answer" in this instance.

As the material in this chapter illustrates, it is not always (or even usually) obvious what the parameters of a population are from eyeballing a sample. Therefore, when encountering statements about populations made from samples, ask questions such as the following: How were the parameters of the population determined? Were they guessed at or were inferential statistics used? If inferential statistics were used, is it possible to check the calculations, or is only the result of the test presented? Interpretations of past cultures and peoples through archaeological materials are most often made from ideas about populations of artifacts rather than from only a sample of artifacts. As we have hopefully learned in this chapter, this information transformation is fraught with difficulty and subject to errors that can reverberate around the research cycle.

INTERPRETING THE ARCHAEOLOGICAL RECORD

III

I F YOU ASK ARCHAEOLOGISTS why they are studying the archaeological record, they will probably tell you that the study of the archaeological record is their way of learning about past peoples and their lifeways. That is, artifacts, features, and other components of the archaeological record are a medium through which archaeologists reconstruct (some would say, construct) past cultures and things like tools and houses that no longer exist in their original form and context. Phrased another way, archaeologists are generally interested in making the move in the research cycle from a focus on sites and artifacts to a focus on past real-world contexts (settlements, tools, cultures, religious systems, and so on).

Chapter 14 provides an introduction to the nature of the interpretations archaeologists produce about events, things, and individual and cultural understandings that may have been present or have taken place in the past. To help us think critically about this information transformation in the upper left quadrant of the research cycle, I refer to an interpretation like this as a theory, a generally accepted word in the social sciences.[1] More tersely, a theory is anything that fills that information component. The purpose of chapter 14 is to introduce readers to the most basic constituents of and the nature of the theories they encounter when they read archaeology.

Chapter 15 examines the four research programs most commonly used by archaeologists. The goal of the chapter is to introduce readers to the assumptions these research programs make and to the types of theories that their use typically produces. The last two chapters in part III review two kinds of arguments commonly associated with theories in archaeology: explanatory arguments (chapter 16) and causal arguments (chapter 17). When archaeologists try to clarify how something came to be or what made it what it is, they are presenting an explanatory argument. A causal argument is a special kind of explanation that attempts to identify the trigger or process that brought about something. An example is the relationship between expanding population sizes of hunter-gatherer societies in a region and an increase in the incidence of warfare among them.

Together, the chapters provide a gentle introduction to the nature and creation of interpretations of the past in archaeology.

Is There a Theory in My Reading?   **14**

A CHARACTERISTIC OF RESEARCH in archaeology is the intent to interpret the archaeological record. To do this, archaeologists typically use concepts like "house," "pottery vessel," "extended family," and "resource scarcity"—that is, concepts that a cultural anthropologist is likely to use in describing and explaining the lifeways of somewhat similar kinds of people living at the time of the study. Note that these concepts as used by archaeologists are about the lifeways of people who lived in the past, of people who can no longer be directly observed and talked to.[1] If archaeologists were to adopt a strictly empirical approach, they would be restricted in their studies to examining the content of the archaeological record. They would limit themselves to the measurement of the thickness of pottery sherds, the weight of projectile points, and the dimensions of below-ground features, along with similar kinds of studies. Therefore, archaeologists interested in understanding the lifeways of people who lived in the past through the medium of the archaeological record make the root assumption that it is possible to make statements about past peoples through the examination of the archaeological record (for the notion of a root assumption in archaeology, see chapter 5). This chapter provides an introduction to how they go about doing this. In the research cycle, statements like these appear in the theory information component located at the top of the cycle (see figure 2.1).

Chapter 14 contains three sections. The first section introduces eight terms that are useful in making sense of the archaeological record; the second distinguishes between two different views of the structure of a theory; and the third outlines the dispute between the philosophical positions of empiricism, social constructionism, and realism and gauges the impact of this dispute on building theories in archaeology. The dispute between these positions is about the nature of the correspondence (connection, association) between theories as interpretations of reality and what they are thought to represent. Although the dispute is commonly ignored in archaeology today, it is a focus of discussion and concern in many scholarly disciplines.

Making Sense of the Archaeological Record

A straightforward, introductory way to explain how archaeologists go about making sense of the archaeological record is to look briefly, but carefully, at the definition of eight terms. The terms are *theory, model, concept, hypothesis, fact*, the *past-in-itself*, the *past-as-reconstructed*, and *research program*.[2]

Theory and Model

A theory is the content of the top information component in the research cycle.[3] A primary reason for creating theories in archaeology is to give meaning to objects and spatial distributions in the archaeological record. Theories do this most often by interpreting the content of the record in terms of familiar objects, systems, and processes, such as grinder, social system, and migration. When an archaeologist excavates a large feature at a site and calls it a "house," she has moved from a statement about something in the archaeological record, such as a large rectangular stain in the ground, to a statement about something in the past like a multifamily longhouse.

Theories in archaeology are the products of the transformation of information about the archaeological record into information about the past using the methodological controls of concept formation, hypothesis formation, and model building. As with other transformations in the research cycle, this transformation represents a shift from one kind of information to another—and, as with other shifts from one kind of information to another in the research cycle, serious errors can occur.

Theories in archaeology vary widely in their scope. Some are particularizing. They are about the lifeways and thoughts of particular groups of people. Others are generalizing. They are about processes and ways of thinking of particular types of societies or the transformation of one kind of society into another. Most readings in archaeology revolve around a particularizing theory. They are about the use that a particular kind of artifact had in the past in a village or cluster of villages, and so on. They are archaeologists' attempts to write ethnography-like descriptions of the life of a people who lived in the past. In contrast, a generalizing theory is about repetitive patterns that seem to hold in all societies of a particular type when certain situations are present. An example is Lewis Binford's study of long-range trends in the evolution of hunter-gatherer societies.[4] In my experience, particularizing and generalizing theories form a continuum, with some particularizing theories becoming so abstract that they begin to grade into a generalizing theory.

In a logical empiricist interpretation of science, the goal is to move up the spectrum from the particular to the general.[5] That may be so in archaeology too. However, at this moment in the development of the discipline, archaeologists are more often than not concerned about getting the particular straight. This involves in part the development of methods that allow them to access with some degree of certainty the stories that can be told in any of the four quadrants. This may seem straightforward, but even the understanding of how an artifact was once used in the past as a tool is proving to be a more involved process than once thought. For example, many so-called projectile points are now understood to have served as multiuse tools.

Large-scale theories in archaeology typically contain references to multiple realms of a past lifeway. Examples are the political, economic, religious, and social systems of a past people, as well as their natural environment. These separate parts of a theory are called models here (see the characterization of a theory as a "family of models" in the following section). Models are typically composed of hypothetical and factual statements, while theories consist in large part of multiple models. For reasons given below, it is the implications of a model rather than a theory that are tested in the research cycle.

Concept

Concepts are the "building blocks" of interpretations of the past-in-itself. They are words and phrases that archaeologists use to make sense of the archaeological record. They can be identities that say what something in the archaeological record was. An example is "This stone artifact was used as a projectile point in the past." A concept can also be a variable like degree of resource intensification or extent of interregional trade. Concepts can likewise refer to processes like migration, population pressure, and intensification of resource exploitation, and to feelings, thoughts, cultural patterns, and other aspects of the content of any of the four quadrants.

In general the source of concepts in the theory information component is the ethnographic record. Thus archaeologists use terms like "camp," "village," "city," "scraper," "house," "gatherer," and so on, rather than mathematical symbols or some other formal language. The use of these terms is based on the assumption that people did things, made things, and thought in certain ways in the prehistoric past for the same reasons that people did things, made things, and thought in certain ways in historically observed societies. This is a root assumption in archaeology known as the principle of cultural uniformitarianism. Of course, the further back in the past portions of the archaeological record date to, the less likely this principle holds. Earlier species of human beings (*Homo erectus*, for example) may have done things and made things for different reasons than modern human beings (*Homo sapiens sapiens*) do. Likewise, their cognitive processes may have been different from ours. Regardless, it is important to remember that an analogy can only be a source of hypotheses rather than of proof (the notion of concepts and their role in theory building and testing are discussed more fully in chapter 19).

Hypothesis and Fact

A hypothesis is a tentative claim, an exploratory conjecture, about some aspect of the past-in-itself. Simple examples are "This artifact is a projectile point" and "The upper component of this site is the remains of a summer planting village" (statements like this are called identities, for they simply say what something is thought to be). More complex hypotheses relate two or more concepts, as in this example: In the Northwoods environment, as the population size of its human occupants increased, more second-line food resources like fish and wild rice were exploited (the hypothesis relates two concepts, "human population size" and "exploitation of second-line food resources"). The presence of hypotheses in the theory component is frequently a sign of an early phase in the interpretation of some aspect of the past-in-itself. It is in this sense a starting point for further investigation of the archaeological record.

Unlike the tentative, exploratory nature of a hypothesis, a fact has demonstrable support, perhaps through tests within the research cycle of what was once a hypothesis.[6] Since there are varying degrees of support for statements about the past-in-itself, it is often difficult to separate hypotheses from facts. Nonetheless, as a principle of good science, all claims about the past-in-itself should be formulated in such a way that they are testable against the archaeological record. In the above hypothesis (that the upper component of a site is the remains of a summer planting village), a test might be the recovery (or not) of plant and animal remains in the food debris that were typically (and mainly) present in the summer, as well as the remains of artifacts associated with planting. Like a hypothesis, a fact can stand by itself or be part of an elaborate story or theory.

Past-in-Itself and Past-as-Reconstructed

The term "past-in-itself" refers to what actually was present, took place, and was thought in the past. Archaeologists' attempts to understand the past-in-itself are best understood as the past-as-reconstructed, for they are always partial reconstructions and may in part be incorrect. An important goal of repeated trips around the research cycle is to make the past-in-itself and the past-as-reconstructed correspond more closely. The distinction between the past-in-itself and the past-as-reconstructed is an important one in reading archaeology critically, for readers can easily slip into the habit of mistaking statements about the past-as-reconstructed for the past-in-itself. Remember, there is nearly always space between the past-in-itself and the past-as-reconstructed. It is a task of critical reading in archaeology to figure out how large that space is.

Research Program

In chapter 5, a research program in archaeology was defined as a recurring cluster of assumptions about proper research objectives, definitions of key terms like "culture" and "evolution," and the very nature of research itself. Clusters of assumptions like these are called research programs because they provide a program of research. They are guides for conceptualizing a problem, for determining what data to collect, and for presenting the results of a study, among many other issues involved in formulating a research strategy. The foundational assumptions of a research program strongly influence the research process itself, for they result in admonitions about what are acceptable procedures, arguments, and results and what are not.

Since the assumptions in research programs influence the research process itself, they guide and constrain the construction of theories too. In a very real sense, the theories archaeologists produce are embedded in a research program—for the unaware reader, an archaeologist's research program is an invisible web that binds the parts of a theory together. For this reason, theories themselves are not globally testable, for they incorporate this assumptive base. It is a statement within a model in a theory that archaeologists test.

Two Views of the Structure of a Theory

As defined above, a theory in archaeology is created in order to explain archaeological data.[7] The theory of evolution by natural selection is a well-known example of a theory of this kind in another discipline. It is an explicit attempt to account for fossils, differences among life forms, and other biological phenomena. Calls for building theories of this kind became part of the rhetoric of processual archaeologists in the 1960s and 1970s, when they decided that the proper approach to the archaeological record was an "explicitly scientific" one.[8] Their attempts to achieve this goal were stymied, however, by their adoption of a syntactic conception of a scientific theory that has its roots in logical positivism. According to this conception, a scientific theory is an axiomatic deductive structure that is partially interpreted in terms of definitions called correspondence rules. Correspondence rules define the theoretical terms of the theory by reference to observational terms. For example, a theoretical term like "population pressure" is partially defined by references to certain measures on the content of the archaeological record and to how those measures are made. In addition, the basic axioms of the theory are considered regularities (laws) of the highest generality from which all other regularities can be derived. The explanation and prediction of archaeological phenomena and past ways of life consist of demonstrating that they follow logically from the governing regularities of the theory. Said more tersely, theories constructed within the ambit of the syntactic conception of a scientific theory are very formal logical systems of concepts and statements whose internal relationships are highly structured.

Since high-level regularities, strict axiomatic structures, formal correspondence rules, and many other aspects of the syntactic conception of scientific theories have proven difficult, if not impossible, to formulate in a satisfactory manner, explicit theory building in this sense in archaeology (and the social sciences more generally) has been largely avoided. Still, when pressed to give a definition of a scientific theory, many archaeologists refer to some version of this conception.

An alternative conception of theories, called the semantic conception, emerged in physics in the 1970s through detailed examination of the actual practice of science. In this generalized, model-based understanding of scientific theories, there is no commitment to formal languages, such as mathematics or logic, or even to the widely held view that science is about the discovery of high-level regularities of nature and society. The views that theories are well-defined entities, that regularities are true statements of universal form, and that science yields knowledge of claims that are universal are all rejected. Instead, the concern is with the construction in more or less everyday language of idealized, abstract systems or interpretations, but interpretations that are nonetheless still called theories. The behavior of theories in this sense depends on assumptions about the behavior of real-world systems, such as human societies.

Theories of this kind are most commonly composed of a family of models distributed among many scientists operating in diverse specialties, such as geology, archaeology, zoology, and psychology. Here the primary representational relationship is between models and particular real systems, between what ways of life might have been like in particular settings at a particular time and what they were actually like. In this view of theories, generalizing across particular real systems still remains a viable goal for archaeologists interested in explaining similarities and differences among past ways of life, but not necessarily the ultimate goal for all archaeologists. A "family of models" conception of theory fits the interdisciplinary nature of archaeological practice and its products much more snugly than does the syntactic conception.

Although the content of this section is a bit abstract, it does provide some guidance in understanding the theories we encounter when we read archaeology.

The Empiricism–Social Constructivism–Scientific Realism Dispute

A continuing dispute in the social and natural sciences is this: What is the relationship between a theory and whatever it is "out there" that it is intended to represent? Is the relationship one of similarity or of identity? And just what does "whatever it is that it is intended to represent" mean? The dispute is about the nature, then, of the correspondence between theories and what they are thought to represent. Even more deeply, it is a dispute about what can be known about the world "out there"—or, in our case, "back then."

For a realist, the intended correspondence between a theory and what it is intended to represent is one of identity. Realists assume that unobservable "things," such as a culture, a past society, and a process, have a reality that people who adopt the position of empiricism find mystical and metaphysical. For the realist, theories are not just useful (heuristic) devices but also descriptions of genuine existing and recurring forms and processes that underlie or are behind the phenomena being studied. There is a multilayered reality "out there" that is both independent of our mind and accessible to inquiry.[9]

Strict empiricists like the philosopher David Hume acknowledge, in contrast, that cultures, social structures, the subjective states of individuals, and underlying forms and processes may exist, but they maintain that it is not the purpose of science to attempt to get behind the phenomena experienced through our senses. Underlying forms and processes are useful analogies or "instruments" that help us think about the patterned social activities of people and things—and that is all. Said another way, for the strict empiricist the correspondence between theories and what they are thought to represent is one of similarity rather than of identity.[10]

Critical readers should be aware of this debate, for it has far-reaching implications for their understanding of the intent and nature of the process of building theories in archaeology and of theorizing in archaeology in general.

But do archaeologists have direct access to the world "out there" as maintained by these two opposed positions? From the perspective of social constructivism, our sense perceptions are fitted with a socially constructed lens. Descriptions of the archaeological record and its interpretation are no more than conventions that shift as worldviews do.[11] This does not mean that "anything goes," for there is still some kind of brute reality (or so it is assumed) that influences what we can sense.[12] Nonetheless, rather than sensing brute reality directly, as maintained by empiricists, or indirectly, as maintained by realists, all people construct "reality" using words and concepts.

A related issue in this debate is the nature of the past that archaeologists study. From the perspective of some moderate postmodern writers, there are many pasts that come into view through different ways of seeing. According to these writers, to assume otherwise—that is, to adopt the naive empiricist view that there is only one past that archaeologists and historians study—is to commit the epistemic fallacy of the myth of the given. If this view is adopted in archaeology, then archaeologists would be required to outline their assumptions about the past that they are studying.[13] So when critically reading archaeology, ask this question: Does the writer assume that there is one past that all archaeologists write about, or is he aware of the charge to be clear about the nature of the past that he is writing about?

Active readers of archaeology should pay attention, then, to the ontological commitments, if any, that archaeologists make to the theories they use and construct.[14] Do they consider their theories only useful devices (in line with the view of empiricism), or do they mean for their theories to describe real forms and processes that lie behind and account for what they are studying (in line with the view of realists)? Do they acknowledge that their views are at least in part social constructions? Do they believe that there are many pasts that come into view through different ways of seeing? In my experience, most archaeologists write like realists—though, like the person who is surprised (and delighted) to learn that she has been writing prose for many years, they would be equally surprised (and perhaps more confounded than delighted) to learn that they are writing like a realist.[15]

Despite the backlash by some postprocessual archaeologists against theory and science in general (see chapter 15), explicit attention to theorizing and the process of building theories in archaeology remains a critical component of the research cycle in the discipline.

Which Research Program Is My Reading an Example Of?

15

As introduced in chapter 5, a research program in archaeology is a cluster of assumptions that provide a program for research.[1] While archaeologists working in one program focus on the inter-relationships of past societies and environments, archaeologists in a different program work to discover the meaning of things to the people who made up those past societies. Since the underlying goals of each program differ, archaeologists who adopt one or the other program will necessarily ask different questions, follow different procedures, and differ in what is considered an acceptable result of a research project. Understanding how research programs affect the arguments and patterns of reasoning of archaeologists is an essential task in reading archaeology critically.

Chapter 15 concentrates on the four main research programs practiced in Western archaeology today: trait-centered, system-centered, agency-centered, and integral archaeology (with an emphasis on North American archaeology). The following sketches of the programs are incomplete because of space limitations. Nonetheless, the sketches provide an indication of how research programs function. The last section asks a question of fundamental importance in archaeology today: Must archaeologists work within a single research program?

Trait-Centered Archaeology

As its name implies, trait-centered archaeology concentrates on identifying the traits of either an archaeological culture (an upper right quadrant focus) or a past culture (a lower left quadrant focus). A well-known example of trait-centered archaeology is cultural historical archaeology as practiced in

North America. The program emerged in the 1930s as a response to the data-poor speculations of nineteenth-century unilinear evolutionists, the need to organize rapidly accumulating artifact collections, and the professionalization of the field of archaeology.[2] For summary purposes, I divide the history of cultural historical archaeology into three phases.

Following their rejection of the speculations of unilinear evolutionism at the end of the nineteenth century, a group of North American archaeologists turned to anthropology for a new organizing principle. The principle they adopted was the concept of culture—the normative concept—that had been developed by Franz Boas and other early twentieth-century cultural anthropologists. This model of culture assumes that human behavior is generally regulated by norms. The following three working assumptions summarize the core of this view of culture: culture is a set of ideas, norms, or rules (that is, something mental) about the nature of the world, such as the proper way to hunt, to make a pot, or to interact with men and women in one's kin group; in principle, a society's norms can be reconstructed by examining its members' behavior and material products (that is, they are retrievable); and, by extension, the artifacts, features, and other contents of the archaeological record are material manifestations of past behavioral norms.

Like Boas and his students, archaeologists developing this new research program concentrated their research on tracing the history and spread of what were called cultural traits in archaeology. The first phase of what came to be known as cultural historical archaeology concentrated on gathering information about cultural traits from their manifestations in the archaeological record and placing those traits in a taxonomic framework. The framework contained local, regional, and transregional scales, for traits like the style of a projectile point or a mode of burial were mobile and moved from one group of people to another through processes like diffusion or acculturation. The taxonomy adopted was W. C. McKern's Midwestern taxonomic method, whose units of increasing spatial spread were the focus, aspect, phase, pattern, and base.[3] As proposed by McKern, the taxonomy purposely lacked the dimension of time, for the chronological age of taxonomic units was poorly understood at the time. This first phase of cultural historical archaeology lasted from the mid-1930s to the late 1940s.

Between the late 1940s and the late 1960s, archaeologists' understanding of the temporal placement of taxonomic units had increased to the extent that the dimension of time now became a dimension in regional taxonomies. This shift is reflected in the widespread adoption of a taxonomy proposed by Gordon Willey and Philip Phillips in 1958.[4] Accompanying that shift was a shift from a view of culture as a "shreds and patches" mixture of traits to a view of culture as a patterned whole characteristic of a group of people. This new view of culture resulted in a waning of interest in the mobility of traits; a concentration on local taxonomic units, such as the phase and tradition (which are considered material manifestations of the culture of a group of people); and a fading of interest in higher-level taxonomic units (as tools for studying the mobility of traits).[5] These shifts define the second phase in the development of cultural historical archaeology.

By the late 1950s, the task of identifying the archaeological (taxonomic) units in most regions of North America had been largely completed.[6] Since that time, archaeologists working in this research program have concentrated on associating components (separate occupations) in newly excavated sites with a named archaeological culture, filling out the range of traits of that archaeological culture, and refining the chronological context of the culture. Another characteristic of this third phase in the development of the program has been a shift from McKern's lower left quadrant focus to an upper right quadrant focus. Increasingly, the rhetoric of the program has been about traits of the archaeological record rather than about traits of past cultures.[7] Throughout these three phases, the research strategy has been consistently empirical in that data are gathered before interpretations are suggested so as not to bias the results of a project by premature speculation. The notion was "Get the facts first!" and "Get the facts right!"

Readers of archaeology will recognize the presence of a cultural historical model in what they are reading by an emphasis on the identification of local archaeological cultures and their traits. This process is commonly carried out by test excavating sites in a search for trait-laden artifacts.[8] The research program is also concerned with the chronological ordering of archaeological cultures and their traits, and with the production of brief ethnography-like sketches of what life in the past was like.

Systems-Centered Archaeology

By the late 1950s and early 1960s, many North American archaeologists began to adopt an ecological approach inspired by Julian Steward's 1955 book *Theory of Culture Change*.[9] Steward's approach to explaining similarities and differences between people's cultures concentrates on lower right quadrant processes. The approach was articulated most vigorously by Lewis Binford in a series of papers in the 1960s.[10] Following Leslie White's 1959 materialist definition of culture as "the extra-somatic means of adaptation for the human organism," Binford adopted a working model of culture that is an amalgam of four research programs—functionalism, general systems theory, cultural ecology, and cultural materialism—whose origins lie outside archaeology. Fundamental assumptions of this approach are that cultural change and, ultimately, cultural evolution stem from changes within the adaptive relationship between culture and environments;[11] cultures can be studied as if they are systems; people constantly try to optimize the cost-benefit relationships involved in satisfying their basic needs, which causes changes in technology; research should focus on technology, for the basic needs of human beings (food, shelter, and bodily comfort, for example) are most directly satisfied by technology; and the focus of cultural studies should be observable human behavior (in contrast to unobservable thoughts, meanings, and dispositions), because this makes the use of objective scientific methods possible in cultural studies. The program became known as the "New Archaeology" and eventually processual archaeology.

The notion of cultural systems adapting in interaction with their environments resulted in a rapid change in research procedures, at least in North America. In contrast to the testing of sites in order to record traits, archaeologists working in the processual program concentrated on the distribution of the range of different types of sites of an archaeological culture within a region and the subsistence-settlement information in those sites.

The magnum opus of processual archaeology is Binford's 2001 *Constructing Frames of Reference: An Analytical Method for Archaeological Theory Building Using Ethnographic and Environmental Data*. In the book, Binford uses statistical techniques to explore the associations of multiple features of hunter-gatherer lifeways, as recorded in a sample of 390 historic-period hunter-gatherer groups from around the world, with a large number of environmental variables. He also develops a hypothetico-deductive model called the terrestrial model based on these data and his own ethnoarchaeological studies of hunter-gatherer groups in several regions of the world.[12] In a large number of propositions, he then states predicted relationships between the environmental variables and aspects of the social organization and settlement-subsistence systems of past people, such as expected group size, degree of group mobility, and gender differences in subsistence tasks, in all parts of the world.

For summary purposes, processual archaeology can be divided into two phases. During the first phase in the 1960s and 1970s, the rhetoric of logical empiricism was a front-and-center component of processual archaeology.[13] The rhetoric promoted the use of the hypothetico-deductive approach, a covering law model of explanation, and the use of multiple working hypotheses, among other methods of this theory of science. Like a fashion fad, logical empiricism as a theory of science swept throughout the social (and many of the natural) sciences at this time. By the late 1970s, both logical positivism and logical empiricism had become ancient history, and the "science wars" (conflicting and contested interpretations of science) had begun. Nonetheless, processual archaeology has remained committed throughout its development to the close study of historic hunter-gatherer groups and the construction of hypothetico-deductive models (complex theories in my sense) of the interrelationships of hunter-gatherer societies through time with aspects of their natural environment.

Processual archaeology can be recognized in your reading by its strong focus on the lower right quadrant, a materialist (culture as adaptive) understanding of the purpose of culture, process, the adaptive link between natural environments and human societies, a comparative study of cultural systems, the explanation of culture change, ethnoarchaeology, middle-range theory,[14] the statistical study of data associations, and the aspiration to "do science."

Agency-Centered Archaeology

Agency-centered research programs concentrate on left-side quadrants, especially the lower left (culture) quadrant. A prominent example is postprocessual archaeology, a program strongly associated with the postmodern critique and the historic turn that came to prominence in Euro-American academia in the 1980s, and the symbolic and interpretive turn that emerged in cultural anthropology in the 1960s and 1970s.[15]

In contrast to processual archaeology, which treats culture as adaptation and portrays culture change as a response to shifts in some aspect of culture-environmental interactions, postprocessualists argue for a more humanistic approach, one that recognizes the primacy of worldview in guiding people's lives. Three presuppositions that capture the core of this approach are as follows: forms and changes in behavior—and its material expression, through pottery styles, burial practices, house forms, and so on—can be understood only in the context of the particular set of cultural values, attitudes, and other beliefs that give the world meaning (that, in fact, constitute or represent the world as known and understood); behavior is meaningfully constituted, and that meaning is expressed through symbols, such as language, the decoration on pottery, and the clothes that people wear; and symbols and their meaning (that is, ideology) are primary and determinative in people's daily lives and in culture change over time.

Postprocessual archaeologists argue that cultural historical and processual archaeologists, by adopting models of culture that emphasize, respectively, ideal norms and adaptive systems, miss the defining attribute of culture and humanity—unlike other creatures, human beings interpret the world around them. According to the cognitive model of culture adopted by postprocessualists, culture is the set of meanings that people construct to make sense of their lives.[16] By saying that "culture is constructed," they portray people as active agents who individually rework learned norms and traditions to construct reworked or reproduced systems of meanings that fit the contexts of their own lives. Postprocessual archaeologists claim that by contrast both cultural historical and processual archaeologists treat the people practicing a culture collectively and passively, rather than as individual, active agents.

In attempting to carry out their project, postprocessual archaeologists have adopted several approaches. An approach favored by Ian Hodder, a founder of postprocessual archaeology, is a contextual archaeology modeled after Clifford Geertz's concept of "thick description." If carried out by a cultural anthropologist, an interpretation would involve the identification of the setting in which actions (meaningful behavior) are being carried out, the actors (individuals) involved, and the meaning of the actions to the actors. A "thick description" of what was going on in this setting is a description of the meaning of the scene to the members of that culture. Like a rising hand, the meaning is not obvious from the behavioral motion itself. The task of the ethnographer is to become aware of the meaning of this and many other everyday scenes in that culture.

When applied to the archaeological record, an interpretation (or reading) has often been attempted through the reenactment method. In this method, an archaeologist learns as much as possible about the conditions, content, and so on of the archaeological culture being studied—a process often enhanced through insights from ethnoarchaeological studies—and then envisages what the meanings were.[17]

The reasons given for culture change in postprocessual archaeology generally refer to internal change models that focus on the decisions of individuals or on the logic of that culture as its implications and contradictions play out over long periods of time. While postprocessualists might refer to processes like diffusion, exchange, and migration, they maintain that people in the past, as today, were active agents who negotiated the process of change, which, because they were determinative, active agents, was not a predetermined outcome. That is, whether a diffusing notion, such as a new way of decorating pottery vessels, was adopted was the result of decisions by individuals in groups. In this view, then, the changes in artifact form and style that can be observed in the archaeological record are the result of conscious decisions by individuals—not the mechanical adjustment of "technology" in a positive feedback loop whose outcome is a more efficient cultural adaptation.

Although quite diverse, the presence of the postprocessual research program in your reading can be recognized by a closer link to the humanities rather than the sciences, concentration on "reading" or "interpreting" the past, a symbolic understanding of culture, a focus on the context-dependent meaning of cultural things, a strong ethnoarchaeological element, an alignment with history rather than anthropology, a lack of interest in the satisfaction of the basic needs component of processual archaeology, a self-reflectiveness about the possibly harmful impact of archaeological interpretations on peoples of the world, and a concern with the distorting influence of the biases and Western agendas of archaeologists on their interpretations of the past.

Integral Archaeology

In integral archaeology, attention is paid to all four quadrants without privileging any one of them. A program that aspires to this ideal is what Christopher Carr and D. Troy Case call thick prehistory.[18] The goal of the program is to produce personalized, ethnography-like descriptions of a past people in their own terms through the medium of the archaeological record. According to the authors, this means "the detailed describing of individuals, social groups, events, actions, patterned behaviors and ideas, and their interrelationships within a local social, cultural, natural, and historical context."[19] Contra processual archaeology, the aim is to "present a people" in a straightforward, descriptive manner rather than to explain their lifeway and its change through time.

In the thick prehistory approach, close attention is paid to a wide variety of evidence, such as animal and plant remains, bioarchaeological (human skeletal) and artifactual remains, and mortuary and ceremonial center architecture in local, regional, and transregional contexts within diverse site types. The goal is to reconstruct settlement-subsistence systems, social systems, leadership roles, gender roles, and ceremonial and burial practices, among other aspects of a past way of life. As anticipated, a multifaceted methodological and theoretical approach is adopted suited to the requirements of a four quadrants approach. Interpretive approaches, for example, include middle-range theory, taphonomy, ethnographic analogy, the direct historic approach, and cross-cultural near universals, all of which are used in an exploratory manner to gain insight into the way of life of past peoples. The result is the amassing of large databases, many of which are attached to publications in CD form.

The view of culture adopted is known as the partitive view. In contrast to the normative view in which norms typify a culture, a partitive view recognizes that "different individuals 'participate in' different aspects of culture at different locations across a region through the varying roles they take on at those different locations."[20] This information is gained by inferring behavior from its objectifications, such as artifacts and architecture, and culture from that reconstructed behavior. As in the normative view of culture, culture from a partitive perspective is considered unobservable and nonmaterial—that is, something mental.

The thick prehistory approach acknowledges that getting at the specific person as an agent is beyond the resolution of the prehistoric archaeological record, so it "moves the analytical unit up one level" to the notion of the social role in a local cultural context. By examining redundant patterning in the associations of artifacts, especially in mortuary settings, social roles that guide the actions of specific individuals as an agent are identified or at least suggested. These roles "guide the actions and interactions of persons in particular positions within a social field by defining or suggesting the mutual rights, duties, actions, responses, and tasks of those persons in a given social context."[21] In this way the situating of individuals in social roles personalizes the archaeological record with individuals in action.

Given the comprehensive goals of thick prehistory, it is a difficult—if not nearly impossible—program to carry out in most regions of the world at the present moment. It requires vast databases, large numbers of "socially and culturally vocal" artifacts, a long-term commitment by a team with diverse skills, large-scale and long-term financial support, and a focused and enduring research agenda. A key assumption is that by immersing oneself in all of this rich detail, the range of reconstructions that can be made will be constrained and, therefore, more likely.

The occurrence of the thick prehistory research program in your reading can be recognized by the presence of very large databases at local, regional, and transregional levels; the intent to write a four-quadrant, ethnography-like description of the way of life of a past people; an express interest in personalizing the archaeological record; and the use of a "social role" approach to identifying social individuals.

Must Archaeologists Work within a Single Research Program?

Most readers would probably agree that research programs in archaeology are complementary rather than competitive, since each addresses different problems—and why can't archaeologists engage in studies that they are most interested in or best at? But if you trace the rhetoric of archaeologists through time, at least in North America, the impression emerges that archaeology has evolved from immaturity to maturity, for successive programs contend that earlier programs are inadequate. Cultural historical archaeologists viewed nineteenth-century evolutionism as overly speculative, processual archaeologists consider cultural historical archaeology "mere description," postprocessual archaeologists consider processual archaeology inadequate because it neglects people, and integral archaeologists claim that postprocessual archaeology is only partial, for it concentrates on one aspect (the symbolic and interpretive) of being human. The question "Must archaeologists work within a single research program?" is an important one, then, for it requires us to think about the reasons for research program change in archaeology.

Is archaeological knowledge progressive, then, or are there other reasons for the emergence of successive programs? For argument's sake, a case can be made that the emergence of the research programs reviewed in this chapter were stimulated as much if not more so by changing ideals of science than by growing maturity within the discipline. It can be argued that cultural historical archaeology mirrors observation-based views of science characteristic of the early twentieth century, early processual archaeology is a manifestation of the emergence in popularity of logical empiricism in the 1960s, the emergence of postprocessual archaeology in the 1980s was a response to the rise to prominence of postmodernism and the historic turn, and integral archaeology seems to be a reflection of the era of the science wars in which no one theory of science is dominant (and all are contested).

Again, for argument's sake, questions can be raised about the role of the reward system in archaeology. Are "revolutions" in social science disciplines consequences of better ways of understanding the subject matter of a discipline or a means for young scholars to gain recognition?[22]

But stop. If I continue in this direction, we will fall down the rabbit hole with Alice and meet the Mad Hatter, the Queen of Hearts, and the smile of the Cheshire Cat.[23] For critical readers, it is sufficient to ask which research program the reading is an example of.

Is an Explanation Offered?　　　**16**

SOME BOOKS ON ARGUMENTATION and critical thinking make a distinction between explanations and arguments. According to this distinction, an argument is an attempt to use one or more statements (premises) that are believed to be true to support the truth of another statement (the conclusion). An explanation may look like an argument, but its purpose is to relate why something occurred, not to support the truth of a statement. Whether you believe that there is a big difference in principle between arguments and explanations, or that an explanation is just a special kind of argument, it is worth examining what an explanation is and what kinds of explanations there are, for processual archaeologists in particular believe that the goal of archaeology is to explain (rather than just describe) what happened in the past. What does it mean, then, to "explain what happened in the past"?

This chapter explores the difference between explanations and arguments, describes common targets of explanation in archaeology, and lists common errors in framing an explanation. It also briefly explores the use of an analogy to explain. The assumption throughout the chapter is that there really is a distinction between explanations and arguments, although I and many other people who have thought about the distinction believe that an explanation is (only) a special kind of argument.[1]

Identifying Explanations

Arguments use evidence or reasons (premises) taken to be true to persuade others to accept a statement or point of view (the conclusion). The words "so," "therefore," "thus," and "hence" are common indicators of the presence of an argument. Explanations, rather than trying to persuade us that a statement is true, provide reasons why something is true. Expressions like "the reason is . . ." and "X caused the . . ." signal the presence of an explanation. Said more briefly, while arguments attempt to prove that something is true, explanations are cause and effect statements.

Arguments and explanations can look like each other. However, with a bit of practice, it is often possible to distinguish between the two.[2] Consider the following example: Let's assume that you are reading two articles about late prehistoric sites around the shores of Clearwater Lake in the northern Great Lakes. The conclusion of the first article is that the inhabitants of these sites were intensive wild rice harvesters, for rice harvesting features and many rice kernels are present throughout the sites. This is an argument, for the writer is trying to persuade us to accept the conclusion that the inhabitants of the sites were intensive wild rice gatherers. The reason: wild rice features and many rice kernels were found throughout the sites.

The author of the second article agrees that the inhabitants of the sites were wild rice harvesters. However, her concern is not whether they were wild rice harvesters, but rather why they harvested wild rice. In her conclusion, she says, "The reason the inhabitants of the sites were wild rice harvesters is that, because of severe external threats, they had grouped together into larger settlements for defense; because of the concentration of large numbers of people together, local resources soon became depleted and they had to intensify their exploitation of the wild rice beds that covered many of the lakes in the region in order to survive."

As in this example, archaeologists present an argument when one or more reasons are given in support of the truth of a statement ("the inhabitants *were* wild rice harvesters"). They offer an explanation when they provide one or more reasons why something is true ("the *reason* they were wild rice harvesters is . . .").

For the sake of clarity, we should be aware as well of the distinction that is often made between explanations and justifications, though they may blend together. For example, let's say we read in a late eighteenth-century manuscript that a voyageur stole a bundle of furs. Why did the voyageur steal the furs? In his diary he explains that he needed money to send to his sick mother in Montreal. He justifies his action by explaining the reason he stole the furs. A justification is an argument, then, that defends (justifies) an action or belief (either in the past or present); the argument is an attempt to make an action or belief seem reasonable and socially or morally acceptable.

But not all explanations are intended to justify an action or belief. Here is an example: A German author may try to explain why many German archaeologists vigorously supported the Nazi Party's view of the prehistory of the German people. The writer may point out that the notion of pure races was common at the time, and so on. These statements provide an explanation for the views of many German archaeologists at the time. In contrast to the previous example, however, they are not an attempt to justify those views. Not enough information is provided to determine the intent of the author, but as given it provides a value-free explanation for a belief.

Distinguishing between explanations intended to justify an action or belief and those that are not is a critical skill for readers of archaeology. Just because an archaeologist provides an explanation of an action or belief does not mean that she has sympathy (or antipathy, for that matter) toward that action or belief. As a critical writer, then, be sure when presenting an explanation that your intent—positive, negative, or neutral—is clear.

Three Targets of Explanation in Archaeology

Since there are six very different kinds of information components in the research cycle in archaeology, you are likely to encounter explanations of different kinds of things in your reading. Three of the most commonly encountered targets of explanations in archaeology are physical things, past behavior, and the function of something. As a critical reader you should be able to recognize these different targets of explanation when you read archaeology.

Explanations of physical objects answer questions like the following: Why did the site slide down the hill? Why doesn't quartz fracture like obsidian during flint knapping? Why did the climate change during the Little Ice Age? What caused the grasslands to expand northward during the Prairie Period? Why is a textile pressed against a copper artifact often preserved in a burial? These questions all require a physical (natural science) explanation, for they refer to physical processes or properties, such as the fracture pattern of quartz, a (natural) change in climate, and so on. The answer will be found in geology, paleoecology, chemistry, physics, and other natural sciences.

A commonly encountered problem in presenting an explanation of something physical is just where to rest the explanation. In explaining the fracture pattern of quartz, we can start with the attributes of quartz as a rock, explain those attributes by referring to the constituent materials of quartz, and explain those by referring to the atomic- and subatomic-level elements that make up those constituents. This is known as the chain of causes problem. The answer to the chain of causes problem may depend on the level of focus of the question. Is the question being asked about a specific event (why did the site slide down the hill?) or about a characteristic of nature in general (why doesn't quartz fracture during flint knapping like obsidian?)? Reference to gravity and local soil conditions may be sufficient to answer the first question, but we would normally move deeper down the chain of causes to answer the second question.

Explanations of past behavior explain why someone did something (what their motive or reasons were) and the reasons for recurring patterns of behavior, such as the (near) universal presence of the incest taboo. Explanations of behavior answer questions like these: Why did the Danubian I farmers move northwestward into Europe? Why are people fascinated by archaeology? Why did people cross the Bering Strait into North America? Why did people start to make pottery vessels? Why did the Anazazi abandon the Four Corners area of the American Southwest? Instead of the natural sciences, these explanations are rooted in disciplines like psychology, economics, anthropology, and other social sciences, as well as historical disciplines like history.

The chain of causes problem is present here, too. In general the explanation should rest at a level appropriate to the question asked, the discipline, and the intended audience.

Explanations of the function of something answer such questions as the following: What's a spear-thrower? Why was the village surrounded by a palisade? What were these artifacts used for? Why did the houses in the village become larger? A question that asks what something is or was used for is asking what the function of that thing is or was. The explanation will answer that question, as in these examples: a spear-thrower is a short implement that is used to increase the speed and power of the impact of a projectile, the village was surrounded by a palisade for defense, and so on. Explanations that explain what the function of something is or was may range along a spectrum from simple to complex. Compare these two questions: What is a spear-thrower? and Why did early states arise in the ancient Near East? Though these questions differ in level of complexity, the explanations proposed to answer them share a similar intent—to explain something's function or purpose.

Argument to the Best Explanation

An archaeologist whose research focus is the relationships between social systems and the natural environment (typically a lower right quadrant concern) is likely to look toward this relationship to explain a change in the subsistence practices of a past people. Perhaps as the number of people living in a region grew through time, families had to diversify their subsistence base to acquire enough food energy throughout the year. An agency-centered archaeologist might explain the same change by suggesting a shift in how neighbors regarded each other (a left-side quadrant concern). Perhaps a feud developed between neighbors, and as a consequence it became too dangerous for groups of two or three hunters to range widely in search of game. As a consequence, families began exploiting more local second-order foods.

Which is the best explanation? As a critical reader, you must be alert to the possibility that an alternative explanation better explains a situation in the past than the explanation offered by a writer. This process of reasoning is called an argument (or inference) to the best explanation.[3] In science, an argument to the best explanation is a very common and powerful reasoning tool, a tool that relies on criteria like those listed in the next section to decide which one of two or more explanations is more likely correct.

Common Errors in Framing Explanations

Even though there is no finite list of hard-and-fast rules that can be applied automatically to evaluate all explanations, some criteria have proven more useful than others in evaluating the explanations of archaeologists.[4] A caution here: Just because an explanation is weak does not mean that it has no value in the research cycle. A weak explanation may be the best one available in the early phases of theory building.

Testability

If archaeologists are intent on saying something true about the past-in-itself, why propose an answer to a question or problem that cannot be tested using archaeological materials? It is a principle of science that statements about the world "out there" should be testable. This does not mean that we are not going to come across statements about the past-in-itself that are not testable in this sense. Here are two examples:

> Archaeologists are heretics, for they believe that the archaeological record was built up over several million years by past human ancestors. We of the faith know, of course, that the world is only six thousand years old—and that all of those artifacts were placed there by the Devil to test our faith.

> Why did the Mayan civilization collapse? I guess it was due to fate.

How could either of these statements be tested? Could the Devil have really placed artifacts in the earth to test our faith? Was the collapse of the Mayan civilization really due to fate (bad karma, let's say)? These questions remind me of a question that Bertrand Russell, the British philosopher, once asked: How could we prove that the world and all our memories were not created five minutes ago? An important point is being made here: science in any quadrant is concerned only with statements that are testable using agreed-upon methods within the context of science. This does not mean that other explanations of the world are not ultimately true.

Noncircularity

If an explanation merely repeats what it is intended to explain, the explanation is circular. This weakness of an argument is often not detected because different words and phrases are being used to say the same thing in both the question asked and the explanation offered. Here's an example:

> [Q] Why did the northern Oneota move southward at the onset of the Little Ice Age? [A] The deterioration of the climate at the beginning of the Little Ice Age caused the northern Oneota to move southward.

Since the climate was deteriorating at the beginning of the Little Ice Age, the northern Oneota moved southward because of the deteriorating climate. The conclusion is repeating what it is intended to explain. This is an untestable or ad hoc explanation, at least as stated, for the reason that the conclusion is just another way of stating the phenomenon to be explained.[5]

Relevance

Not all explanations are relevant to the question being asked.[6] If a student asks why the quartz used to make arrowheads in the northern lakes area fractures like it does, an irrelevant answer would be because quartz was the only tool stone readily available in that area. It may be the case that quartz was the only tool stone readily available in that area, but that explanation is not an explanation for why quartz fractures the way it does. This appears on the surface to be an error that should be easily avoided. However, in a long article or a book, the question may get lost among all the other information provided.

A test for relevance is the ability of the explanation to predict the phenomenon to be explained. Does "quartz was the only tool stone readily available in that area" predict the fracture pattern of quartz? Certainly not. An explanation that provides details of the molecular structure of quartz would.

Freedom from Excessive Vagueness

The vagueness of a key word or expression in an explanation violates the acceptability criterion of a good argument for several reasons.[7] First, a premise containing an imprecise word or expression may provide no or only weak support for an explanation. Consider this example: If a student asks an archaeologist why he believes the Wilford site is a village and he answers, "Because there are a lot of pottery sherds at the site," how is the student to understand "a lot of"? Now the Wilford site may well be a village site and have a pottery sherd profile typical of village sites in the region. But "a lot of" just might mean that more pottery sherds were recovered from the site than is typical for most sites sample excavated in the region, but the reason there are more pottery sherds at the site is because the site was occupied more frequently by small numbers of seminomadic people. The phrase "a lot of" provides only weak support for the explanation.

Reliability

An unreliable explanation produces predictions that, when tested, prove to be false. Here is an example:

> Protohistoric people in the valley aggregated into large palisaded villages about A.D. 1600. Professor Morris explains that it was due to an increase in interregional warfare. However, recent investigations, which found no evidence for warfare, point to the spread of contagious disease as the more likely explanation. That is, to protect their populations, leaders used palisades to stop infected people from entering their village.

Since no evidence has been found in support of Professor Morris's explanation, it is an unreliable explanation. The lesson of this example is that all explanations in archaeology, no matter how persuasive and elegant, must be tested—and a route to their testing is through the predictions embedded in them.

Explanatory Power

A principle of a good scientific theory is that it explains more than competing theories. Of course, an archaeologist may only be interested in explaining what she has found in the archaeological record without further generalization. Nonetheless, here is an example of this weakness in action.

Let's say, for example, that according to the archaeological evidence, there were two tribes of people living in southern Mexico hundreds of years ago and that they both seem to have disappeared at about the same time. Anthropologist A comes up with a theory that explains what may have happened to one tribe, but this theory is irrelevant to the other tribe. Anthropologist B comes up with a theory that explains what may have happened to both tribes. Even if both theories are equal on all other grounds and both are equally supported by the physical evidence, the explanation offered by anthropologist B has the edge over that of anthropologist A on the grounds of greater explanatory power—it simply explains more.

Freedom from Unnecessary Assumptions

In the natural sciences, an explanation that requires fewer assumptions is preferred to one that requires more assumptions, for all the reasons pointed out in chapter 5. This is also the case in the social sciences and in archaeology, regardless of whether the explanation is about unique or general phenomena. In some instances the unnecessary assumptions concern dubious methods of acquiring information about the past-in-itself, at least from the point of view of professional archaeologists. For example:

> In a local newspaper two explanations are presented for the collapse of the Mayan civilization. One explanation points to the possible presence of environmental deterioration and increased regional warfare that led to the abandonment of ceremonial centers. The other accepts the presence of environmental deterioration and increased regional warfare but argues that the ceremonial centers were abandoned when the inhabitants fled across the Atlantic Ocean to resettle in the Near East and Africa, thus leading to the collapse of the Mayan civilization. A few similarities in artifact form and decoration between these continents are cited as evidence.

The first explanation is based on two reasons: environmental deterioration and increased regional warfare. An additional reason is offered in support of the second explanation: the Mayans (or at least the Mayan elite) fled across the Atlantic Ocean. The second explanation requires that we agree that a flight across the Atlantic is a reasonable premise—which seems an unnecessary (and likely wacky) assumption. The first explanation is preferred.

Consistency with Well-Established Theory

As a rule in archaeology and the sciences more generally, an explanation should be consistent with well-established theory. Of course, there are examples of theories that were once considered well established that later proved false. Until the discovery of Paleoindian projectile points in association with the bones of Ice Age animals, archaeologists were in general agreement that the first *Homo sapiens* entered the New World after the last Ice Age. Still, there are many more examples of explanations that challenge well-established theory that are more likely false than true. Back to the Kensington rune stone:

> Olaf Torgen, the foremost student of Minnesota's Kensington rune stone and a strong believer in its authenticity, admits that the presence of thirteenth-century Norsemen in Minnesota challenges standard archaeological reconstructions.

If Torgen has only the rune stone as evidence for the presence of an early Norse presence in the state, then we should be suspicious of the authenticity of the rune stone, for the standard archaeological reconstruction of the prehistory of the state has been built up through the analysis of thousands of sites, all of which lack evidence of a Norse presence.

Absence of Alternative Explanations

What could account for the presence of a Norse rune stone in early Minnesota? Could it be a prank that has gotten out of hand? As another rule of good research practice, be open to alternative explanations of a phenomenon, even (and perhaps especially if) the prevailing explanation is considered well established. For example:

> Oneota people moved southward out of the Upper Mississippi River Valley not long after the onset of the Little Ice Age. Was the explanation a deteriorating climate that limited agricultural production? Maybe. But then maybe the movement of the Oneota southward and the onset of the Little Ice Age were not causally related to each other at all. Perhaps rising warfare associated with aggression by their neighbors to the north was the cause.

Using an Analogy to Explain

Some explanations in archaeology are based on an analogy between two or more societies (let's say), at least one of which is better known than the other(s). If the societies share some critical traits in common, then it seems likely the lesser-known society will have other traits of the better-known society, or at least that is the argument. For instance, in an article an archaeologist explains why hunter-gatherers in late prehistoric Minnesota became village horticulturalists by comparing them to a well-described ethnographic example of this kind of shift in South America.

Experience has shown that it is difficult to prove these kinds of analogies. Because of these difficulties, archaeologists generally maintain that analogies are better considered as a source of hypothesis than of proof.

Is There a Causal Argument?   **17**

A CAUSAL ARGUMENT IS an attempt to support a causal claim or a causal hypothesis. A causal claim is a straightforward statement that one thing caused or causes another thing. A causal hypothesis makes the same kind of claim but more tentatively. In reading archaeology, a critical reader is most likely to encounter a causal claim in the theory information component of the research cycle and a causal hypothesis in the predictions or test implications component. Here are some examples of causal claims, with causal hypothesis wording in parentheses:

- Prehistoric warfare caused (may have caused) population aggregation.
- The artifacts are scattered across the field because they were spread (may have been spread) there by the plow.
- Climatic change caused (may have caused) northern Oneota groups to move southward.
- Increased moisture on the northern Plains resulted (may have resulted) in an increase in the size of buffalo herds during the late prehistoric period.
- Shifts in the distribution of wild grasses in the Near East at the end of the last Ice Age led (may have led) to the first domestication of wild plants.

Causal arguments are liberally sprinkled throughout the archaeological literature. Classic causal arguments have been advanced to explain the collapse of the Mayan civilization, the domestication of plants and animals, the disappearance of northern mastodons at the end of the last Ice Age, and many other events in the past. Since causal arguments are an integral part of reasoning in archaeology, the critical reader should pay attention to this form of argument. In this chapter we review the arguments that are most commonly used to support causal claims and causal hypotheses in archaeology.[1]

Causation among Specific Events

Archaeologists frequently reason that one event caused another event or that one event may have caused another. All but the first example above are of this kind. For instance, one event, a change in climate in a region, caused another event, the movement southward of northern Oneota groups. How do we reach a conclusion (that is, establish a causal claim) that one specific event or occurrence caused some other specific event or occurrence? In this section we discuss the two most frequently employed types of arguments (patterns of reasoning) designed to reach such conclusions.[2]

Only-Relevant-Difference Reasoning

Oneota groups living in the Upper Mississippi River Valley in Minnesota and Wisconsin moved southward into the present state of Illinois about A.D. 1250. Why? Well, they seemed to be content living there until something different happened. A change at the time was the onset of colder weather (the beginning of the Little Ice Age). As the length of the growing season became shorter, it became increasingly difficult (perhaps) to grow sufficient amounts of native maize (corn). Was climatic change the only relevant difference between the time the Oneota lived in the upper valley and when they lived in Illinois? Let's assume that it was or that it likely was the case. The deterioration of the climate must, then, have caused the Oneota to shift location (a causal claim), or so it seems (a causal hypothesis).

The type of reasoning illustrated by this example has an obvious name: only-relevant-difference reasoning. Since this is a common type of causal reasoning in archaeology, critical readers should become familiar with the structure of this pattern of reasoning. The pattern of reasoning is as follows:

1. One item (culture, regional environment, artifact type, and so on) has a feature (called the feature in question) other similar items lack.
2. There is only one relevant difference between the item that has the feature in question and the items that do not have the feature in question.
3. Therefore, the relevant difference is the cause of the feature in question (or at least one can hypothesize that it is).

Let's review the Oneota relocation example to see whether it fits this pattern:

> The northern Oneota lived contentedly in the northern Mississippi Valley before the climate became harsher for maize horticulturalists. They moved southward into Illinois after the climate deteriorated. Therefore, the change in climate was responsible for their southward movement.

First, let's identify the feature in question. It's the southward movement of the northern Oneota. Now let's identify the only relevant difference. The difference seems to be a deterioration of regional climate. The reason: these Native American horticulturalists relied for much of their food energy on a maize (corn) species vulnerable to prolonged cold weather.

In this example the only relevant difference is a before-and-after comparison, the southward movement of the northern Oneota following the deterioration of regional climate. Only-relevant-difference reasoning can also be found in side-by-side comparisons. Here is an example:

> One northern Oneota village cluster lasted longer in the Upper Mississippi River Valley than all other northern Oneota village clusters. The gardens of the longer-lasting cluster were in the broad alluvial plain of the Mississippi Valley, where the soils were moister than upland soils and soils along smaller tributaries. Therefore, the moister soils allowed (caused) this northern Oneota village cluster to last longer in the upper valley than all other northern Oneota village clusters.

Two conditions must be satisfied in only-relevant-difference reasoning. First, there must be a feature in question that separates one thing (let's say an event) from similar kinds of things. And, second, the feature in question must not only be relevant to the difference between the one thing and similar kinds of things, but it must also be the only relevant difference.

The results of only-relevant-difference reasoning run the gamut from fairly certain to less certain. Here's an example of a fairly certain argument, at least by today's standards in archaeology:

> A CRM survey crew finds artifacts widely scattered across a field, but test excavations indicate that the artifacts below the plow zone are concentrated in only one part of the field. After talking with the farmer, they conclude that repeated plowing had dispersed artifacts from within the plow zone across the field.

True, it is possible that wind, water running across the field during a flash flood, gravitation, and other processes could have dispersed the artifacts across the field. So the reasoning isn't absolutely secure. But based on years of observation, the reasoning is strong enough for the survey crew to conclude in their report that plowing caused the dispersal of artifacts across the field.

Compare the above example of a fairly certain argument to this less certain example:

> The longer-lasting Oneota cluster near moister alluvial soils might have had hardier strains of maize or relied more on fishing than the other northern Oneota clusters.
>
> There may be all sorts of relevant differences between this Oneota cluster and the others besides planting their gardens on moister soils.

Of course, in any real-life situation some parts of an argument are always open to debate. In this complex, interdependent world, what are the chances that there is only one relevant difference in an only-relevant-difference argument? Indeed, how is the word "relevant" being used in this form of argument? In most instances it merely means that a difference between something and similar things may be a relevant difference. Stated this way, the statement becomes a causal hypothesis.

But let's assume for the moment that there is only one or at least one best relevant difference in a claim about the past-in-itself. It is a task for researchers to provide reasons why that difference is the only or best relevant difference in that claim. This is why the successive tasks of the research cycle in archaeology are of fundamental importance. Let's suppose that for theory-building purposes an archaeologist makes the causal claim that the northern Oneota moved southward because of a deterioration in local climate. What evidence might show that this claim is false? To find out, the archaeologist draws out test implications of the claim and subjects them to test. And so question and answer follow one another in (it seems) never-ending trips around the research cycle.

Only-Relevant-Common-Thread Reasoning

Sometimes archaeologists notice multiple occurrences of something, such as populations aggregated in five different places at different times. What caused the aggregation of these populations? A review of the archaeological literature in all five places shows that warfare was on the rise at the time in all five instances. The answer to our question seems to be warfare.

The pattern of reasoning in only-relevant-common-thread reasoning is as follows:

1. Multiple occurrences of a feature (the feature in question) are united by a single relevant common thread (the common thread in question).
2. Therefore, the common thread in question is the cause of the feature in question.

Of course, the thought processes involved in only-relevant-common-thread reasoning are open to question, too. For instance, the five examples of population aggregation may have shared other events or processes in common, or they may each be the result of unique events, and so forth. Again, the more we know about each example of population aggregation, the better we are able to weed out common threads or unique events that are irrelevant.

As with only-relevant-difference reasoning, only-relevant-common-thread reasoning in its causal claim and causal hypothesis forms play different roles in the research cycle. While the claim is a feature of the theory information component, the hypothesis is a feature of the prediction/test implication component. Just because the only-relevant-common-thread reasoning results in a causal claim does not mean, at least as regards the research cycle, that it is not hypothetical in nature. The reason should be obvious. Does the writer know for sure that the feature in question resulted from that common thread? Are there other shared similarities among the things in question that may have been the actual cause of the feature in question? And so on.

Common Mistakes in Causal Reasoning

The strength (reliability) of causal reasoning of the two varieties just considered depends on avoiding some common mistakes.[3] The likely mistakes in only-relevant-difference reasoning are as follows:

The major difference we take to be the cause of the feature in question might not be a relevant difference. Remember, when an author says a difference is relevant, she most likely means that it is not unreasonable to suppose that the difference might have caused the feature in question. In the Oneota example, the change in climate recorded at the time of the shift southward of northern Oneota groups may not have been severe enough to lessen the productivity of their gardens.

The difference we take to have caused the feature in question might be a relevant difference, but not the only relevant difference. Perhaps both climatic deterioration and an increase in the intensity of warfare caused the southward movement of the Oneota.

Sometimes the difference we're looking at is the effect rather than the cause of the feature in question. Perhaps population aggregation was the result of internal social reorganization. Given their greater concentrated numbers, these newly aggregated communities began raiding distant smaller communities, which caused a general increase in the intensity of warfare throughout this geographical area.

Perhaps the difference did not cause the feature in question, but rather the difference and feature in question are both effects of a third underlying cause. In the example above, maybe competition between populations developed in response to increased trading opportunities with a distant chiefdom. Some people aggregated into village clusters, while others remained dispersed and concentrated around key economic resources. However, all of these people began fighting each other for control of the regional resources that the chiefdom wished to trade for.

Similar questions need to be asked with regard to only-common-thread reasoning. Here again is the case of population aggregation:

> Populations aggregated in five different places at different times. What caused the aggregation of these populations? A review of the archaeological literature in all five places shows that warfare was on the rise at the time in all five instances. The answer to our question seems to be warfare.

Assuming that the author is not mistaken in saying that all five populations aggregated, we need to ask the following:

Is the common thread relevant to the feature in question? For example, each population may have aggregated for locally unique reasons.

Is the common thread the only relevant common thread? For example, all five populations may have aggregated because of centralization in social organization. Perhaps the thread the author focused on (let's say the deterioration of regional climate) had nothing to do with the feature in question or, more likely, was only one of a number of contributing causes.

Could the author have reversed cause and effect? In this example, did population aggregation result in an increase in regional warfare?

Did the author overlook a possible common cause of the common thread and the feature in question? Were both population aggregation and a rise in regional warfare a response to the appearance of traders from a more complex social system? Was a third thing or occurrence actually responsible for both the feature in question and the proposed only relevant common thread? Since real-life situations are often quite complex, was a fourth or fifth thing or occurrence involved as a cause as well? Be aware, then, that while our minds seem to seek simple solutions, the world is complex and interdependent.

Is the feature in question such that it might not have required a common cause to begin with? For example, each of the five populations may have aggregated for different reasons, because of social centralization in one case, for defense in another, to have a sufficient number of people for large-scale animal drives in still another, and so on. It may be true that warfare was on the increase in all five instances, but was that only coincidence? Just because multiple communities aggregated at roughly the same time, does that necessarily imply that they all aggregated because of the same cause? Coincidences do occur (see below). So when evaluating an instance of only-relevant-common-thread reasoning, ask whether it could be coincidence.

To recap, when evaluating only-relevant-common-thread reasoning, ask the following questions: Is the common thread relevant to the feature in question? Is the common thread the only relevant common thread? Could the author have reversed cause and effect? Did the author overlook a possible common cause of both the common thread and the feature in question? Is the feature in question such that it might not have required a common cause to begin with?

Post Hoc, Ergo Propter Hoc

I have listed several questions to consider when you encounter only-relevant-difference and only-relevant-common-thread reasoning in your reading. When an archaeologist doesn't consider one or more of these questions, he could be committing the mistake or fallacy known as post hoc, ergo propter hoc (for short, the post hoc fallacy). "Post hoc, ergo propter hoc" means "After this, therefore because of this," or, more informally, "This happened after that happened; therefore this must have happened because that happened." To reemphasize, just because one thing happened after another thing happened does not mean that the first thing necessarily caused the second. Just because the northern Oneota moved southward shortly after a deterioration in climate does not mean they moved southward because of the change in climate.

Overlooking the Possibility of Coincidence

If you carefully examine the common mistakes in causal reasoning listed in this section of the chapter, you may notice that some of the proposed cause-and-effect links could in fact be just a coincidence. Briefly defined, a coincidence occurs when two or more things coincide in time or follow one another in time but there is no causal relationship. How do we as readers decide what is the case? Was there a causal relationship or was coincidence at play? This is an important question, for both cause-and-effect relationships and relationships that are only coincidences occur all the time.

So in situations in which one event occurs before another, a causal relationship between the two must still be established. It cannot be assumed just because of the before-after link. Perhaps the relevant difference identified is not the only relevant difference. Perhaps it is a coincidence and not a relevant difference at all.

Another situation in which coincidence is common occurs when a feature in question, a feature shared by all instances being considered, is not the result of the common thread proposed in a study. Perhaps the feature in question was caused by a common thread not yet identified. For example, population aggregation and an increase in warfare may both have occurred in the five cases in the study, but both are a response to the appearance of new trading opportunities with a distant chiefdom.

A third common situation in which this confusion occurs is when multiple effects occur that seem similar in kind (let's say the aggregation of multiple communities). It is tempting to assume in occurrences like this that there must be a common thread. In reality, the multiple effects may not have been caused by a single common thread. Perhaps all five of the populations in the different cases aggregated for different reasons. It is just coincidence that warfare was also on the rise in each area at the time.

Remember, then, that what appear to be cause-and-effect relationships could in reality be the result of coincidence.

Causation in Populations

Many causal claims in archaeology concern populations, not individual things or events like the southward movement of the Oneota.[4] The claim "Warfare causes population aggregation in preindustrial societies," for example, should not be interpreted as meaning that warfare will cause any particular preindustrial population to aggregate, or even that warfare will cause the majority of these populations to aggregate. The claim is that warfare is a causal factor for population aggregation in preindustrial societies—that is, there would be fewer instances of aggregated populations among preindustrial societies if there was less warfare. Phrased more formally, if something A causes something B in a population, the more members of the population that are exposed to A, the more B there will be in the population (this is a small hint of what an argument in formal logic looks like).

The principles underlying causation in populations have been established using both experimental and nonexperimental investigations. Since only nonexperimental effect-to-cause studies are encountered when reading archaeology, a few cautions should be mentioned. First, remember that what may appear to be a cause-and-effect relationship may in fact be the result of coincidence. So ask the following: Is other evidence besides the correlation between the purported cause and the effect presented in support of the causal claim? And second, as with nonexperimental cause-to-effect studies, it is difficult in nonexperimental effect-to-cause studies to control for the presence of other relevant differences or relevant threads. So again, less confidence is placed in this type of nonexperimental test than in experimental tests.

Use of Anecdotal Evidence in Causal Reasoning

Appeals to anecdotal evidence are commonly encountered in causal reasoning in archaeology. The appeal is a mistake because it violates the sufficiency criterion of a good argument.[5] In this appeal an archaeologist cites an example or two in which an effect followed exposure to a causative factor to claim that the causative factor did cause the effect. An example would be a claim that an increase in warfare leads to population aggregation in preindustrial societies simply because the writer knows of an example or two in which this was the case. This is another common form of hasty generalization and, as such, is a weak argument (see chapter 12). The argument would be just as weak if it were turned around and the claim became that an increase in warfare does not cause population aggregation because the writer knows of a few examples in which this was not the case.

As with hasty generalizations in general, there is insufficient evidence to justify the claim. It may be the case that preindustrial societies did (or did not) aggregate their populations when exposed to warfare, but the author has been too hasty in making the claim based on one or two examples that he knows about. As a consequence, this is a fallacy of missing evidence often called the fallacy of insufficient sample, for there is simply not enough evidence to establish the claim.

Although another somewhat dense chapter, it is worth our effort as critical readers to understand the basics of causal reasoning, for archaeologists frequently refer to causes in their writing.

EVALUATING INTERPRETATIONS IV
OF THE ARCHAEOLOGICAL RECORD

THINKING TASKS IN DIFFERENT PARTS of the research cycle normally involve different forms of reasoning. As we learned in chapter 12, inductive generalization is involved in the transformation of sample summaries to population estimates; in this use of inductive reasoning, statements about known samples are transformed into statements about unknown populations. Stated more broadly, inductive arguments of this kind involve reasoning from specific instances to general conclusions. By contrast, when archaeologists test a proposed theory about the past of one kind or another, they draw out implications of the theory using deductive reasoning. They then make new observations on the archaeological record to test the implications. If the new data match the test implications (predictions), they conclude that the theory has factual support.[1]

Drawing out and testing implications of a theory about the past is obviously an integral process in the research cycle. In fact, the confrontation of a theory about the past with factual data (as problematic as it may be) is what makes archaeology a "science" rather than a Hollywood storytelling venture. Among the questions that critical readers might ask about this process of confrontation are the following: Do the implications an archaeologist has drawn from a theory about the past logically follow from the content and form of the theory itself? Is the theory itself so poorly developed or internally contradictory that logically incompatible implications can be drawn from it? Does the reasoning move from general premises to specific conclusions or from one specific relationship to another? If an archaeologist is serious about testing ideas about the past (and not all archaeologists are involved in producing theories about the past-in-itself), then these and related questions are fundamental to the research process.

The chapters in part IV concern the transformations involved in archaeology in this testing process. Chapters 18 and 19 ask, "Are deductively valid conclusions drawn?" and "Are concepts given archaeological interpretations?" The final chapter, chapter 20, asks, "Are the conclusions reasonable?" If you have worked your way through this book this far, you will have some grasp of the effort involved in becoming an effective critical reader. So the postscript asks, "Is critical reading worth the effort?"—and by now you sense what that answer is!

Are Deductively Valid Conclusions Drawn?   **18**

FORMAL LOGIC CONCENTRATES almost exclusively on deductive reasoning. For the most part, textbooks on formal logic are filled with abstract symbols and, for us, not very useful examples. Nonetheless, deductive reasoning has an ineludible role in the research process in archaeology, for it draws out claims for testing from theories. This "drawing out" takes place in the upper right part of the cycle (see figure 2.1). Our goal in this chapter is to get a sense of the issues that critical readers should be aware of when encountering predictions from theories about the past-in-itself and of deductive reasoning more generally.

Deductive versus Inductive Strength of Arguments

In quick review, a key difference between a deductive argument and an inductive one is the certainty of a correctly formed deductive argument. If the argument is correctly formed, its conclusion follows with logical certainty from the premises. It was this difference in relative strength that led New Archaeologists in the 1960s and 1970s to champion the use of the hypothetico-deductive approach—and to castigate culture historians for favoring a "weaker" inductive approach. In a correctly formed deductive argument, if the premises are true, the conclusion cannot be false. A deductive argument that is correctly formed is called a valid argument. In contrast, inductive reasoning expands known information from a sample to another sample or to a larger population. It makes claims that cannot be known to be true.

Archaeologists (including myself) rarely use formal deductive arguments to demonstrate the truthfulness of their interpretations of the past-in-itself. Rather, if interpretations are tested at all, the predictions are less formally formulated. Consequently, if a prediction does not deductively follow from the premises of the interpretation, a test of the prediction may not have anything useful to contribute to the validation of the interpretation. Likewise, although there are exceptions, archaeologists seldom develop their interpretations of the past-in-itself in such a manner that the premises are clearly stated and logically complete. The critical reader should be acutely aware of the implications of this practice and of the specific weaknesses that signal its presence. The following sections, while brief and ultimately inadequate, provide some insight into the skills that are necessary to make these judgments.

Some Common Patterns of Deductive Arguments

When using deductive reasoning to draw out implications for testing, errors in the form of the argument can occur. As critical readers, we should become familiar with common forms of valid and invalid deductive arguments. The techniques of categorical logic are used in critical thinking to differentiate between these valid and invalid forms. Categorical logic is a system of logic based on the relations of inclusion and exclusion. A categorical statement claims that something is included (or not) in a category or categories, such as "All students are members" (of, say, the Minnesota Archaeological Society) and "Some members are students." It is easy to substitute whatever claim you want, such as "all Oneota village sites," "alongside river banks," and "horticultural sites." Although useful in the examination of arguments, categorical logic is much too involved to review here in detail. Nonetheless, the following common examples of valid and invalid deductive arguments provide a glimpse of the value of this sort of reasoning.[1] In reading these examples, think of the conclusion as a prediction that follows (or not) from the premises of an interpretation of the past-in-itself.

Here are three valid patterns that you should make an effort to remember (in this group "P" and "Q" stand for any claims you want them to).

- *Modus ponens* (affirming the antecedent): If P, then Q. P is present or occurred. Therefore, Q.

Example: If Jones bought the flotation machine, then a crate would be outside the lab (If P, then Q). She bought the flotation machine (P is present). Therefore, a crate would be outside the lab (Q).

- *Modus tollens* (denying the consequent): If P, then Q. Not-Q. Therefore, not-P.

  Example: If Jones bought the flotation machine, then a crate would be outside the lab (If P, then Q). A crate is not outside the lab (not-Q). Therefore, she didn't buy it (not-P).

- *Chain argument*: If P, then Q. If Q, then R. Therefore, if P, then R.

  Example: If Jones bought the flotation machine, then a crate would be outside the lab (If P, then Q). If a crate is outside the lab, then we will see the flotation machine in the lab (If Q, then R). Therefore, if Jones bought the flotation machine, we will see it in the lab (Therefore, if P, then R).

Here are two related but invalid patterns:

- *Affirming the consequent*: If P, then Q. Q is present or has occurred. Therefore, P.

  Example: If Jones bought the flotation machine, then a crate would be outside the lab (If P, then Q). A crate is outside the lab (Q is present or has occurred). Therefore, she bought the flotation machine (Therefore, P).

- *Denying the antecedent*: If P, then Q. Not-P. Therefore, not-Q.

  Example: If Jones bought the flotation machine, then a crate would be outside the lab (If P, then Q). She didn't buy the machine (not-P). Therefore a crate won't be outside the lab (Therefore, not-Q).

Here is another group of commonly encountered argument patterns, two of which are valid and two of which are invalid (in this group, X and Y stand for classes of things):

- *Valid conversion 1*: No Xs are Ys. Therefore, no Ys are Xs.

  Example: No students are members (No Xs are Ys). Therefore, no members are students (Therefore, no Ys are Xs).

- *Valid conversion 2*: Some Xs are Ys. Therefore, some Ys are Xs.

  Example: Some students are members (Some Xs are Ys). Therefore, some members are students (Therefore, some Ys are Xs).

- *Invalid conversion 1*: All Xs are Ys. Therefore, all Ys are Xs.

  Example: All students are members (All Xs are Ys). Therefore, all members are students (Therefore, all Ys are Xs).

- *Invalid conversion 2*: Some Xs are not Ys. Therefore, some Ys are not Xs.

  Example: Some students are not members (Some Xs are not Ys). Therefore, some members are not students (Therefore, some Ys are not Xs).

A related form deserves special emphasis because it is so common:

- *Unnamed invalid inference*: Some Xs are Ys. Therefore, some Xs are not Ys.

  Example: Some students are members (Some Xs are Ys). Therefore, some students are not members (Therefore, some Xs are not Ys).

It is also invalid to run the last argument in reverse, where "Some Xs are not Ys" is followed by "Therefore, some Xs are Ys."

Example: Some students are not members (Some Xs are not Ys). Therefore, some students are members (Therefore, some Xs are Ys).

In this last group (below) of commonly encountered valid and invalid argument patterns, X, Y, and Z stand for classes of things:

- *Valid syllogism 1*: All Xs are Ys. All Ys are Zs. Therefore, all Xs are Zs.

  Example: All students are members (All Xs are Ys). All members are archaeology majors (All Ys are Zs). Therefore, all students are archaeology majors (Therefore, all Xs are Zs).

- *Valid syllogism 2*: All Xs are Ys. No Ys are Zs. Therefore, no Xs are Zs.

  Example: All students are members (All Xs are Ys). No members are archaeology majors (No Ys are Zs). Therefore, no students are archaeology majors (Therefore, no Xs are Zs).

- *Invalid syllogism 1*: All Xs are Ys. All Zs are Ys. Therefore, all Xs are Zs.

  Example: All students are members (All Xs are Ys). All archaeology majors are members (All Zs are Ys). Therefore, all students are archaeology majors (Therefore, all Xs are Zs).

- *Invalid syllogism 2*: All Xs are Ys. No Zs are Xs. Therefore, no Ys are Zs.

  Example: All students are members (All Xs are Ys). No archaeology majors are students (No Zs are Xs). Therefore, no members are archaeology majors (Therefore, no Ys are Zs).

Since readers more commonly mistake invalid patterns for valid patterns, the usual advice in critical thinking books is to concentrate first on recognizing the invalid patterns. So concentrate first when reading this book on recognizing the seven invalid patterns sketched out above. That makes the task of learning all patterns somewhat easier. The exception among valid patterns is *modus tollens* (denying the consequent), which is often mistakenly thought to be an invalid pattern.

An Example of Deductive Reasoning in Archaeology

In the following case study, we step back from our concentration on deductive reasoning to look more broadly at how deductive reasoning functions in the testing of an actual interpretation of the past. There will be considerable review along the way. We will review some of the fundamental assumptions of processual archaeology, a systems-centered research program; show how a particular perspective within that approach to interpretation in archaeology (evolutionary archaeology) has been developed; demonstrate the role of research program–based assumptions in developing interpretations of the past; and examine how test implications (predictions) may be deductively drawn from those interpretations.

Contemporary evolutionary archaeology is an interpretation-building component of systems-centered archaeology. Evolutionary archaeology explores the implications in theory building of applying neo-Darwinian evolutionary theory to general archaeological issues. It is this theory (neo-Darwinism) that supplies the operational assumptions in the theory-building process. Before looking more closely at neo-Darwinian theory, let's review some of the basic assumptions of systems-centered archaeology.

Although repetitive, this review will help us understand more clearly why this version of evolutionary archaeology fits comfortably within systems-centered archaeology as a research program.

As a research program, systems-centered archaeology is based upon a set of research program–defining assumptions that include the following:

1. The focus of research in archaeology should be observable human behavior or its by-products (in contrast to unobservable thoughts), because it makes number 2 below possible.
2. To be scientific, research studies must adopt methods that are firmly anchored in ("brute") reality.
3. Culture is the primary means by which human societies adapt (with varying degrees of efficiency) to their external environment, which has physical, biological, and cultural components.
4. Culture change—and, ultimately, cultural evolution—stems from changes within this adaptive relationship between culture and environment.
5. People constantly try to optimize cost-benefit relationships in satisfying their basic needs for food, shelter, comfort, and so on. This results in changes in "technology"—that is, in those aspects of culture that are nearest nature.
6. Changes in technology cause changes in social organization and ideology—that is, in the upper levels of a base-superstructure model of culture that has technology at its broad base.
7. The goal of systems-centered archaeology is to explain (rather than to understand) the similarities and differences among all cultures—that is, to contribute to the general goals of social science when conceived of as a science.
8. The latter goal can be achieved by developing general theories that identify those underlying processes that affect all cultures (or at least all cultures of a certain kind) and their change.

Contemporary evolutionary archaeology is based upon these assumptions or at least upon versions of these assumptions.[2] It provides in addition, however, processes derived from neo-Darwinian evolution that serve as the driving force of this type of model. Among the basic presuppositions of Neo-Darwinian evolution as applied to the study of human beings in the past are the following:

1. The behavior of all organisms is shaped through natural selection. By extension, evolutionary theory is applicable to people.
2. Human behavior has evolved in response to changes in the physical and social environment.
3. Archaeological phenomena can be thought of as products of Darwinian evolution.
4. Human behavior and the products of human behavior are aspects of the human phenotype.
5. Humans have been selected to be enormously opportunistic in their responses to change in the (physical, biological, and cultural) environment.
6. Humans have been selected to seize opportunities that are likely to enhance their relative reproductive fitness.
7. Phenotypes—and behavior a fortiori—are ways of adapting different strategies in different environments using the same sets of genes, and phenotypes themselves are products of natural selection.
8. Neo-Darwinian theories of culture are selectional rather than transformational, and the focus of selection is the individual.

As a branch of systems-centered archaeology, a neo-Darwinian evolutionary perspective applied to the history of cultures as viewed through the archaeological record is in a fledgling stage. Considerable disagreement exists over its secondary presuppositions and how best to proceed. Rather than a hindrance, these first steps and disagreements provide readers critical insights into what the formation of a research program looks like in print. What is involved, then, in the development of a research program?

First, before archaeologists can use biological evolution as an analogy (a process) in modeling, they must identify and define cultural and archaeological equivalents of key concepts in biological evolution. They must also determine how change is to be identified and measured, how Darwinian processes as expressed in the archaeological record are to be identified and measured, what in culture or human behavior evolves, what is meant by Darwinian evolution, and so on. As in most research programs, these are continuing rather than short-term goals. This transference of core notions from one domain of inquiry (here biological evolution) to another (archaeology) and their redefinition at an operational level (for instance, when applied to the archaeological record) are characteristic features of research program development. Similar transferences and redefinitions occurred with the adoption by processual archaeologists of core notions from general systems theory, cultural ecology, and logical empiricism (the methodology of science adopted).

Second, as with all research programs, evolutionary archaeology will have its own vocabulary that must be learned. Some new terms, such as "phenotype," will be introduced into archaeology, while otherwise familiar terms will be redefined. An example of a familiar term that has been redefined in this research program is "culture," which now designates the particular and elaborate system of behavior associated with humans. Examples of other concepts associated with evolutionary archaeology are natural selection, genetic change, culturally transmitted behaviors, energetic models, energetic cost-and-benefit data, coevolutionary interaction, variation generation, information transmission, fitness, replicative success, and sorting processes.

Third, evolutionary archaeologists will argue among themselves about how best to proceed. While some of these arguments will involve relatively low-level problems, such as the most valid measure of a concept, others will involve the core concepts of the program.

Kenneth Russell's *After Eden: The Behavioral Ecology of Early Food Production in the Near East and North Africa* (1988) demonstrates the potential of evolutionary archaeology as a research program and some of the directions that it is taking. *After Eden* is an evolutionary cost-and-benefit approach to the analysis of cultural energetics in this region of the world during the period of early food production. More specifically, the study explores the applicability of behavioral ecology to archaeological issues involving the evolution and adoption of alternative food production strategies in the Near East and North Africa. Behavioral ecology is one means of applying neo-Darwinian concepts to actual field situations. Among the presuppositions of Russell's study are the following:

1. Significant advances in understanding the evolution and adoption of food production strategies are unlikely unless human–animal–plant relationships are investigated within the context of general theories that address the underlying principles affecting subsistence behavior.
2. Since energy fuels reproduction, an organism that captures energy more efficiently than its competitors would enjoy a relative reproductive advantage.
3. Patterns of subsistence behavior that enhance *reproductive success* due to the efficiency of energy capture are expected to persist and spread at the expense of those that do so less effectively.

4. The goal of foraging behavior is to maximize the rate of energy capture.
5. The ability to ensure or increase the productivity and reliability of plant and animal resources would have been a desirable (and perhaps necessary) goal under conditions of environmental and demographic stress.
6. Since energy derived from food fuels reproduction, organisms that maximize their foraging efficiency, as measured by their rate of energy capture, would generally enjoy a relative reproductive fitness.
7. All else being equal, foraging strategies that are more effective in rate of energy capture should be favored by natural selection and would persist at the expense of those that are less efficient.

Russell's research goal was to test the hypothesis that food production strategies were adopted in his area of study when the mean foraging return rate fell equal to or below the mean return rate for alternative food production options. Furthermore, available food production options should have been adopted according to their ranking by relative return rate. The main hypothesis is an implication drawn from his general theory—that is, it is a test implication and, therefore, a research move that is characteristic of the next information transformation in the research cycle (the move from theory to test implication).

An evolutionary cost-and-benefit approach is used in *After Eden* to measure and analyze the cultural energetics (the energy pluses and minuses of various subsistence options) of the situation. A main problem of his study was how to measure energetic costs and benefits in a manner suited to the archaeological record—a problem whose discussion fills the bulk of his manuscript. The energetic expectations (predictions) of his hypothesis include (but are not limited to) the following:

1. Meat plus milk pastoral strategies would not have become marginal to the average cereal subsistence option until the advent of animal traction tillage (an innovation).
2. If milk production was not significant in the evolution of early pastoral strategies, archaeological evidence should reflect the agricultural exploitation of marginal dry-farming environments before the appearance of alternative pastoral societies.
3. If milk production was significant in the evolution of early pastoral strategies, archaeological evidence should reflect the agricultural

exploitation of marginal dry-farming environments only after the appearance of alternative pastoral societies.
4. The order in which habitats or habitat types were occupied should have varied directly with the net energy return rates gained from exploiting them.

To test his predictions, which are deductive implications of his premises, Russell carried out energetic analyses using simple energy optimization models derived from behavioral ecology. Examples of these types of model are optimal diet models and path-choice models. Some of the results of his tests on archaeological collections are listed below:

1. The identification of anomalies (events not predicted by the theory). Examples include the out-of-order domestication of camels and the seemingly late appearance of strategies of cattle use and domestication.
2. The identification of counterintuitive expectations. Examples include the development of "marginal" environments and the appearance of profitable camel strategies.
3. The identification of additional factors that were apparently significant in the evolution of early food production strategies but have been ignored. An example is the importance of game drivelines and corrals.

Regardless of one's views of evolutionary archaeology, Russell's model (1) provides a more extended example of the theory-building process in archaeology, (2) illustrates the role of fundamental assumptions in model development, (3) demonstrates how test implications may be drawn from a model, and (4) introduces some of the problems involved in testing theories in archaeology, such as providing adequate archaeological measures for real-world (ethnographic) words like "foraging return rate" and "milk production." Because of the formal development of his argument, the rudiments of theory building and the role of deductive reasoning in theory evaluation are more clearly displayed to the reader in *After Eden* than they are in most reading in archaeology.

Like inductive reasoning, deductive reasoning has its own crucial role to play in the research cycle in archaeology. Critical readers should be able to recognize and evaluate this form of reasoning when they read archaeology.

Are Concepts Given Archaeological Interpretations?

19

A CRITICAL AND DIFFICULT PHASE of the research process that archaeologists must grapple with involves the transformation of statements about the past-in-itself into statements about the present archaeological record. This transformation means that archaeologists can only test their interpretations of the past indirectly. Chapter 19 examines the nature of this transformation. The first section reviews the process of transforming a prediction to a test implication, and the second the reliability and validity of indicators in test implications. The third section looks at several examples of this transformation in action.

Preparing Predictions for Testing

In quick review, every interpretation of the past in the research cycle makes some predictions about the content of that past world. For example, the statement "This is a projectile point" implies that a particular artifact was once bound to a shaft and propelled through the air when used. These two predictions are contained in the definition of projectile point. Like sample summaries, logical predictions are not true information transformations. Since they are already in the interpretations of the past from which they have been deduced, they are "drawn out" rather than transformed to a new kind of information, with all the uncertainty that the word "transformation" implies.

The theories (interpretations of the past) from which predictions are deduced through the methodological control of deduction are generally statements of knowledge about past peoples, their culture, and the world they lived in. Since the history of archaeology indicates that many of these statements are most likely false, or at least inadequate in some way, we need a process for identifying true and false, and better and worse, statements of knowledge. In science, this is most definitively accomplished by devising confrontations between the consequences of statements of knowledge (theories) and fresh experience, whether on the right or left side of the four quadrants. In archaeology this does not necessarily mean new excavations or even new sets of artifacts. It might just mean fresh experiences—that is, experiences not used in constructing the theory.

Another way to think about scientific knowledge is that it is knowledge capable of refutation—although, as we know from our review of the postmodern critique, this is a problematic and uncertain enterprise. One of the necessary characteristics of predictions in archaeology, then, is that they have test implications—that is, that they say something about the reality of the remnants of the past—and some predictions are more difficult to test than others. For instance, a prediction that refers, say, to the meaning a particular kind of Lower Paleolithic stone axe had to its makers (a left quadrant prediction) is less likely to produce convincing testable implications than a prediction about the specific contents of their diet (an upper right quadrant prediction), although it may be the case that the first kind of prediction is the more important of the two in a particular interpretation of the past.

In this context, it is necessary to distinguish between two meanings of the word "true." Interpretations of the past in archaeology are considered true or at least potentially true when their test implications are not falsified by empirical observations on the archaeological record (the falsification approach to theory testing); they might also be considered true when they are confirmed (supported) by fresh observations on the archaeological record (the confirmation approach to theory testing). Alternatively, logical statements are considered true if they are contextually and thus necessarily true—that is, if they are true by definition. For instance, in the argument "[P] All men are mortal and [P] Binford is a man; therefore [C] Binford is mortal," the statement "Binford is mortal" is contextually true because it necessarily follows from the premises of the argument (it is a tautology, which is a statement that is true by definition).

The unwary reader is often misled by tautological arguments into accepting as true what may be false. Consider the following example: "[P] The economic base of all Neolithic societies was food production and [P] X was a Neolithic society; therefore [C] the economic base of society X was food production."

If we accept this definition of the word "Neolithic" and conclude that a component of a site is Neolithic (say the component is considered Neolithic because it contains a polished stone axe), then we must (logically) conclude that its inhabitants were food producers. No empirical evidence of food production is necessary to arrive at this conclusion, for it is true by definition—even though "the economic base of society X was food production" may be a false statement.

In archaeology, terms within test implications nearly always refer to characteristics of the past-in-itself, such as past sociopolitical systems, human groups, or environments. Therefore, it is necessary to interpret the concepts and relationships in these statements in terms of phenomena on which observations can be made. A switch must be made back to archaeological context. This abstractive transformation raises challenging methodological problems in archaeology.

To connect abstract notions with observational data, the abstract notions must be given interpretations that refer to empirical things or relationships in the archaeological record. In this regard, it is useful to think of a concept as having three parts: a name, a theoretical definition, and an operational definition. A theoretical definition gives meaning to a concept, a name labels it, and an operational definition indicates what is actually measured or observed when an instance of the concept is identified in the archaeological record. Operational definitions do not provide concepts with meaning. Rather, they are rules for interpreting concepts in terms of things and relationships in the archaeological record, and are therefore ways of indirectly testing the truth or falsity of statements about the world in the past.

Cultural anthropologists and archaeologists share the names and theoretical definitions of many concepts. However, they measure or operationalize these same concepts using different operational definitions. An example is the concept of matrilocality. One theoretical definition of this concept is "postmarital residence that locates the married pair in the domiciliary group of the wife's mother." Cultural anthropologists identify the practice by actually talking to married couples, observing who lives where, and other direct approaches. Archaeologists necessarily use indirect approaches. A definition that we will look at in more detail later in the chapter is "a living floor area of the average house in a society of greater than six hundred square feet."

Another example is the concept warfare. One theoretical definition of this concept is "activity undertaken by a political unit to weaken or destroy another." A simple operational definition of this term is "presence of mutilated skeletons" in the archaeological record. As this example illustrates, operational definitions in archaeology are frequently incomplete: they capture only part of the intended meaning of a concept or relationship. Operational definitions like "presence of mutilated skeletons" are mere indicators, in the same manner that "presence of exotic objects," such as foreign flints or seashells, is merely an indicator of the possible presence of trade. For this reason, archaeologists frequently use multiple indicators to provide together a more convincing operational definition of a concept. In the warfare example, the indicators "defensive walls," "ditches," "towers," and "presence of mutilated skeletons" (as present in the archaeological record) together provide a more convincing operational definition of warfare than any does by itself.

If indicators like these are quantified, they can even be used in measuring the intensity or degree of an activity besides merely denoting its presence in the past.

The Reliability and Validity of Indicators

Moving from predictions to empirical interpretations in the cycle of science is a true information transformation. Like the transformation of empirical generalizations to theories (interpretations about something that existed in the past), it is an example of abstractive thinking that connects concepts and relationships in theories by abstraction to objects and relationships in the archaeological record for at least some of their relevant scope. The movement from statements about the archaeological record to statements about the past-in-itself (on either side of the four quadrants) and back again is at the core of archaeology when practiced as a science.

Notwithstanding the fundamental importance of this movement, there are many reasons in archaeology why these transformations are less than perfect. One reason is that in moving from predictions to empirical interpretations, there is usually a low correspondence between theoretical and operational definitions. A few of the reasons why this is so are mentioned here. First, operational definitions that completely capture all of the meaning of a theoretical definition are very difficult to think of in archaeology. What, for example, would be a complete operational definition of such terms as "population pressure" and "degree of social interaction"? Second, archaeologists typically pay little explicit attention to operational definitions. They either do not formulate operational definitions at all or do not make explicit just what definitions they have in mind. As a result, tests of predictions are often not directly and explicitly comparable or additive to one another, for there is no guarantee that they are measuring the same concept.

Third, archaeologists normally do not make their theoretical definitions of concepts explicit. Consequently, it is unclear to the reader just what operational definition would be appropriate. Think, for example, of all of the definitions of the concept "agriculture." Unless we are explicitly told, it is frequently difficult to determine what is meant. Are the statements "Agriculture first appeared in area Alpha ten thousand years ago" and "Agriculture first appeared in area Beta five thousand years ago" referring to the same phenomenon? How would we know? Finally, archaeologists are not in the habit of systematically evaluating the validity of their operational definitions. As a result, inadequate or weak measures are perpetuated.

Since many archaeologists tend to breeze through the transformation of test implications into empirical interpretations in the right side of the research cycle, the critical reader should be particularly alert for errors in this transformation. A useful way to evaluate the adequacy of this transformation is to rate the reliability and validity of the indicators that are given in empirical interpretations—if this transformation has been made at all. (It is not uncommon to read a report that lacks explicit tests of interpretations about something in the past against the archaeological record. A jump has been made instead to the observation information component.)

The reliability of a measurement refers to the likelihood that the results of a measurement would be the same if repeated by the same or another archaeologist. The smaller the swing in value of the same measure, the more reliable the measure is. Standard radiocarbon dates are less reliable in this sense because of their degree of statistical error. By contrast, measurements of the length of a projectile point with a caliper are normally more reliable. Measurement can be made more reliable by improving the instruments of measurement and in some cases by standardizing the procedures of measurement.

The validity of a measurement is the extent to which the indicators that are measured correspond to the concept archaeologists want to measure. Phrased another way, if an operational definition completely captures the meaning of a theoretical definition of a concept, then it is a completely valid measure of that concept. Think of the problems in the last section of finding an operational definition of "warfare" that completely captures the meaning of that concept when defined as "activity undertaken by a political unit to weaken or destroy another."

To grasp why reliability and validity are problems in archaeology, let's look at three basic types of measurements: fundamental, derived, and fiat or proxy. A fundamental measurement involves the straightforward measurement of something like length, height, width, or weight. A derived measurement is a straightforward relationship between fundamental measures, such as a length–height ratio. In contrast, a fiat measurement is a proxy measure of something more elusive, such as degree of social stratification. Fiat measurements of something like degree of social stratification are obviously more prone to problems of measurement validity and reliability than are the length and length–height ratio of a projectile point. As a rule, then, archaeologists should try to check the reliability and validity of their measurements, but especially their fiat measurements.

A useful way of thinking about validity and reliability is to think of an imaginary scale that ranges from zero to ten. A measurement corresponding to ten on the scale would represent identity between a theoretical definition and its operational interpretation: the measure repeatedly captures the complete meaning of the concept. A zero is the reverse. Most fundamental and derived measurements in archaeology fall near the upper end of this imaginary scale of validity and reliability, while the great majority of fiat measurements undoubtedly fall in the lower half of the scale. The reason for this discrepancy should be obvious. Fiat measures are indirect measures; they are measures of underlying variables that are also poorly defined in many cases.

The validity and reliability of the measures that archaeologists use to test the implications of their interpretations of the past deserve more serious attention, for how they rank on the zero-to-ten scale can affect the evaluation of a test. Since most fiat measures in archaeology have a rank of only three or four (in my opinion), what does a positive test of a hypothesis mean? Should archaeologists reject the hypothesis if it is falsified by the test? These are vexing problems that are due in part to the neglect of this transformation process.

Evaluating Archaeological Indicators

As archaeologists, we should learn to evaluate archaeological indicators rather than merely accept them as tools in our methodological toolbox. One of the first steps we can take to remedy this situation is to ask explicit questions about the indicators that we and other archaeologists use. Among the many questions that we might ask about the archaeological indicators we confront are the following: How valid are they (on our zero-to-ten scale)? Which of two indicators is better and why? What are the assumptions underlying these indicators? How are indicators to be evaluated?

If we decide that an indicator has a validity of three or four on the zero-to-ten scale, then it is a task for archaeologists to explicitly develop an indicator for that concept that is higher on the scale. This research task in archaeology is rarely explicitly recognized for what it is. As a result, this portion of the cycle of research in archaeology has languished in development. However, when one's attention is drawn to the creation of increasingly more valid indicators in archaeology, it is seen for what it is: a difficult but rewarding and necessary enterprise.

The following two examples of archaeological indicators demonstrate more clearly their nature and how they might be evaluated logically and factually.

An Archaeological Indicator of Matrilocal versus Patrilocal Residence

A classic example of an explicit attempt to develop an archaeological indicator of a social practice is Ember's criterion for differentiating between matrilocal and patrilocal residence.[1] A cultural anthropologist, Ember's concern was that if cultural anthropologists and archaeologists were to work on similar problems, then they must explore, systematically and comparatively, how the behavioral and material realms they work with may be correlated.

Matrilocal residence means that a couple lives with or near the wife's kin, normally her parents. The couple lives with or near the groom's kin, normally his parents, where patrilocal residence is the rule. Since residence rules are usually associated with subsistence pattern and other sociocultural traits, they have been of particular interest to processual (systems-centered) archaeologists. Using random samples drawn from the more than eight hundred societies in the Human Relations Area Files (HRAF) that have information on patterns of residence, Ember found that matrilocal and patrilocal residence patterns could be simply and accurately predicted from the size of the living floor area of the average house in a pre-European contact society: patrilocal societies have an average living floor area of less than 550–600 square feet, whereas matrilocal societies tend to have living floor areas of more than 550–600 square feet.

What problems might exist with Ember's archaeological indicators for matrilocal and patrilocal residence? What could lower their degree of validity and reliability? Consider the following issues: First, sampling error. How representative of all past societies are the eight hundred societies examined in the HRAF files? Second, how was the "average house in the society" identified? What does "average" mean? Was this criterion applied uniformly to all eight hundred societies in the sample?

Third, what is "living floor area"? Are storage and work areas included in "living floor area"? Were the criteria used to make this decision uniformly applied in all eight hundred cases? How is "the floor space" of "the average house" identified and measured?

Fourth, there may be confusion with other residence patterns. The size of living floor areas for both neolocal residence (in which couples live in a residence apart from either of their kin) and bilocal residence (in which couples can live with or near either of their kin) overlaps that of matrilocal and patrilocal residence. Neolocal residence is most frequently associated with commercial or monetized exchange (so the presence of coins might be an indicator of the presence of full-time specialists). Bilocality is frequently associated with recent depopulation because of disease, warfare, and similar catastrophes. In applying Ember's indicator, one would have to make sure that these possibilities were excluded. These issues are part of the larger problem of domain of application, which for Ember is pre-European contact societies that have neither a bilocal nor a neolocal residence pattern.

Ember's indicator seems to rank high on the scale of validity, for all but one patrilocal and all matrilocal societies in his sample fit the size requirement. Because of definitional and possible sampling problems, it probably rates a seven or eight on the zero-to-ten scale.

Mammalian Taphonomy and Taxonomic Diversity

Archaeologists frequently include the entire bone assemblage in a sample from a site in their studies of the subsistence practices of the occupants of those sites. One indicator of the subsistence practice of a site's occupants is taxonomic diversity. Were the occupants of the site hunter-gatherers with a generalized (diverse) broad-spectrum subsistence strategy, or were they specialists who exploited a narrow range of animal species? A basic, fundamental question is asked in these kinds of studies: Is the taxonomic diversity of the entire bone assemblage from several sites a valid indicator of which of these subsistence strategies was followed?

Schmitt and Lupo demonstrate that the presence of noncultural bone in an assemblage can severely reduce the validity and reliability of the use of taxonomic diversity as a measure of subsistence practices.[2] Noncultural bone is usually the remains of small and medium-sized animals, such as foxes, gophers, and snakes, that lived in (or at least died in) the soil matrix of a site. Since the site's human occupants did not eat these animals, their bones must be removed from the assemblage before a taxonomic diversity study is undertaken. When analyzed, the entire bone assemblage in Schmitt and Lupo's study indicated that the site's inhabitants had practiced a generalized, broad-spectrum subsistence strategy. When the noncultural bone was removed and the diversity measure recalculated, a different, narrower subsistence pattern was revealed.

In conclusion, when reading archaeology you should make a practice of noting whether an effort was made to remove noncultural bone from an assemblage before subsistence practices were reconstructed. And remember, of all the transformations of information in the research process in archaeology, the way in which concepts are given archaeological interpretations is one of the most neglected.

Are the Conclusions Reasonable? **20**

WITHIN THE RESEARCH CYCLE in archaeology, a conclusion is drawn with each transformation of one kind of information to another. When the data in the sample summaries component are transformed into a generalization about unknown populations in the empirical generalizations component, a conclusion is proposed. When the generalizations in that component are transformed into a theory using concept-, hypothesis-, and model-formation techniques, a conclusion is formed. And so on. There are issues and claims associated with each of these transformations. Whether there is a sound argument or whether errors in reasoning are present is to be determined.

These are important, even pivotal, junctures of reasoning in archaeology, for an erroneously constructed transformation can skew the entire reasoning chain in the cycle. Nonetheless, archaeologists pay the most attention to the soundness of conclusions in the theory information component, for they are conclusions about past peoples and the worlds they lived in. The creation of the content of this component involves the transformation of statements about the archaeological record to statements about past peoples and their lifeways, and the throwing back again of these statements onto the archaeological record for testing. Chapter 20 focuses upon these kinds of conclusions, although many of the procedures mentioned can be applied to the evaluation of conclusions reached in other information transformations, too.

There is good news and not-so-good news in evaluating conclusions in the theory component. First the good news. Because theories in archaeology most often take the form of a story, terms in a theory tend to be familiar ones to readers who have read a few ethnographies written by anthropologists. Examples are "grinding stone," "pottery vessel," "long house," "a subsistence economy," "migration," and "resource scarcity." Terms like these describe the nature of the settlements that people lived in, their material world, the typical activities of their daily life, and the processes and thoughts that shape their life, among other aspects of their cultural and natural world.

Now the not-so-good news: The stories archaeologists tell about people who lived in the past tend to be unsystematic in presenting the detail of information transformations from one component to another. Thus, links between chains of reasoning are frequently not mentioned, particularly regarding how generalizations about the archaeological record (the empirical generalizations component) were made and what the archaeological definition of a term in a theory (the empirical interpretations component) is. Together, these issues make the evaluation of a conclusion in the theory component difficult. As a result, different procedures are necessarily involved in the evaluation of the stories told by archaeologists as compared to those used to evaluate theory laid out in axiomatic form. This chapter suggests several approaches to this kind of evaluation. But first let's raise this question: Are the conclusions true?

Are the Conclusions True?

When we begin reading archaeology, it is natural to assume that the conclusions are either true or false. But conclusions in archaeology are not as simple as that scenario suggests. Let's start by asking what truth is. In a research discipline like archaeology, it is commonly assumed that "truth" means "in accord with fact or reality."[1] Once again, like the person who was surprised to learn that she had been speaking prose all her life, archaeologists (with few exceptions) would be surprised to learn that they are adherents of the correspondence theory of truth. As in the dictionary definition of truth cited above, this theory assumes that conclusions are intended to be in agreement with fact or reality. An advantage of this view is that the truth or falseness of a conclusion can be determined by how well it fits with objective reality—and in fact that is what the testing of a theory in archaeology nearly always means.

This is the ideal. However, if you read chapter 9 carefully, you have already realized that there are potential problems with this view. Rather than repeating the arguments in that chapter, two examples suffice here. One is that we create our world of "things" out there and inside ourselves by dividing up what is an indivisible field of energy by using words. Another is that many words in a people's language are difficult to perfectly translate into other languages. As a consequence, people who speak different languages live in somewhat different objective realities. This does not mean that there is not some kind of brute reality "out there," but it does mean that we approach it differently depending on our historical, cultural, and linguistic context.[2] Closer to actual practice, then, archaeologists adopt what is called the consensus theory of truth.[3] According to this theory, truth is whatever we agree it is, given the historical, cultural, and linguistic context in which we live. It is within this context that archaeologists are objective and that statements can be determined to be true or false.

I have wandered a bit from this chapter's topic ("Are the conclusions reasonable?"), but for a purpose. Archaeologists generally practice their trade rather naively. Adopting the correspondence theory of truth, they assume (again, with some exceptions) that they can test their theories about life in the past by comparing them with objective reality—a problematic concept, for sure. Still, readers of archaeology do not have to become involved in adjudicating between conflicting theories of truth. Their task is to be aware of the assumptions behind this way of thinking in archaeology and of what it implies about the nature of the conclusions archaeologists draw.

Assessing the Truth Value of Conclusions: A Four-Step Approach

Theories in archaeology rarely have an axiomatic deductive structure whose soundness can be assessed with logical rigor (the syntactic conception of a scientific theory discussed in chapter 14). Consequently, an alternative, somewhat looser approach more suited to the evaluation of a family of models conception of theory tends to be adopted when archaeologists assess theories. Suggestions in critical reasoning texts on how to assess the truth value of conclusions in a family of models theory can be summed up in the following four-step approach: understand the reading, reconstruct the argument, assess the truth value of the conclusion, and write an argument commentary.

Understand the Reading

The purpose of the first step is to ensure that we thoroughly understand the content of what we are reading when we read archaeology. This task is most easily carried out by asking lots of questions about a reading. Some examples follow: What kind of archaeology is it? Which quadrant or combination of quadrants is the research positioned in? What are the issue and the claim? Is there an argument? What are the assumptions? Is the writing clear enough to understand the intended meaning of the writer? Are (deceptive) rhetorical devices and fallacies present? Is there a skeptical postmodern theme in the argument? Is there an inductive or causal argument? Is an explanation offered? Are facts clearly distinguished from opinions and other claims? Which research program is the reading an example of? Are more than one research program combined in the reading? Are the procedures adopted in the research project and the types of information generated appropriate to the research program that is adopted? And so on. Many critical readers find it useful to prepare a checklist of questions like these that they can refer to when critically reading an article or a book.

Reconstruct the Argument

Once you have a firm grasp of the content of a reading, go back through it and reconstruct in standard form the main argument or arguments that run through the reading.[4] For example, the issue in an article may be why the hunter-gatherer people whose material remains are now called the Brainerd culture began harvesting wild rice almost four thousand years ago. The conclusion of the article is that as the size of the human population in the region grew to a critical level, it was no longer possible to rely mainly on large game hunting for food energy; as a consequence, local populations began exploiting secondary foods like fish and wild rice. Here is a simple reconstruction of the argument in standard form:

> [P1] The size of the regional hunter-gatherer population had grown to a critical level; [P2] a regional hunter-gatherer population of that critical size can no longer be supported by a concentration on large game hunting; [P3] hunter-gatherer populations that rely mainly on hunting large game animals for food energy typically diversify their subsistence quest where possible when a critical population size is reached; and [P4] wild rice was an available secondary food source. Therefore, [C] Brainerd people began harvesting wild rice when their population passed a critical level.

Assess the Truth Value of the Conclusion

The third step asks two questions about the conclusions in the theory component of the research cycle: How certain are they? How abstract are they?[5] The first question concerns the degree of certainty of the conclusions. Is there sufficient evidence to support the author's stated degree of certainty?

How convincing is the evidence? Because of the looser construction of the stories archaeologists tell, critical readers have little recourse but to ask questions about the chain of reasoning that occurred within the research cycle. Examples of relevant questions are as follows: On what basis were the attributes in the observations information component chosen (that is, were they explicitly chosen for testing purposes or not)? Are the sample summaries appropriate to the testing process? If there is a population estimate, how was it made? Are the statements in the theory component closely associated with the information in the sample summaries and empirical generalizations components or are the statements more speculative? Are deductively valid test statements drawn from the statements in the theory component? Are concepts given archaeological interpretations? Are explicit tests of the statements in the theory component proposed or carried out? And so on. Again, many critical readers find it useful to prepare a checklist of questions that they can refer to in assessing the certainty of the statements in the theory information component.

In the wild rice harvesting example given above, a critical reader might begin the assessment of the truth-value of the conclusion by asking questions like the following: How is the critical population level defined [P1]? What evidence is there that that critical population level had been reached [P1]? What evidence is there that a regional hunter-gatherer population of that size cannot continue to maintain a nourishing subsistence base by continuing to concentrate on large game hunting [P2]? What evidence is there that hunter-gatherer populations that rely mainly on the hunting of large game animals for food energy actually do diversify their subsistence quest when the critical population size is reached [P3]? Was wild rice actually available to harvest in that region at that time [P4]? In some instances, subsidiary arguments will be made in the reading to support some of these truth claims. These arguments should be reconstructed in standard form too. For example, the argument for the availability of wild rice in the region at the time might be reconstructed in the following manner:

> [P1] Pollen diagrams for the region show that wild rice was present at that time, and [P2] wild rice phytoliths are present within the food residue adhering to the inside surface of Brainerd pottery vessels. Therefore, [C] wild rice was available for harvesting at the time.

Some of the other premises may be supported by ethnographic and theoretical modeling by other archaeologists whose studies are cited in the article. In some cases a premise will be assumed to be agreed-upon knowledge among archaeologists and thus not explicitly supported in the article.

For all of the reasons given above, it is generally too simple to think in terms of true or false in assessing conclusions in the theory component of the research cycle. In my own critical reading, I find it useful to think in terms of the reasonableness of the conclusions along a scale of zero to ten. I call this the zero-to-ten scale of reasonableness (as readers will note, a zero-to-ten scale is used for similar purposes elsewhere in the research cycle). In a majority of cases, what we read when we read critically will fall somewhere in the middle of the scale.

There are a number of reasons why this is so. In many cases insufficient evidence is provided about the chain of reasoning in the research cycle. There is a great gulf, too, between the realm of the archaeological record and the realm of the past-in-itself, and just how the transformation from one realm to the other and back again was made may be obscure. Steps around the research cycle may have been skipped (or perhaps they are just not mentioned in the reading). Should we accept the author's word that the premises are well supported? As a critical reader, we should as a matter of principle suspend judgment on the soundness of a conclusion when the argument of which it is a conclusion remains weak, at least within that reading. Besides incompletely presented arguments, there may be errors of reasoning in the writing. With some training in critical thinking and reading, perhaps these authors will become critical writers, too, who are sensitive to the requirements of the presentation of a sound argument. As a tool for critical writing, they will benefit by keeping the zero-to-ten scale of reasonableness in mind. A critical writer is careful in not assigning too high a degree of certainty to her conclusions when it is not warranted.

Assigning a score for a reading on the scale of reasonableness should not be considered a negative undertaking. Rather, it exposes weaknesses in the content of a text that authors should be made aware of—and readers who become writers will benefit greatly from these kinds of close readings.

The question "How abstract are the conclusions?" concerns the degree of generalization of the conclusions. Knowledge claims are made at varying levels of generalization. In his excavations of nine fall season Sandy Lake sites along the shores of a lake, an archaeologist found evidence of wild rice harvesting in each site. In a review essay on the Sandy Lake culture, he includes a tenth, as yet unexcavated, Sandy Lake culture site along the shores of the lake within a list of fall season wild rice harvesting sites. Is this generalization warranted? Critical readers should constantly be alert to the practice of overgeneralization in archaeology. Remember, there is a difference between making a prediction and making a statement of certainty.

Of course, readers of archaeology do not evaluate the conclusions of everything they read at this level of detail. To do so would be prohibitive. Rather, most readers have one or a few special interests that they are willing to read more closely. A graduate student writing a thesis, for example, will critically read a few books and perhaps a dozen articles at this level of detail. Professionals with a special research interest will critically read articles and books related to that interest in detail, but read other articles and books in archaeology less closely. My own experience suggests, however, that with constant practice the principles of critical reading become ingrained in one's consciousness. As one's skill in critical reading increases, one begins to read critically without making a conscious effort to do so.

Another issue that critical readers should be aware of in assessing the truth value of the conclusions in a reading is the wide difference in the background of the readers themselves. A professional archaeologist who has an intimate understanding of the archaeology of a region may find the conclusions in an article more rationally persuasive (and thus rank the truth value of the conclusion higher on the scale of reasonableness) than a reader who lacks that background. As a consequence, the argument can be unconvincing for one reader but convincing for another.

Write an Argument Commentary

The fourth step in assessing the truth value of a conclusion in the theory component of the research cycle is to write a prose commentary that summarizes the argument and your analysis of it.[6] The purpose of your commentary is to clarify the strengths and weaknesses of the argument. In what form was the argument originally presented in the reading? How did you reconstruct it? Was the argument valid or inductively forceful? What conclusions did you reach about the truth content of the premises that were used to support the argument? Are there errors in reasoning in the argument?

Again, not every critical reader need write an argument commentary for everything they read when they read archaeology. However, it should be a regular part of our critical reading practice when we read articles and books that are central to thesis writing or a study by a professional archaeologist.

Common Errors in Drawing Conclusions

Critical readers of archaeology should be aware of some of the common errors that are committed when conclusions are drawn. Several of these errors are hinted at in the above discussion of evaluating conclusions in archaeology. Five are stressed here.

Being Overly Certain

Perhaps it is merely a case of being careless in one's wording, but it is not uncommon for archaeologists to state their conclusions as if they were certain they are true. As a principle of critical writing, authors should make it a habit of carefully gauging the degree of certainty of their conclusions. Are they meant to be speculative? How strongly do the reasons given in support of a conclusion support that conclusion? What uncertainties exist in stating a conclusion? Clear answers to these and related questions in a reading are a sign of the presence of an author who writes critically.

Overgeneralizing

A second principle of critical writing is to carefully gauge the degree of generalization that is warranted by the evidence in stating a conclusion. Is the conclusion too abstract for the evidence provided? If an author feels that a conclusion can or should be generalized beyond the evidence available, then that generalization should be stated in the form of a hypothesis or prediction.

Omitting Conflicting Evidence

A third principle of critical writing is the obligation to explicitly mention and confront evidence that seems to contradict a conclusion that is being drawn. It is a critical writer's obligation to become aware of evidence that might contradict the conclusions he would like to draw. More basically, it is sound scholarship to be in accord with evidence that is generally accepted within a discipline.

Not Discussing Alternative Theories

Like omitting conflicting evidence, it is generally considered a practice in critical writing to mention the strengths and weaknesses of alternative answers to an issue. To do so actually strengthens one's own conclusion, for writers assume that their own alternative conclusion is better than, or at least as good as, other proposed conclusions.

Presenting a Foggy Argument

A variation of the degree of certainty error, this error occurs when a conclusion is drawn without offering much evidence in support of it. In other words, the argument is foggy. Sometimes authors who are not trained in critical writing are so focused on presenting their conclusions that they do not think of them as arguments that require support. This manner of writing in archaeology is most often encountered in overviews of the archaeology of an area or of an archaeological culture, where it is not considered an error of reasoning. It is, however, when it is presented as the outcome of an examination of evidence. In cases like this, critical writers will present sufficient citations that critical readers can examine for themselves.

Remember: The Research Cycle Is a Cycle

In archaeology the research cycle *is* a cycle. Initial attempts to reconstruct the settlement and subsistence systems of a past people, for example, will normally be less systematic and have a lower degree of certainty than later attempts. In my own field of Minnesota archaeology, I am part of a third generation of professional archaeologists addressing many of the same issues identified by the first generation. I believe that we have a more defensible understanding of many of these issues than did earlier generations—but we still know much, much less about the lifeways of people who lived in this region of North America in the past than we believe we know. For instance, many more trips around the research cycle are necessary before we can say with some degree of certainty that we understand the details of the settlement and subsistence systems of a past people who lived in the state. It is useful, then, when evaluating the conclusions in the theory component of a reading, to have some understanding of the history of an issue. It will make the position of conclusions along the scale of reasonableness more comprehensible.

Coda: Is Critical Reading Worth the Effort?

EARNING CRITICAL READING SKILLS requires practice and still more practice. A good place to start is with a standard critical thinking textbook, such as Brooke Noel Moore and Richard Parker's *Critical Thinking* (2004). Like other critical thinking textbooks, *Critical Thinking* contains numerous exercises on identifying issues, claims, conclusions, fallacies, unstated assumptions, inductive thinking, deductive thinking, and many of the other topics introduced in this book. By working through the exercises in a textbook like *Critical Thinking*, you develop critical reading skills—and you learn that developing those skills takes large doses of time, patience, and effort.

So, is learning critical reading skills in order to read archaeology critically worth the effort? The answer depends in part on why you are reading archaeology. If it is because, as a pleasant pastime, you enjoy reading about life in ancient Egypt or Peru, then developing critical reading skills is less important. If you are an aspiring professional archaeologist or a strongly committed nonprofessional, then you should have at least an introductory-level understanding of critical reading skills. From my perspective, there is an urgent reason why archaeology should be read critically by both professional and committed nonprofessional readers. A case can be made that large-scale trends in human lifeways throughout the last one hundred thousand years are responsible for many of the crises in the world today like global warming, the population explosion (at present, one billion more people are added to the world's total population every twelve years), and terrorism.[1] It may be crucial to the survival of our species, then, to understand these trends—and to do so with sound reasoning. It is from this latter perspective that I have written this book.

Notes

Introduction

1. The question-asking format that I use for the titles of chapters in the book was inspired by Daniel Flage's *The Art of Questioning: An Introduction to Critical Thinking* and M. Neil Browne and Stuart Keeley's *Asking the Right Questions: A Guide to Critical Thinking*. Other books on critical thinking that I have found particularly useful in writing *Critically Reading the Theory and Methods of Archaeology* are Brooke Noel Moore and Richard Parker's *Critical Thinking*, Tracy Bowell and Gary Kemp's *Critical Thinking: A Concise Guide*, and Anne Thomson's *Critical Reasoning: A Practical Introduction*. For reviews of the history and philosophy, respectively, of the critical thinking movement, see Fasko (2003) and Scriven (2003).

Chapter 1: What Kind of Archaeology Is It?

1. John Staeck, *Back to the Earth: An Introduction to Archaeology* (2001).

2. *Webster's Seventh New Collegiate Dictionary* (1963).

3. Frank Eddy, *Archaeology: A Cultural-Evolutionary Approach* (1991).

4. Carol Ember and Melvin Ember, *Anthropology*, 4th ed. (1973).

5. C. Renfrew and P. Bahn, *Archaeology: Theories, Methods and Practice*, 3rd ed. (2000).

6. B. Fagan, *Archaeology: A Brief Introduction*, 7th ed. (1999).

7. L. Binford, "Archeological Perspectives" (1968).

8. Julian Thomas, *Interpretive Archaeology: A Reader* (2000).

9. Martin Hall, *Archaeology and the Modern World* (2000).

10. Martin Hall, *Archaeology and the Modern World* (2000).

11. See Ken Wilber's *The Marriage of Sense and Soul* (1998).

12. For a still useful overview of both skeptical and moderate postmodern positions, see Pauline Rosenau's *Post-modernism and the Social Sciences* (1992).

13. See Wilber's *A Brief History of Everything* (2000).

14. See Wilber's *The Marriage of Sense and Soul* (1998:155–58).

15. The concept of "material culture" is problematic for at least two reasons. First, just what part of the material world is considered material culture has varied through time and varies among archaeologists. And second, what we "see" in the "material world" is unavoidably interpretive (see chapter 9). I use the expression "archaeological record" throughout this book with these cautions in mind. For a critique of the concept of an archaeological record, see Patrik's (1985) much-cited article.

Chapter 2: What Kind of Investigation Is It?

1. The figure is adapted from figure 2.1 in my *Anthropological Archaeology*. The research cycle in archaeology is an adaptation of the "scientific method." Besides a concentration on the archaeological record, there is a strong historical focus in the research cycle of archaeology that is not typical of the application of the scientific method *sensu stricto*. For introductions to the scientific method, see Carey (2011) and Gower (2002).

2. The use of the term "theory" is awkward here in my view, for it is rarely used in archaeology in this sense. Awkward or not, the term is used deliberately in this book to stress that interpretations in archaeology are no different in principle than interpretations (called theories) in the other social sciences. As such, they are subject to the same standards of scholarship as in those other disciplines (in other words, the claims that archaeologists make within any of the four quadrants must be rigorously tested).

3. This transformation is not a straightforward movement from the archaeological record to notions about the past-in-itself, for all kinds of ideas enter the research cycle at this juncture from outside the cycle. For this reason, the traditional idea of a "logic of discovery" from data to theory via induction has fallen into disfavor. The argument in brief is that it is impossible (when you think about it) to infer the concepts and models of a theory (see chapter 14) inductively from observational reports on the archaeological record alone. Rather, induction plays its indispensable role in the cycle of research in the justification of proposed theories. For these arguments, see chapter 4 ("Induction, Prediction, and Evidence") in Curd and Cover's (1998) *Philosophy of Science: The Central Issues*.

4. Rick, Erlandson, and Vellanoweth (2001).

5. Binford and Binford (1966).

6. Kooyman et al. (2001).

7. Binford (1982).

Chapter 3: What Are the Issue and the Claim?

1. For kinds of issues and their identification, see Browne and Keeley (2001:15–18).

2. The five Ws are basic questions whose answers are considered basic information in information gathering in research, police investigations, and journalism, among other avenues of inquiry.

3. For claims (conclusions) and their identification, see Bowell and Kemp (2005:12–16), Capaldi (1987:26–32), Crews-Anderson (2007:99–104), Flage (2004:58–62), and van den Brink-Budgen (2010a:33–41; 2010b:1–10). The clues are taken from Browne and Keeley (2001:18–26). It is useful to remember that claims "are either true or false, and no proposition [claim] can be both true and false" (Crews-Anderson 2007:94–104).

4. For a thorough introduction to the art of framing questions, see White (2009).

5. Also known as the fallacy of the complex question or loaded question, the fallacy occurs when "more than one question is being asked in what appears to be a single question" (Damer 2001:102).

Chapter 4: What Is the Argument?

1. Most critical reading texts contain chapters on identifying and evaluating an argument. Both Anne Thomson's *Critical Reasoning: A Practical Introduction* and Stella Cottrell's *Critical Thinking Skills: Developing Effective Analysis and Argument* include especially accessible introductions to these skills. Also see Bowell and Kemp (2005:168–225), Browne and Keeley (2001:27–40), Capaldi (1987:23–44), Cottrell (2011:37–50), Crews-Anderson (2007), Flage (2004:43–98), Moore and Parker (2004:259–91), van den Brink-Budgen (2010a:2717–23; 2010b:20–32, 39–56), and chapters 1 and 2 in Salmon (2013). Crews-Anderson (2007:404–18) stresses the distinction between the form and the content of an argument. While the form of an argument is its logical structure, the content is the group of statements that comprise an argument. An argument is true or false based on its content, not its form.

2. Premises are also called reasons and propositions in the critical thinking literature, though the word "proposition" is also commonly used as another name for a claim.

3. For identifying the presence of an argument, see Thomson (2002:5–14) and Salmon (2013:752–59).

4. For the distinction between an argument and a nonargument, see Cottrell (2011:51–62).

5. I borrow the phrasing of these two questions from Moore and Parker (2001:252).

6. For a useful and straightforward introduction to the concepts "valid" and "invalid," see the "validity" entry in Beth Black's *An A to Z of Critical Thinking* (2012:174–76).

7. Useful arguments like this whose conclusion is thought to be probably true are sometimes said to be relatively strong (see, for example, Moore and Parker 2001:237).

8. For examples of checklist questions for evaluating arguments, see Black (2012:70–72), Bowell and Kemp (2005:105–7), and Thomson (2002:39–76).

9. A non sequitur ("it does not follow") is an argument with irrelevant premises—that is, the conclusion does not follow from the premises. The argument thus violates the relevance criterion of a good argument. See Damer (2001:51).

10. For these and other codes of conduct for effective rational discussion, see chapter 1 in Damer's *Attacking Faulty Reasoning* (2001).

11. For unstated assumptions, see chapter 5 of this book.

Chapter 5: What Are the Assumptions?

1. For useful, introductory discussions of the role of assumptions in the structure of an argument, see Browne and Keeley (2001:59–90), Cottrell (2011:85–104), Thomson (2002:25–37), and van den Brink-Budgen (2010b:33–38).

2. Like most social scientists and historians, archaeologists are generally unaware that they have adopted a specific epistemological or metaphysical position. As Alexander Rosenberg (2012:78–85) says, "Social scientists must take sides on philosophical problems, whether they like it or not, even whether they know it or not." This applies as well to archaeologists who do not consider themselves social scientists: they have no choice but to adopt (consciously or not) one epistemological or metaphysical position rather than another. Consequently, it seems best to make the decision with a clear understanding of just what the implications are in adopting one position or another.

Chapter 6: Is the Writing Clear?

1. On clear writing relevant to critical writing, see Kallan (2012) and Rybacki and Rybacki (2012). Many critical thinking texts also contain chapters on clear writing. Examples that I found useful in writing this chapter are Browne and Keeley (2001:41–58), Cottrell (2011:63–84), Fisher (2001:61–78), Moore and Parker (2004:41–83), and van den Brink-Budgen (2010a:595–602).

2. Kroeber and Kluckhohn (1952).

3. For a discussion and examples of the fallacies of composition and division, see Damer (2001:112–15).

4. For spotting and clarifying ambiguities in your reading, see Bowell and Kemp (2005:22–25, 191–94), Browne and Keeley (2001:41–58), Damer (2001:85–87), and Salmon (2013:1661–68).

5. Damer (2001:93) defines the *fallacy of misuse of a vague expression* as an attempt "to establish a position by means of a vague expression or in drawing an unjustified conclusion as a result of assigning a very precise meaning to another's word, phrase, or statement that is quite imprecise in its meaning or range of application." We all use vague expressions in everyday conversation; they become a fallacy when they are misused in an argument. On vagueness in argumentation, see Bowell and Kemp (2005:25–27, 194–98) and Salmon (2013:1795–1804).

Chapter 7: Are (Deceptive) Rhetorical Devices Used?

1. For overviews of common rhetorical devices used to persuade, see Bowell and Kemp (2005:113–67), Moore and Parker (2004:124–51), and chapter 4 in Crews-Anderson (2007).

2. For euphemisms and dysphemisms, see Keith Allan and Kate Burridge's *Euphemism & Dysphemism*, R. W. Holder's *How Not to Say What You Mean*, Ralph Keyes's *Euphemania*, and Hugh Rawson's *Dictionary of Euphemisms and Other Doubletalk*.

3. Persuasive definitions commonly display an error in reasoning called "begging the question." See chapter 8 for a fuller discussion of this fallacy. Definitions that fail to have merit because they are overly broad, use obscure or ambiguous language, or contain circular reasoning are called fallacies of definition. On definition, see Salmon (2013:1856–64) for a useful discussion within the context of critical thinking.

4. A loaded question is a common fallacy that violates the acceptability criterion of a good argument (see chapter 8).

5. For an informative introduction to contemporary weaselers, see Wasserman and Hausrath's *Weasel Words: The Dictionary of American Doublespeak* (2005).

6. The beet example is delightfully adapted from Moore and Parker (2004:139).

Chapter 8: Is There a Fallacy in the Reasoning?

1. Beth Black in *An A to Z of Critical Thinking* (2012:84) defines a fallacy as "an argument which is flawed not by its form but by its content." Books on critical thinking, such as those mentioned in note 1 of the introduction, contain extended discussions of common fallacies. Also see *Thinker's Guide to Fallacies* (2008) by Richard Paul and Linda Elder and *The Fallacy Detective: Thirty-Eight Lessons on How to Recognize Bad Reasoning* (2009) by Nathaniel Bluedorn and others. When first exposed to the notion of a fallacy, critical readers often see fallacies everywhere in their reading, even where they do not exist (much like medical school students who think they have every disease they learn about). Be aware, then, of this tendency toward "fallacy frenzy."

2. For extended discussions of each of these categories (and of common fallacies), see the most recent edition of T. Edward Damer's *Attacking Faulty Reasoning: A Practical Guide to Fallacy-Free Arguments*.

3. An attempt to persuade through the length of an exposition is called proof by verbosity, or *argumentum verbosum*.

4. A post hoc fallacy is a special case of a *non sequitur* (Latin for "it does not follow"). A related fallacy is *cum hoc ergo propter hoc*, which assumes that a correlation necessarily implies a causal relation.

Chapter 9: Are There Skeptical Postmodern Themes in the Argument?

1. In my view, Pauline Rosenau's *Post-modernism and the Social Sciences* (1992) remains the most relevant and accessible review of the issues as they relate to the social sciences in general. Matthew Johnson's *Archaeological Theory: An Introduction* (2010) and Ian Hodder's *The Archaeological Process: An Introduction* (1999) are readable, moderate postmodern introductions to reasoning in archaeology. Skeptical postmodernism is more rarely encountered in archaeology than it is in the humanities. When encountered in archaeology, skeptical postmodernism is most frequently associated with the postprocessual/interpretive research program.

2. See my "What Does an Observation Mean in Archaeology?" (1989b).

3. See Norwood Russell Hanson's *Patterns of Discovery* (1958). In this book he makes the useful distinction between "seeing as" and "seeing that."

4. For many of these skeptical views, see Keith Jenkins's *Re-thinking History* (2004) and *Refiguring History* (2003).

5. Hawking's *A Brief History of Time* (1998).

6. Binford (1989:35).

7. I write from a moderate postmodern position firmly rooted in the lower right quadrant. In contrast, most archaeologists who adopt a moderate postmodern position work in left-side quadrants.

Part II: From Observations to Population Estimates

1. Utts (1999:3).

Chapter 10: Are Facts Clearly Distinguished from Opinions and Other Claims?

1. In the sense used here, a fact (from the Latin *factum*) is (merely) an assertion that something is a "true fact," where a true fact is "something that has really occurred or is the case" (*OED* 2nd ed., 1989, "Fact"). In other words, factual claims in archaeology have to be verified. See the discussion of "fact" in *The Stanford Encyclopedia of Philosophy* (online) and the *Oxford Companion to Philosophy*.

2. I use the same kind of scale for another reason in chapter 19.

3. See Browne and Keeley (2001:115).

4. For discussions of kinds of evidence and their differing degree of credibility, see Browne and Keeley (2001:111–45), Cottrell (2011:125–46), Crews-Anderson (2007:2036–42), Fisher (2001:93–106), Flage (2004:99–123), van den Brink-Budgen (2010b:98–107), and chapter 14 in Godfrey-Smith (2003).

5. For the role of analogies in critical thinking, see Damer (2001:123–25), Flage (2004:252–79), van den Brink-Budgen (2010b:83–88), and chapter 3.3 in Crews-Anderson (2007). Also see note 2 in chapter 12.

6. These basic questions are from Browne and Keeley (2001:132–33).

Chapter 11: How Are the Observations Summarized?

1. For introductions to descriptive and inferential statistics in archaeology, see Baxter (2010), Drennan (2010), and VanPool and Leonard (2011).

Chapter 12: Is There an Inductive Argument?

1. For introductory reviews of inductive reasoning, see Ian Hacking's *An Introduction to Probability and Inductive Logic* (2001) and Aidan Feeney and Evan Heit's *Inductive Reasoning: Experimental, Developmental, and Computational Approaches* (2007). Sections of this chapter are modeled after Moore and Parker's (2004:357–93) discussion of inductive reasoning. Also see Bowell and Kemp (2005:80–112), Flage (2004:251–318), van den Brink-Budgen (2010a:175–20), chapter 3 in Crews-Anderson (2007), chapter 3 in Godfrey-Smith (2003), and chapters 3, 4, and 6 in Salmon (2013). As Crews-Anderson (2007:79–94) usefully stresses, "All arguments are either *deductive* or *inductive*, and an understanding of this distinction is required for criticism." As a consequence, critical readers should gain experience in distinguishing deductive from inductive reasoning.

2. Analogical reasoning is one of the most common methods of argumentation. It is often used to clarify something unknown or poorly known by comparing it to something better known. A faulty analogy (or false analogy) violates the acceptability criterion of a good argument. For arguments from analogy and their evaluation, see chapter 3 in Crews-Anderson (2007) and Salmon (2013:3775–82).

3. For inductive errors, biases, and fallacies, see Crews-Anderson (2007:805–17), Salmon (2013:3775–82), and Walton (1989:198–238).

4. Three related errors in reasoning are *card stacking*, in which facts are selectively used; *false generalization*, in which an argument becomes so abstract that the facts of the matter become lost; and *sweeping generalization*, in which exceptions to the generalization are disregarded.

5. See Popper's *Conjectures and Refutations* (1963:33–39). On Popper's view of science, see chapter 4 in Godfrey-Smith (2003).

Chapter 13: Is There a Population Estimate from a Sample?

1. This example comes from Shennan (1997).

Part III: Interpreting the Archaeological Record

1. See note 2 in chapter 2.

Chapter 14: Is There a Theory in My Reading?

1. Thus, archaeologists are ultimately interested in "unobservables," a concept whose ontological nature (ontology) and means of study (epistemology) continue to be of central concern in the philosophy of science. In the early years of the rise of science, strict empiricists argued that unobservables are not a proper subject for scientific study, a position that has proven to be impractical in modern sciences like physics. For the most part, archaeologists are interested in what are called practical unobservables—that is, events, processes, and things that could be directly studied (as cultural anthropologists do today), but practical difficulties get in the way (i.e., the subject matter for archaeologists [past peoples and their cultures and societies] is no longer present for study).

2. Numerous terms are used in the natural and social sciences for the components of interpretations of natural and social reality, and for their construction. The few terms used here reflect, I believe, the essence of the content and the process of information formation in the past-as-reconstructed component of the research cycle in archaeology.

3. Social scientists define the word "theory" in numerous, usually conflicting ways. For some social scientists, a theory is "a set of statements about the relationship(s) between two or more concepts or constructs" (Jaccard and Jacoby 2010:28), while, for others, "a theory is simply a set of statements or sentences" (Simon and Newell 1956:67). For our purposes, a theory in archaeology will be simply defined as a set of statements in the theory information component that are intended to make sense of the archaeological record by relating it to the past-in-itself. For an overview of the use of the word "theory" in archaeology, see Gibbon (2012c).

4. Binford (2001).

5. For logical positivist and logical empiricist understandings of science, see my *Explanation in Archaeology* (1989a) and chapter 2 ("Logic Plus Empiricism") in Godfrey-Smith (2003).

6. For a more extensive discussion of the word "fact," see chapter 10.

7. Sections of this chapter were previously published in my "Theory in Archaeology" review essay in *The Oxford Companion to Archaeology*, which was edited by Neil Asher Silberman (2nd ed., 2012).

8. See, for example, *Explanation in Archeology: An Explicitly Scientific Approach* (1971) by Watson, LeBlanc, and Redman. For an extensive discussion of the embrace by early New Archaeologists of logical positivism and logical empiricism, see Gibbon (1998a).

9. For this dispute in the philosophy of science, see chapter 9 in Curd and Cover (1998). For a realist perspective in archaeology, see chapter 7 in Gibbon

(1989a). For a realist philosophy of social science, see Manicas (2006), and in the sciences more generally, see chapter 12 in Godfrey-Smith (2003).

10. As summarized by Jim Baggott in *A Beginner's Guide to Reality* (2006:233), "There is simply no purpose to be served by seeking to describe a reality beyond our immediate senses." Science proper deals with the facts and not with forms like culture and reality that may lie behind them. Obviously, an archaeology based on strict empiricism would be confined to observations on the archaeological record, as mentioned earlier in the chapter.

11. See Kenneth J. Gergen's *An Invitation to Social Construction* (2009) for an accessible introduction to social constructionism in a more radical sense.

12. As phrased by Baggott (2006:238), "Gravity is a brute empirical fact, but theories of gravity are social constructions."

13. See Gibbon (2012b) for an expression of this view.

14. An ontological commitment as used here refers to what a person believes or assumes (in the context of a research program) exists. Ontology is the study of what exists or at least of the positions on existence that have been adopted.

15. The default position in the social sciences today is what may be called pragmatic realism (see Jaccard and Jacoby's *Theory Construction and Model-Building Skills*). Although scientists demanding hard evidence find no justification for realism (Baggott in *A Beginner's Guide to Reality* [2006:239] asks, "What is the justification for this position?" and answers, "There is none"), most working scientists still adopt that position, but now not naively. Assumptions have to be spelled out and terms in theories defined. The rationale for pragmatic realism is that the "obdurate character of our social and physical environment" will be a deciding factor in separating good from bad interpretive theories (Jaccard and Jacoby 2010:33). These emerging positions in the social sciences challenge archaeologists to think more critically about what they are doing when they engage in theorizing and theory building.

Chapter 15: Which Research Program Is My Reading an Example Of?

1. For an overview of the concept of a research program (and paradigm), see chapters 5 through 7 in Godfrey-Smith (2003). There are many reasons for the selection of one research program or another. If anthropology is the science of culture, for example, then an anthropological archaeologist will select a program that has a focus on the lower left quadrant (culture), as in early cultural historical archaeology. The emergence of processual and postprocessual archaeology was an attempt in part to more centrally locate archaeology as a research discipline.

2. Late nineteenth-century unilinear evolutionists speculated that human cultures evolved along a single or unilinear path from, for example, savagery to barbarism to civilization. For histories of cultural historical archaeology, see Willey and Sabloff (1993) and Trigger (1989).

3. For McKern's conception of the program, see McKern (1939); also see Gibbon (2007).

4. Willey and Phillips (1958). The main taxonomic units in their taxonomy are phase, tradition, culture, and stage.

5. The shift to an integrated view of culture was influenced in part by Ruth Benedict's popular *Patterns of Culture* (1934). The "that thing of shreds and patches" description of culture comes from Robert Lowie (1920:441). In the same paragraph, he refers to "that planless hodgepodge."

6. The career of many archaeologists who were active between the 1930s and the late 1950s was focused on completing this task. A typical example is Lloyd Wilford's (1937, 1941, 1955, 1960) long-term development of a space-time grid of archaeological units for Minnesota.

7. This shift was more in line with the dominant theory of science at the time, logical positivism, which was suspicious of entities like culture that lie behind observables. According to Godfrey-Smith (2003:582–86), for logical positivists "the sole aim of science is to track patterns in experience." In other words, there is only surface. For the empiricist tradition in general, see Garrett and Barbanell's *Encyclopedia of Empiricism* (1997).

8. In Minnesota, Wilford's field strategy was to sample excavate sites in as many areas of the state as possible during a season. He rarely spent more than a few days at any one site.

9. For Steward, the diversity of cultures resulted from different adaptations to different environments, not necessarily from evolutionary differences (contra the nineteenth-century evolutionists). At the University of Wisconsin–Madison, my advisor, Dr. David Baerreis, inspired by Steward's book, was promoting the reconstruction of the environmental context of past peoples by 1960.

10. See, for example, Binford (1962, 1964, 1968).

11. This assumption does not imply environmental determinism, for cultures and environments interact on each other.

12. For the importance of ethnoarchaeological fieldwork in Binford's processual program, see Binford (1976, 1978a, 1978b, 1980). For an application of ideas in Binford's *Constructing Frames of Reference* (2001) to the archaeology of a state, see Gibbon (2012a).

13. For an example, see Watson et al. (1971). As I believe I demonstrate conclusively in *Explanation in Archaeology* (1989a), the principles of logical empiricism as a coherent theory of science were never applied in processual archaeology. For an introductory overview of the logical empiricist theory of science, see chapter 2 in Godfrey-Smith (2003). For two very popular philosophy of science texts at the time, see Hempel (1965, 1966).

14. The archaeological record cannot be connected directly to theories because of cultural and natural transformation processes and other processes that distort this link. Middle-range theory is intended to work through this connection. Ethnoarchaeological studies are often a component of this process. For a still-useful review, see Raab and Goodyear (1984).

15. Postprocessualists generally agree that the term "postprocessual" is inadequate, for it does not describe what their program is about—other than "post" or "above" processual archaeology. Nonetheless, the term lingers on in general use, despite attempts to introduce alternative labels, such as symbolic or interpretive archaeology. For a popular postprocessual primer, see Ian Hodder and Scott Hutson's *Reading the Past*. Symbolic anthropology—the study of the social construction and social effects of symbols—was prominently practiced at the time by cultural anthropologists like David M. Schneider and Clifford Geertz. Geertz's *The Interpretation of Culture* (1973) has been particularly influential in archaeology. In contrast to the other research programs reviewed here, there is a very diverse array of viewpoints in agency-centered archaeology.

16. For Hodder, artifacts are full participants in culture, not just objectifications of culture.

17. For the importance of ethnoarchaeological studies in postprocessual archaeology, see Hodder (1982a, 1982b).

18. Carr and Case (2005, 2008). The people studied in the two volumes are the Hopewell peoples who lived in the Scioto Valley and neighboring areas in Ohio in the first centuries A.D. Although hunter-gatherer-horticulturalists, these peoples built eighty-acre earthworks aligned to solar and lunar events and large community burial houses, and they also crafted large numbers of finely made, highly "socially and culturally vocal" works of art.

19. Carr and Case (2008:3).

20. Carr and Case (2008:7).

21. Carr and Case (2005:45).

22. These views differ from Thomas Kuhn's (1996) well-known notion that program change is due to "anomaly and crisis." For Robert Merton's still-useful discussion of the reward system in science and the importance of recognition, see Merton's *The Sociology of Science* (1973).

23. This scenario is a reference to the new interdisciplinary field of science studies in which one can move from hard-line empirical views to increasingly questioning and doubting views that end in skeptical postmodernism. For the field of science studies, see Biagioli's *The Science Studies Reader* (1999). For overviews of the science wars, see Gross and Levitt's *Higher Superstitions* (1994) and Koertge's *A House Built on Sand* (1998). The Mad Hatter, the Queen of Hearts, and the smile of the Cheshire Cat epitomize positions encountered in the science wars. The belief that science is progressive is a key assumption of Enlightenment thought.

Chapter 16: Is an Explanation Offered?

1. For types of explanation and their history, see Salmon (2006), Pitt (1988), and chapter 13 in Godfrey-Smith (2003). For examples of their use in critical thinking, see Flage (2004:33–41, 294–308), Moore and Parker (2001:217–58), and van den Brink-Budgen (2010b:11–19). For their use in accounting for human

action, see chapter 3 in Rosenberg (2012). For the difference between explanation and understanding, see chapters 1 and 3 in Manicas (2006).

2. For discussions of the difference between an argument, an explanation, and a justification, see Black (2012:566–76), Bowell and Kemp (2005:18–20, 37, 215), Crews-Anderson (2007:1617–25), Fisher (2001:42–44, 46), and Moore and Parker (2001:1217–58).

3. For an argument (inference) to the best explanation, see Black (2012:61–69), Flage (2004:53–56, 294–308, 478), and Lipton (2000, 2001). The reasoning is also called abduction and hypothetical induction.

4. For criteria for evaluating explanations and spotting weak explanations, see Browne and Keeley (2001:159–60), Flage (2004:294–308), Moore and Parker (2004:426–28), and Thomson (2002:68–72).

5. Here is a slightly altered example from the critical thinking literature that refers to life as a graduate student writing a dissertation: "[Q] Why can't I finish my dissertation? [A] I sit at my computer, but I simply cannot think of a thing to write. It's because I have writer's block." In this case, he may as well have said that he can't write because he can't write. For circular reasoning (arguing in a circle), see Damer (2001:98–100). The fallacy is a begging the question fallacy that violates the acceptability criterion of a good argument.

6. For the relevance principle in argumentation, see Damer (2001:2325).

7. On vagueness, see note 5 in chapter 6.

Chapter 17: Is There a Causal Argument?

1. For an extensive academic overview of the concept of causation, see Beebee et al. (2012). Sources consulted while writing this chapter include Babbie (2001:68–87), Browne and Keeley (2001:147–64), Capaldi (1987:153–72), Damer (2001:150–61), Fisher (2001:138–53), Jaccard and Jacoby (2010:137–76), Moore and Parker (2004:394–447), Pearl (2000), and chapter 5 in Salmon (2013). For Mill's five rules for investigating causes, see Crews-Anderson (2007:1806–73).

2. The *locus classicus* in the critical thinking literature on informal causal reasoning is Moore and Parker's *Critical Thinking*. For these two basic patterns of causal reasoning, see Moore and Parker (2004:395–99).

3. For common mistakes in causal reasoning, see Moore and Parker (2001:425–32). Many of these mistakes are considered causal fallacies that violate the sufficiency criterion of a good argument (Damer 2001:150–61).

4. For causation in populations, see Moore and Parker (2001:407–17), who cite Giere (1991) as a source.

5. For anecdotal evidence and its problems, see Black (2012:207–15) and Damer (2001:28–29).

Part IV: Evaluating Interpretations of the Archaeological Record

1. The role of prediction differs here from its usual use in the natural sciences. In the natural sciences prediction is an ideal goal. If scientists can predict what will occur in the natural world, then they understand it, more or less. In archaeology and the social sciences more generally, a prediction is part of the movement around the research cycle—and no more. For instance, in archaeology a prediction tests whether the pictures archaeologists draw about the past-in-itself are consistent with (or supported by) the archaeological remnants of that past. For the role of prediction in the natural sciences and the general absence of that intent in the social sciences (except in some lower right quadrant studies), see Rosenberg's *Philosophy of Social Science* (2012).

Chapter 18: Are Deductively Valid Conclusions Drawn?

1. For categorical logic and deductive argumentation more broadly, see Bowell and Kemp (2005:43–79), Crews-Anderson (2007:437–81), Flage (2004:141–99), Halpern (1996:118–66, 212–40), Moore and Parker (2004:261–356), van den Brink-Budgen (2010a:372–78), and chapters 3 and 4 in Salmon (2013).

2. For overviews of evolutionary archaeology, see Broughton and Cannon (2009), Lyman and O'Brien (1998), O'Brien and Lyman (2000), and Leonard (2001).

Chapter 19: Are Concepts Given Archaeological Interpretations?

1. Ember (1973).
2. Schmitt and Lupo (1995).

Chapter 20: Are the Conclusions Reasonable?

1. Merriam-Webster's Online Dictionary, http://m-w.com/dictionary/truth (accessed 2012). For a collection of classic Western conceptions of truth, see Simon Blackburn and Keith Simmons's *Truth* (eds., 1999). Also see Kirkham (1992), Horwich (1988), Field (2001), and Shapin (1994). For an implicit defense of the correspondence theory of truth, see chapter 7 ("Truth, Knowledge and Belief") in Bowell and Kemp (2005).

2. Jaccard and Jacoby (2010:8) refer to this brute presence as "the obdurate character of the empirical world." Also see their useful discussion of the nature of reality (Jaccard and Jacoby 2010:7–10).

3. Other theories of truth include the coherence theory of truth, the constructivist theory of truth, the pragmatic theory of truth, deflationary theories of truth, the performative theory of truth, redundancy theories of truth, and pluralist theories of truth. See the references in note 1 above for descriptions of these notions of truth. Perhaps this overview can be summed up by saying that truth is not a simple concept. The literature on "truth" is complex and conflicted.

4. Examples of useful discussions of argument reconstruction include Bowell and Kemp (2005:168–225), Crews-Anderson (2007:1663–70), Flage (2004:43–98), Moore and Parker (2004:226–60), Salmon (2013: 418–34, 1628–29), and Thomson (2002:5–37).

5. For an extended discussion of these questions within the context of the evaluation process, see chapter 7 in Wallace and Wray's *Critical Reading and Writing for Postgraduates* (2006). The books cited in note 4 above also contain chapters on the assessment of arguments.

6. For a discussion of and examples of argument commentaries, see Bowell and Kemp (2005:244–53) and Crews-Anderson (2007:1808–22).

Coda: Is Critical Reading Worth the Effort?

1. For this argument, see Gibbon (2012a:209–11). Here is a last point for critical readers to think about: researchers can accept a theory because they believe it is likely true or pursue a theory because, if the idea were true, it would have huge importance. My interest in this theory is for the latter reason. For the useful distinction between the acceptance and the pursuit of theories, see Larry Laudan's *Progress and Its Problems* (1977).

Bibliography

(Note: Many of the books I used in writing this book are continuously being republished in new editions. In purchasing a book, check the title for the most recent edition.)

Allan, Keith, and Kate Burridge. 1991. *Euphemism & Dysphemism: Language Used as Shield and Weapon*. New York: Oxford University Press.

Babbie, Earl. 2001. *The Practice of Social Research*. 9th ed. Belmont, CA: Wadsworth.

Baggott, Jim. 2006. *A Beginner's Guide to Reality: Exploring our Everyday Adventure in Wonderland*. New York: Penguin.

Baxter, Michael J. 2010. *Statistics in Archaeology*. Hoboken, NJ: Wiley.

Beebee, Helen, Christopher Hitchcock, and Peter Menzies (eds.). 2012. *The Oxford Handbook of Causation*. New York: Oxford University Press.

Benedict, Ruth. 1934. *Patterns of Culture*. New York: Houghton Mifflin.

Biagioli, Mario (ed.). 1999. *The Science Studies Reader*. New York: Routledge.

Binford, Lewis R. 1962. Archaeology as Anthropology. *American Antiquity* 28(2):217–25.

Binford, Lewis R. 1964. A Consideration of Archaeological Research Design. *American Antiquity* 29:425–41.

Binford, Lewis R. 1968. Archaeological Perspectives. In *New Perspectives in Archaeology*, ed. S. R. Binford and L. R. Binford, 5–32. Chicago: Aldine.

Binford, Lewis R. 1976. Forty-Seven Trips: A Case Study in the Character of Some Formation Processes of the Archaeological Record. In *Contributions to Anthropology: The Interior People of Northern Alaska*. Mercury Series 40, ed. E. S. Hall Jr., 299–351. Ottawa: National Museum of Man.

Binford, Lewis R. 1978a. Dimensional Analysis of Behavior and Site Structure: Learning from an Eskimo Hunting Stand. *American Antiquity* 43:255–73.

Binford, Lewis R. 1978b. *Nunamiut Ethnoarchaeology*. New York: Academic Press.

Binford, Lewis R. 1980. Willow Smoke and Dogs' Tails: Hunter-Gatherer Settlement Systems and Archeological Site Formation. *American Antiquity* 45:4–10.

Binford, Lewis R. 1982. The Archaeology of Place. *Journal of Anthropological Archaeology* 1(1):5–31.

Binford, Lewis R. 1989. *Debating Archaeology*. New York: Academic Press.

Binford, Lewis R. 2001. *Constructing Frames of Reference: An Analytic Method for Archaeological Theory Building Using Hunter-Gatherer and Environmental Data Sets.* Berkeley and Los Angeles: University of California Press.

Binford, Lewis R., and Sally R. Binford. 1966. A Preliminary Analysis of Functional Variability in the Mousterian of Levallois Facies. *American Anthropologist* 68(2):238–95.

Black, Beth (ed.). 2012. *An A to Z of Critical Thinking*. New York: Bloomsbury.

Blackburn, Simon, and Keith Simmons (eds.). 1999. *Truth*. New York: Oxford University Press.

Bluedorn, Nathaniel, Hans Bluedorn, Rob Corley, and Tim Hodge. 2009. *The Fallacy Detective: Thirty-Eight Lessons on How to Recognize Bad Reasoning*. Muscatine, IA: Christian Logic.

Bowell, Tracy, and Gary Kemp. 2005. *Critical Thinking: A Concise Guide*. 2nd ed. New York: Routledge.

Broughton, Jack M., and Michael D. Cannon (eds.). 2009. *Evolutionary Ecology and Archaeology: Applications to Problems in Human Evolution and Prehistory*. Salt Lake City: University of Utah Press.

Browne, M. Neil, and Stuart Keeley. 2001. *Asking the Right Questions: A Guide to Critical Thinking*. 6th ed. Englewood Cliffs, NJ: Prentice Hall.

Capaldi, Nicholas. 1987. *The Art of Deception: An Introduction to Critical Thinking*. Amherst, NY: Prometheus Books.

Carey, Stephen S. 2011. *A Beginner's Guide to Scientific Method*. 4th ed. Belmont, CA: Wadsworth.

Carr, Christopher, and D. Troy Case. 2005. The Gathering of Hopewell. In *Gathering Hopewell: Society, Ritual, and Ritual Interaction*, ed. Christopher Carr and D. Troy Case, 19–50. New York: Kluwer Academic/Plenum.

Carr, Christopher, and D. Troy Case. 2008. Documenting the Lives of Ohio Hopewell People: A Philosophical and Empirical Foundation. In *The Scioto Hopewell and Their Neighbors: Bioarchaeological Documentation and Cultural Understanding*, ed. D. Troy Case and Christopher Carr, 3–34. New York: Springer.

Cottrell, Stella. 2011. *Critical Thinking Skills: Developing Effective Analysis and Argument*. 2nd ed. New York: St. Martin's.

Crews-Anderson, Timothy A. 2007. *Critical Thinking and Informal Logic*. Penrith, UK: Philosophy Insights, Humanities-ebooks.

Curd, Martin, and J. A. Cover. 1998. *Philosophy of Science: The Central Issues*. New York: Norton.

Damer, T. Edward. 2001. *Attacking Faulty Reasoning: A Practical Guide to Fallacy-Free Arguments*. 4th ed. Belmont, CA: Wadsworth/Thomson Learning.

Drennan, Robert D. 2010. *Statistics for Archaeologists: A Common Sense Approach*. 2nd ed. New York, Plenum.

Eddy, Frank W. 1991. *Archaeology: A Cultural-Evolutionary Approach*. Englewood Cliffs, NJ: Prentice Hall.

Ember, Carol, and Melvin Ember. 1973. *Anthropology*. 4th ed. New York: Appleton, Century, Crofts.

Ember, Melvin. 1973. An Archaeological Indicator of Matrilocal versus Patrilocal Residence. *American Antiquity* 38(2):177–82.

Fagan, Brian. 1999. *Archaeology: A Brief Introduction*. 7th ed. Englewood Cliffs, NJ: Pearson/Prentice Hall.

Fasko, Daniel, Jr. 2003. Critical Thinking: Origins, Historical Development, Future Directions. In *Critical Thinking and Reasoning: Current Research, Theory, and Practice*, ed. Daniel Fasko Jr. Cresskill, NJ: Hampton.

Feeney, Aidan, and Evan Heit. 2007. *Inductive Reasoning: Experimental, Developmental, and Computational Approaches*. New York: Cambridge University Press.

Field, Harty. 2001. *Truth and the Absence of Fact*. New York: Oxford University Press.

Fisher, Alec. 2001. *Critical Thinking: An Introduction*. New York: Cambridge University Press.

Flage, Daniel E. 2004. *The Art of Questioning: An Introduction to Critical Thinking*. Englewood Cliffs, NJ: Pearson/Prentice Hall.

Garrett, Don, and Edward Barbanell. 1997. *Encyclopedia of Empiricism*. Westport, CT: Greenwood Press.

Geertz, Clifford. 1973. *The Interpretation of Culture*. New York: Basic Books.

Gergen, Kenneth J. 2009. *An Invitation to Social Construction*. 2nd ed. Thousand Oaks, CA: Sage.

Gibbon, Guy. 1984. *Anthropological Archaeology*. New York: Columbia University Press.

Gibbon, Guy. 1989a. *Explanation in Archaeology*. Malden, MA: Blackwell.

Gibbon, Guy. 1989b. What Does an Observation Mean in Archaeology? *International Journal of Moral and Social Studies* 4:1–9.

Gibbon, Guy. 2007. McKern's Science. *Wisconsin Archeologist* 85(2):18–23.

Gibbon, Guy. 2012a. *Archaeology of Minnesota: The Prehistory of the Upper Mississippi River Region*. Minneapolis: University of Minnesota Press.

Gibbon, Guy. 2012b. Lifeways through Time in the Upper Mississippi River Valley and Northeastern Plains. In *The Oxford Handbook of North American Archaeology*, ed. Timothy Pauketat, 325–35. New York: Oxford University Press.

Gibbon, Guy. 2012c. Theory in Archaeology. In *Oxford Companion to Archaeology*, ed. Neil Asher Silberman. 2nd ed. New York: Oxford University Press.

Giere, Ronald N. 1991. *Understanding Scientific Reasoning*. 3rd ed. Fort Worth, TX: Holt, Rinehart, and Winston.

Godfrey-Smith, Peter. 2003. *Theory and Reality: An Introduction to the Philosophy of Science*. Chicago and London: University of Chicago Press. Kindle edition.

Gower, Barry. 2002. *Scientific Method: A Historical and Philosophical Introduction.* New York: Routledge.

Gross, Paul R., and N. Levitt. 1994. *Higher Superstition: The Academic Left and Its Quarrels with Science.* Baltimore: Johns Hopkins University Press.

Hacking, Ian. 2001. *An Introduction to Probability and Inductive Logic.* New York: Cambridge University Press.

Hall, Martin. 2000. *Archaeology and the Modern World: Colonial Transcripts in South Africa and Chesapeake.* New York: Routledge.

Halpern, Diane F. 1996. *Thought & Knowledge: An Introduction to Critical Thinking.* 3rd ed. Mahwah, NJ: Erlbaum.

Hanson, Norwood Russell. 1958. *Patterns of Discovery: An Inquiry into the Conceptual Foundations of Science.* New York: Cambridge University Press.

Hawking, Stephen. 1998. *A Brief History of Time: The Updated and Expanded Tenth Anniversary Edition.* New York: Bantam.

Hempel, Carl. 1965. *Aspects of Scientific Explanation and Other Essays in the Philosophy of Science.* New York: Free Press.

Hempel, Carl. 1966. *Philosophy of Natural Science.* Englewood Cliffs, NJ: Prentice Hall.

Hodder, Ian. 1982a. *The Present Past: An Introduction to Anthropology for Archaeologists.* New York: Pica Press.

Hodder, Ian. 1982b. *Symbols in Action: Ethnoarchaeological Studies of Material Culture.* Cambridge: Cambridge University Press.

Hodder, Ian. 1999. *The Archaeological Process: An Introduction.* Malden, MA: Blackwell.

Hodder, Ian, and Scott Hutson. 2004. *Reading the Past: Current Approaches to Interpretation in Archaeology.* 3rd ed. New York: Cambridge University Press.

Holder, R. W. 2003. *How Not to Say What You Mean: A Dictionary of Euphemisms.* New York: Oxford University Press.

Horwich, Paul. 1988. *Truth.* 2nd ed. New York: Oxford University Press.

Jaccard, James, and Jacob Jacoby. 2010. *Theory Construction and Model-Building Skills: A Practical Guide for Social Scientists.* New York: Guilford.

Jenkins, Keith. 2003. *Refiguring History: New Thoughts on an Old Discipline.* New York: Routledge.

Jenkins, Keith. 2004. *Re-thinking History.* New York: A Taylor & Francis e-book, first published by Routledge in 1991.

Johnson, Matthew. 2010. *Archaeological Theory: An Introduction.* 2nd ed. Malden, MA: Wiley-Blackwell.

Kallan, Richard. 2012. *Renovating Your Writing: Shaping Ideas into Clear, Concise, and Compelling Messages.* Boston: Pearson.

Keyes, Ralph. 2010. *Euphemania: Our Love Affair with Euphemisms.* New York: Little, Brown.

Kirkham, Richard L. 1992. *Theories of Truth.* Cambridge, MA: MIT Press.

Koertge, Noretta (ed.). 1998. *A House Built on Sand: Exposing Postmodernist Myths about Science*. New York: Oxford University Press.

Kooyman, B., M. E. Newman, C. Cluney, M. Lobb, S. Tolman, P. McNeil, and L. V. Hills. 2001. Identification of Horse Exploitation by Clovis Hunters Based on Protein Analysis. *American Antiquity* 66(4):686–91.

Kroeber, A. L., and C. Kluckhohn. 1952. *Culture: A Critical Review of Concepts and Definitions*. Papers of the Peabody Museum of Archaeology and Ethnology, Harvard University, vol. 47, no. 1.

Kuhn, Thomas S. 1996 [1962]. *The Structure of Scientific Revolutions*. 3rd ed. Chicago: University of Chicago Press.

Laudan, Larry. 1977. *Progress and Its Problems: Toward a Theory of Scientific Growth*. Berkeley: University of California Press.

Leonard, Robert D. 2001. Evolutionary Archaeology. In *Archaeological Theory Today*, ed. Ian Hodder, 65–97. Malden, MA: Polity.

Lipton, Peter. 2000. Inference to the Best Explanation. In *A Companion to the Philosophy of Science*, ed. W. H. Newton-Smith, 184–93. Malden, MA: Blackwell.

Lipton, Peter. 2001. *Inference to the Best Explanation*. New York: Routledge.

Lowie, Robert. 1920. *Primitive Society*. New York: Liveright.

Lyman, R. L., and M. J. O'Brien. 1998. The Goals of Evolutionary Archaeology: History and Explanation. *Current Anthropology* 39:615–52.

Manicas, Peter T. 2006. *A Realist Philosophy of Social Science: Explanation and Understanding*. New York: Cambridge University Press. Kindle edition.

McKern, Will C. 1939. The Midwestern Taxonomic Method as an Aid to Archaeological Culture Study. *American Antiquity* 4(4):301–13.

Merton, Robert K. 1973. *The Sociology of Science: Theoretical and Empirical Investigations*, ed. Norman Storer. Chicago: University of Chicago Press.

Moore, Brooke Noel, and Richard Parker. 2001. *Critical Thinking*. 6th ed. Mountain View, CA: Mayfield.

Moore, Brooke Noel, and Richard Parker. 2004. *Critical Thinking*. 7th ed. New York: McGraw-Hill.

O'Brien, M. J., and R. L. Lyman. 2000. *Applying Evolutionary Archaeology: A Systematic Approach*. New York: Plenum.

Patrik, L. 1985. Is There an Archaeological Record? In *Advances in Archaeological Method and Theory*, vol. 8, ed. M. Schiffer. New York: Academic Press.

Paul, Richard, and Linda Elder. 2008. *Thinker's Guide to Fallacies: The Art of Mental Trickery and Manipulation*. Tomales, CA: Foundation for Critical Thinking.

Pearl, J. 2000. *Causality: Models, Reasoning, and Inference*. New York: Cambridge University Press.

Pitt, Joseph C. (ed.). 1988. *Theories of Explanation*. New York: Oxford University Press.

Popper, Karl. 1963. *Conjectures and Refutations*. London: Routledge and Kegan Paul.

Raab, L. M., and A. C. Goodyear. 1984. Middle Range Theory in Archaeology: A Critical Review of Origins and Application. *American Antiquity* 49:255–58.

Rawson, Hugh. 2003. *Rawson's Dictionary of Euphemisms and Other Doubletalk: Being a Compilation of Linguistic Fig Leaves and Verbal Flourishes for Artful Uses of the English Language*. Secaucus, NJ: Castle Books.

Renfrew, Colin, and Paul Bahn. 2000. *Archaeology: Theories, Method and Practice*. 3rd ed. New York: Thames & Hudson.

Rick, T. C., J. M. Erlandson, and R L. Vellanoweth. 2001. Paleocoastal Marine Fishing on the Pacific Coast of the Americas: Perspectives from Daisy Cave, California. *American Antiquity* 66(4):595–613.

Rosenau, Pauline. 1992. *Post-modernism and the Social Sciences: Insights, Inroads, and Intrusions*. Princeton, NJ: Princeton University Press.

Rosenberg, Alexander. 2012. *Philosophy of Social Science*. 4th ed. Boulder, CO: Westview Press.

Russell, Kenneth. 1988. *After Eden: The Behavioral Ecology of Early Food Production in the Near East and North Africa*. BAR International Series 391. Oxford: B.A.R.

Rybacki, Karyn Charles, and Donald Jay Rybacki. 2012. *Advocacy and Opposition: An Introduction to Argumentation*. 7th ed. Boston: Allyn & Bacon.

Salmon, Merrilee H. 2013. *Introduction to Logic and Critical Thinking*. 6th ed. Boston: Wadsworth, Cengage Learning. Kindle edition.

Salmon, Wesley. 2006. *Four Decades of Scientific Explanation*. Pittsburgh, PA: University of Pittsburgh Press.

Schmitt, Dave N., and Karen D. Lupo. 1995. On Mammalian Taphonomy, Taxonomic Diversity, and Measuring Subsistence Data in Zooarchaeology. *American Antiquity* 60(3):496–514.

Scriven, Michael. 2003. The Philosophy of Critical Thinking and Reasoning. In *Critical Thinking and Reasoning: Current Research, Theory, and Practice*, ed. Daniel Fasko Jr. Cresskill, NJ: Hampton.

Searle, John R. 1995. *The Construction of Social Reality*. New York: Free Press.

Shapin, Steven. 1994. *A Social History of Truth: Civility and Science in Seventeenth-Century England*. Chicago: University of Chicago Press.

Shennan, Stephen. 1997. *Quantifying Archaeology*. 2nd ed. Edinburgh, UK: Edinburgh University Press.

Simon, H. A., and A. Newell. 1956. Models: Their Uses and Limitations. In *The State of the Social Sciences*, ed. L. D. White, 61–83. Chicago: University of Chicago Press.

Staeck, John. 2001. *Back to the Earth: An Introduction to Archaeology*. New York: McGraw-Hill.

Steward, Julian. 1955. *Theory of Culture Change*. Urbana: University of Illinois Press.

Thomas, Julian. 2000. *Interpretive Archaeology: A Reader*. Leicester, UK: Leicester University Press.

Thomson, Anne. 2002. *Critical Reasoning: A Practical Introduction.* 2nd ed. New York: Routledge.

Trigger, Bruce. 1989. *A History of Archaeological Thought.* Cambridge: Cambridge University Press.

Utts, Jessica. 2004. *Seeing through Statistics.* 3rd ed. Belmont, CA: Thomson Brooks/Cole.

Van den Brink-Budgen, Roy. 2010a. *Advanced Critical Thinking Skills.* Oxford: How to Books. Kindle edition.

Van den Brink-Budgen, Roy. 2010b. *Critical Thinking for Students: Learn the Skills of Analysing, Evaluating and Producing Arguments.* Oxford: How to Books.

VanPool, Todd L., and Robert D. Leonard. 2011. *Quantitative Analysis in Archaeology.* Malden, MA: Wiley-Blackwell.

Wallace, Mike, and Alison Wray. 2011. *Critical Reading and Writing for Postgraduates.* Thousand Oaks, CA: Sage.

Walton, Douglas N. 1989. *Informal Logic: A Handbook for Critical Argumentation.* New York: Cambridge University Press.

Wasserman, Paul, and Don Hausrath. 2005. *Weasel Words: The Dictionary of American Doublespeak.* Sterling, VA: Capital Books.

Watson, Patty Jo, Steven A. LeBlanc, and Charles L. Redman. 1971. *Explanation in Archaeology: An Explicitly Scientific Approach.* New York: Columbia University Press.

White, Leslie. 1959. *The Evolution of Culture.* New York: McGraw-Hill.

White, Patrick. 2009. *Developing Research Questions: A Guide for Social Scientists.* New York: Palgrave Macmillan (St. Martin's Press).

Wilber, Ken. 1998. *The Marriage of Sense and Soul: Integrating Science and Religion.* New York: Broadway Books.

Wilber, Ken. 2000. *A Brief History of Everything.* Rev. ed. Boston: Shambhala.

Wilford, Lloyd A. 1937. *Minnesota Archaeology, with Special Reference to the Mound Area.* PhD diss., Department of Anthropology, Harvard University.

Wilford, Lloyd A. 1941. A Tentative Classification of the Prehistoric Cultures of Minnesota. *American Antiquity* 6(3):231–49.

Wilford, Lloyd A. 1955. A Revised Classification of the Prehistoric Cultures of Minnesota. *American Antiquity* 21(2):131–43.

Wilford, Lloyd A. 1960. The First Minnesotans. In *Minnesota Heritage,* ed. L. M. Brings, 40–79. Minneapolis: T. S. Denison.

Willey, Gordon, and Philip Phillips. 1958. *Method and Theory in American Archaeology.* Chicago: University of Chicago Press.

Willey, Gordon, and Jeremy Sabloff. 1993. *A History of American Archaeology.* 3rd ed. London: Thames & Hudson.

Index

abstract words/phrases, 60
acceptability criterion, 78–81
ad hoc explanations, 166
affirmation of antecedent/consequent
    pattern, 184–85
After Eden (Russell), 190–92
agency-centered archaeology, 155–57,
    165
agendas of archaeologists, 5
aims of archaeology, 7–10, 15–16. *See
    also* research programs
alternatives: analogies, 102;
    conclusions, 210; explanations, 169
ambiguity of language, 56–62
analogical arguments, 123–24, 221n2
analogies, 101–2, 169
anecdotal evidence, appeal to, 125,
    179
anthropology, 8–9, 152
appeals: to anecdotal evidence, 125,
    179; to authority, 78; to common
    opinion, 77; to ignorance, 81; to
    pedantry, 78; to recentness, 78–79;
    to tradition, 79
Archaeological and Historic
    Preservation Act, 15
archaeological record questions, 29

Archaeological Resources Protection
    Act, 15
arguments: to best explanation,
    164–65; commentaries of, 209;
    explanations compared to, 161;
    identifying, 35–39; patterns of, 49–
    50, 184–87; reconstructing, 206;
    tautological, 194–95. *See also* causal
    arguments; claims; conclusions;
    deductive arguments; evaluation of
    arguments; inductive arguments;
    questions
argumentum ad hominem, 83
argumentum ad novitatem, 78–79
argumentum ad verecundiam, 78
argumentum verbosum, 219n3
Asking the Right Questions (Browne
    and Keeley), 48
assumptions: differences in, 5–6;
    factual claims as, 99; functions
    of, 46–47; locating, 48–50;
    methodological, 47–48, 52;
    relationships with conclusions and
    premises, 45–46; types, 47–48;
    unnecessary, 168. *See also* research
    programs
authorities' testimonials, 100–101

authority, appeals to, 78
availability bias, 126
averages, 64–65, 113–15

Baconian error, 32
bar charts, 111
begging the question, 79, 219n3
behavioral ecology, 190–92
"best practices" projects, 24–25
bias, 104, 121–23, 125–27; biased
    generalizations, 125–26
Binford, Lewis, 23, 91, 143, 154
Binford, Sally, 23
black-and-white fallacy, 80
Boas, Franz, 152
A Brief History of Time (Hawking), 90
Bronze Age cemetery study, 135–37
Browne, M. Neil, 48
burden of proof principle, 43

Carr, Christopher, 157
Case, D. Troy, 157
case studies, 101, 103
categorical logic, 184
causal arguments, 171–79; errors in,
    175–78; only-common-thread
    reasoning in, 176–77; only-
    relevant-common-thread reasoning
    in, 174–75, 177; only-relevant-
    difference reasoning in, 172–74
causal claims, 171
causal hypotheses, 171
certainty of conclusions, 206–8, 210
chain argument, 185
chain of causes problem, 164
checklist for evaluating arguments,
    41–44
chronophonism, 89–90
circular arguments, 79
circular explanations, 166
claims, 27, 30–34, 97–99, 130
clarity principle, 43
Clovis hunters investigation, 24

coincidence, 177–78
common opinion fallacy, 77
common sense and meanings, 61
communal confirmation/rejection, 102
composition, fallacy of, 58
concepts, 143–44, 195
conceptual relativity, 92
conclusions: ambiguity in, 60;
    arguments and, 35–39; difficulties
    of, 203–4; errors in, 209–11;
    factual claims offered for, 99;
    four-step approach for assessing,
    205–9; identifying, 30–32; proof vs.
    support of, 105; relationship with
    assumptions, 45–46; truthfulness of,
    204–5. See also deductive arguments
confirmation bias, 126–27
consistency with theory, 168–69
Constructing Frames of Reference
    (Binford), 154
The Construction of Social Reality
    (Searle), 91–92
constructivism, 10–11
contemporary evolutionary
    archaeology, 187–89
context: of discovery, 22; historical,
    27, 33–34; of justification, 22; in
    meanings, 59
contextualism, 11
contradictory results, 103, 210
correspondence rules, 146
correspondence theory of truth, 92,
    204–5
cost-benefit approaches, 191–92
counterevidence, denial of, 82–83
critical thinking, 1–2, 103, 205–6, 213
Critical Thinking (Moore and Parker),
    213
cultural historical archaeology, 151–
    53, 159
cultural relativism, 69
cultural resource management (CRM),
    8, 14–15, 30

cultural uniformitarianism, 144
culture: as constructed, 156; defined,
    9, 190; models of, 152; partitive
    view of, 158
cum hoc ergo propter hoc, 219n4
cycle of research, 211

Daisy Cave investigation, 23
data: averages, 113–15; displaying,
    108–11, 109–10*t*, 112*f*; measuring,
    107–8, 115–17, 115*f*; shifting to
    generalizations, 129–30
deductive arguments: defined, 119–20;
    example of, 187–92; inductive
    arguments compared to, 183–84;
    patterns in, 184–87
defective arguments, 1–2
definitions of archaeology, 7–10
denial: of antecedent pattern, 185; of
    consequent pattern, 185, 187; of
    counterevidence, 82–83
dependent variables, 131
derived measurements, 197–98
descriptive conclusions, 99
descriptive phase of empirical research,
    95–96
descriptive questions, 29–30
descriptive statistics. *See* data
descriptive studies, 22
dictionary definitions, 61–62
direct apprehension/experience, 102
distortions, 104
diversion fallacy, 83
division, fallacy of, 58–59
downplayers, 71–73
dysphemisms, 67–68, 70

either-or fallacy, 79–80
Ember, Carol R., 199–200
Ember, Melvin R., 199–200
empirical generalizations, 18–20, 129–
    30, 196–98
empirical research, 22

empiricism, 148, 154–55
epistemology, 88, 222n1
equivocation, fallacy of, 80–81
errors: in conclusions, 209–11; of false
    dichotomous questions, 32–33; in
    framing explanations, 165–69; in
    framing questions, 27, 32–33; of
    many questions, 32; of metaphysical
    questions, 33; in reasoning, 221n4;
    of semantical questions, 33; of
    tautological questions, 33. *See also*
    fallacies
estimation of populations, 133–34
ethnographic records, 143–44
euphemisms, 67–68, 70
evaluation of arguments: checklist
    for, 41–44; for circularity, 79; for
    defects, 1–2; for fogginess, 210–11;
    for incomplete presentation, 36;
    reasons for, 39; for soundness, 39–
    41, 76. *See also* arguments; fallacies
evidence: evaluating, 97–99; research
    studies as, 102–5; types of, 100–
    105. *See also* data
evolutionary archaeology, 187, 190
experimental tests, 178–79
explanations: arguments compared
    to, 161; arguments to the best
    of, 164–65; errors in framing,
    165–69; greater power in, 167–68;
    identifying, 161–63; persuasive, 69;
    targets of, 163–65
exploratory investigations, 22–23
external projects, 24–25
external realism, 92

factual claims, 97–99, 144–45, 220n1
faint praise, 70
fallacies: acceptability criterion
    violations, 78–81; of composition,
    58; defined, 219n1; of definition,
    219n3; of division, 58–59; hasty
    generalizations, 179; of inductive

arguments, 124–27; of missing evidence, 179; post hoc, 219n4; in reasoning, 75–76; rebuttal criterion violations, 82–84; relevance criterion violations, 76–79; sufficiency criterion violations, 81–82; of vague statements, 218n5
fallibility principle, 43
false alternatives fallacy, 79
false analogies, 221n2
false cause-and-effect fallacy. See post hoc fallacy
false cause fallacy. See post hoc fallacy
false dichotomous questions, error of, 32–33
false dilemma fallacy, 79–80
falsifiability criterion, 126–27
family of models, 143, 147
fiat measurements, 198
flatland modernism, 10–11
foggy arguments, 210–11
frequency distributions, 111, 113–15
function-of-something explanations, 164
fundamental measurements, 197–98

gambler's fallacy, 126
Geertz, Clifford, 156
generalizations: about attributes, 19–20; errors in, 104, 125, 179, 208, 210, 221n4; exceptions to, 42; inductive, 120–23
generalizing theories, 142–43
genetic fallacy, 77–78
greater explanatory power, 167–68
grouping ambiguity problem, 58

Hanson, Norwood Russell, 87
hasty generalization fallacy, 125, 179
Hawking, Stephen, 90
histograms, 111
historical contexts, 27, 33–34
Hodder, Ian, 52–53, 156

"how-to" questions, 28–29
Hume, David, 148
hyperbole, 73
hypotheses: distinguishing assumptions from, 52–53; facts and, 144–45; statistical inference, 133, 134–35; testing, 24, 135–37
hypothetico-deductive approach, 183

idealism, 87
identities, 144
ignorance, appeals to, 81
incompletely presented arguments, 36
independent variables, 131
indicator evaluation, 198–201
indicator words, 31
inductive arguments, 120–27, 183–84
inductive generalizations, 120–23
inferences, 129, 130–34
inferential phase of empirical research, 95–96
inferential statistics. See samples
informal logic, 1
innuendo, 70, 71
instrumental injunctions, 102
instrumental-nomological investigations, 24
insufficient sample fallacy, 179
integral archaeology, 157–58, 159
intellectual contexts, 33–34
internal projects, 22–24
interpretive/theoretical studies, 23
interval scale, 108
intuition, 100
invalid conversion patterns, 186
invalid patterns, 185–87
invalid syllogism patterns, 187
investigations in archaeology, 22–25, 26. See also research cycle; theories
issues, 27, 28–30, 60, 211. See also questions

justifications, 162–63

Keeley, Stuart M., 48
Kluckhohn, Clyde, 57–58
knowledge, 92, 193–94
Kroeber, Albert, 57–58

labels, 69–70
Lakatos, Imre, 51
language: ambiguity of, 56–62;
    indeterminacy of, 87–88; multiple
    meanings in, 55–56; unfamiliar
    words/phrases, 65; vagueness, 62–
    63, 64. *See also* writings
legislation, 14–15
linguistic indeterminacy, 87–88
loaded questions, 71, 219n4
logical empiricism, 154–55
logical predictions, 193
logic of everyday discourse, 1
Lupo, Karen D., 200–201

material culture, 216n15
matrilocality example, 195, 199–200
McKern, W. C., 152
meanings of words. *See* language
mean of frequency distribution,
    114–15
measurement scales, 108
measures of reliability/validity, 115–
    17, 115*f*, 197–98
median of frequency distribution, 114
metaphysical questions, error of, 33
meta-questions, 29
methodological questions, 29–30
methodological rules, 51–52
Midwestern taxonomic method, 152
missing evidence fallacy, 179
models, 142–43, 147
mode of frequency distribution,
    113–14
modernism, 85. *See also* flatland
    modernism
modus ponens pattern, 184–85
modus tollens pattern, 185, 187

Moore, Brooke Noel, 213
Mousterian investigation, 23
myth of the given, 10–11

National Environmental Policy Act,
    15
National Historic Preservation Act, 15
natural variability, 131
neo-Darwinism, 187, 190
New Archaeology. *See* processual
    archaeology
nominal scale, 108
noncircularity, 166
nonexperimental tests, 178–79
non sequiturs, 42, 218n9
null hypotheses, 134–37
Nunamiut Eskimos, 25

objectivity, 41–42, 91, 92, 204–5
observation, 18–20, 86–87, 88, 91,
    101. *See also* data
omissions of information, 63–64
only-common-thread reasoning,
    176–77
only-relevant-common-thread
    reasoning in, 174–75, 177
only-relevant-difference reasoning,
    172–74
ontology, 88, 222n1
operational definitions, 196–98
operationalization, 21
opinions, 31, 77
opposition, identifying with, 49
ordinal scale, 108
overgeneralizations, 208, 210
oversimplifications, 104
overstatements. *See* hyperbole

paradigmatic questions, 29–30
Parker, Richard, 213
particularizing theories, 142–43
past-as-reconstructed, 145
past-behavior explanations, 164

past-in-itself, 29, 143, 145, 165–66,
174, 195. *See also* deductive
arguments
patrilocality, 199–200
patterns: of arguments, 49–50, 184–87;
descriptions of, 19; of residence,
199–200
pedantry, appeal to, 78
peer reviews, 103
percentages, 111
persuasion, 68–69
petitio principii, 79
phenomenalism, 87
Phillips, Philip, 153
physical object explanations, 163–64
pictorial displays of data, 108–11,
109–10*t*, 112*f*
places, study of, 25
plasticity of words, 57–58
point of view, 48–49
Popper, Karl, 126–27
population. *See* samples
populations, causation in, 178–79
post hoc, ergo propter hoc, 177
post hoc fallacy, 81–82, 177, 219n4
postmodernism, 10–11, 90–91. *See also*
skeptical postmodernism
Post-modernism and the Social Sciences
(Rosenau), 93
pragmatic realism, 223n15
predictions, 21, 193–96, 227n1
premises: ambiguity in, 60;
assumptions supporting, 48; of
deductive arguments, 184; errors
in reasoning and, 75–76; as false/
unacceptable, 42; identifying
arguments with, 35–39; mistaking
for assumptions, 50; relationship
with assumptions, 45–46
prescriptive conclusions, 99
preservation legislation, 14–15
presuppositions in research, 93–94
primary analyses, 25

probabilities, 131
processual archaeology, 91, 154–55,
156, 159
proof by verbosity, 219n3
proof surrogates, 73–74
proxy measurements, 198
publication outlets, 25
puzzling comparisons. *See* vagueness

quadrants, 11–16, 102–3, 133, 153,
155, 157. *See also* theories
questions, 27–30, 32–33, 71, 206–9;
"W" questions, 28. *See also* issues

random variation in samples, 122–23
range of distributions, 116
ratio scale variable, 108
Reading the Past (Hodder), 52–53
realism, 92, 147–48, 223n15
reality assumptions. *See* research
programs
reasonableness of conclusions, 208
reasoning errors. *See* fallacies
rebuttal criterion violations, 82–84
reconsideration principle, 44
reconstruction of arguments, 206
reconstruction of cultural history, 9
red herring fallacy, 83
relativism. *See* postmodernism
relevance, 76–79, 166, 175
reliability, 167, 196–98
representationalism, 87
representations, 92
research cycle, 17–25, 18*f*
research programs, 50–53; agency-
centered archaeology, 155–57,
165; cultural historical archaeology,
151–53, 159; development of,
189–90; evolutionary archaeology,
187, 190; integral archaeology,
157–58, 159; presuppositions and,
93–94; processual archaeology, 91,
154–55, 156, 159; systems-centered

archaeology, 153–55, 187–89; trait-centered archaeology, 151–53
research studies as evidence, 102–5
residence patterns, 199–200
resolution principle, 43
reverse role-play, 60–61
rhetorical devices: defined, 67; downplayers, 71–73; euphemisms/dysphemisms, 67–68, 70; hyperbole, 73; innuendo, 70, 71; loaded questions, 71, 219n4; persuasion, 68–69; proof surrogates, 73–74; sarcasm, 73; stereotypes, 69–70, 72; weaselers, 71
root assumptions, 47–48, 144
Rosenau, Pauline, 93
Rosenberg, Alexander, 218n2
Russell, Kenneth, 190–92

samples, 19, 121–23, 130–34. *See also* data; inductive generalizations
sarcasm, 73
Schmitt, Dave N., 200–201
science *vs.* humanities debates, 7–8
scientific method, 216n1
S.D. (standard deviation), 116–17
secondary analyses, 25–26
self-contradictory arguments, 41
semantical question, error of, 33
semantic conception of theories, 146–47
skeptical postmodernism, 10–11, 85, 86–94
slanters. *See* rhetorical devices
social constructivism, 148
sound arguments, 39–41, 76
"so what?" questions, 32
standard deviation (S.D.), 116–17
statistics: defined, 95; statistical inference, 19–20, 130–35; statistical significance, 132–34. *See also* data
stereotypes, 69–70, 72
Steward, Julian, 153

straw person fallacy, 83–84
study of places, 25
subsistence practices example, 200–201
sufficiency criterion violations, 81–82
surrogate proof, 73–74
suspension of judgment principle, 43
symbols, 88
syntactic conception of theories, 146
systems-centered archaeology, 153–55, 187–89. *See also* neo-Darwinism

taken-for-granted assumptions, 70–71
tautological arguments, 194–95
tautological questions, error of, 33
taxonomy, 152, 200–201
temporal succession, 81–82
testability of explanations, 165–66
testimonials, 100–101
theoretical definitions of concepts, 196–98
theories: acceptance and pursuit of, 228n1; building/testing, 20–21, 22, 216n3; confrontation process, 181–82; consistency with, 168–69; disputes in, 147–48; evaluating conclusions in, 203–4; in research programs, 145; terminology for, 142–43, 216n2, 222n3; of truth, 204–5, 228n3
Theory of Culture Change (Steward), 153
thick descriptions, 156
thick prehistory, 157–58
titles of books, 28
trait-centered archaeology, 151–53
transformation of statements: evaluating indicators, 198–201; predictions for testing, 193–96; reliability/validity, 196–98. *See also* conclusions
trivial assumptions, 49
truth: corresponding to facts, 92; in premises, 40–41; skeptical

postmodern presuppositions, 90; theories of, 204–5, 228n3; two meanings of, 194–95
truth-seeking principle, 43
Type I/II errors, 135
types of archaeology. *See* aims of archaeology

unfamiliar words/phrases, 65
unknown populations, 19–20
unnamed invalid inference pattern, 186
unnecessary assumptions, 168
unobservables, 222n1
unreliability of explanations, 167
unwarranted inferences, 84

vagueness, 62–63, 64, 167, 218n5
validity, 13–14, 40–41, 183, 185–86, 196–98. *See also* deductive arguments; inductive arguments

valid patterns, 184–85
valid syllogism pattern, 186
value assumptions, 47–48. *See also* research programs
value-free explanations, 163
variables, 108, 131
verbosity, proof by, 219n3
vicious circles, 79, 219n3

warfare example, 195
weaselers, 71
White, Leslie, 153–54
Wilber, Ken, 11
Willey, Gordon, 153
worldview of Searle, 91–92
writings: clarifying, 65–66; comparison issues, 63–65; critical questioning of, 205–9; organization/style, 56; point of view, 48–49; reasons for, 9–10; titles of, 28. *See also* language

About the Author

Guy Gibbon is professor emeritus at the University of Minnesota. He is the author of a number of books, including *Anthropological Archaeology*, *Explanation in Archaeology*, and *The Sioux*.